# Programming with Enterprise JavaBeans™, JTS, and OTS:

## Building Distributed Transactions with Java™ and C++

Andreas Vogel
Madhavan Rangarao

Wiley Computer Publishing

John Wiley & Sons, Inc.
NEW YORK • CHICHESTER • WEINHEIM • BRISBANE • SINGAPORE • TORONTO

*To my loving family, Radhika, Divya, and Adit*
*—Madhavan*

Publisher: Robert Ipsen
Editor: Robert M. Elliott
Assistant Editor: Pam Sobotka
Managing Editor: Angela Murphy
Electronic Products, Associate Editor: Mike Sosa
Text Design & Composition: Benchmark Productions, Inc.



This book is printed on acid-free paper. ♾



Published by John Wiley & Sons, Inc.

Published simultaneously in Canada.



***Library of Congress Cataloging-in-Publication Data:***

ISBN 0-471-31972-4

Printed in the United States of America.

10 9 8 7 6 5 4 3 2

# Contents

# Foreword

Without question, confusion exists in today's middleware market. The causes of such confusion are many; some technological and some simply market positioning. The large number, and varied mix, of services provided by most middleware tools is the technical reason. Cross-network and cross-language integration, event/message delivery, application state management, and security control generally head the list. But what makes all of these services come together? Why do they fit? Are middleware tools simply a conglomeration of some operating system guru's favorite tools, or is there some unifying theme?

Transparency is the key word that draws together middleware services. Since the dawn of "high-level language" programming (that would be FORTRAN and Lisp, in the late 1950s) and even earlier to EDSAC's first linkers and loaders, system specialists have attempted to simplify the delivery of business applications. "Business logic" for the average early FORTRAN programmer consisted of "merely" mathematical equations—but think about how those equations would have been expressed in some assembly language (e.g., IBM 650) if not for FORTRAN! Language compilers brought "instruction set transparency"—the ability to code mathematical "business logic" in a portable way without regard for the underlying assembly language or instruction set architecture. A powerful feature indeed.

Since then, the tide of system transparencies has continued to roll in. Various standardized mathematical libraries provided relief from coding (or even understanding!) common statistical and mathematical methods. POSIX was, in effect, an attempt to provide operating system transparency. But perhaps this was the wrong level of transparency to provide. Middleware has aimed at locality and distribution transparencies instead—removing from the business logic supplier the need to deal with the vagaries of parallelism. While those of us who have designed and built parallel systems realize this can never be perfect (the prayer,

"Deadlock, thy name is Illiac IV" comes to mind), for the average business application programmer life can be made much better in general.

The new term "application server" is intended to express this group of general services which provide insulation for the business programmer from the details of networking, state management, transactional integrity, and message delivery. I have flippantly defined application server in the past as "what we used to call libraries." This isn't far from the truth—but the impact is in fact quite a bit more widespread than providing portability. In heterogeneous distributed systems, application server also aim to provide interoperability.

The cornerstone of this evolution in business application delivery is transaction management. The delivery of applications with transactional integrity is vital to the operations of any organization; but the complexity of two-phase commit in a distributed setting, with persistence being managed by many, separately delivered services ranging from file systems to database management systems, is not to be ignored. Application programmers wish to be delivered from that complexity while enjoying the fruits of its functionality.

Just as parsers delivered compiler writers from the drudgery of something that could be completely automated (LALR1 language parsing), application servers deliver the application programmer from the drudgery of managing state and transactions. This book gives a detailed, focused view of how this is achieved using the CORBA Object Transaction Service and the related Enterprise JavaBeans transaction services, with abundant examples. Why should you ever deal with ACID properties again?

Richard Mark Soley, Ph.D.
Chairman and CEO
Object Management Group, Inc.

# Acknowledgments

First of all, we want to thank those people who assisted us in writing this book. These are our editor at John Wiley and Sons, Robert Elliott, and his assistants Pam Sobotka and Emilie Herman. Thanks also to Angela Murphy and the Wiley production team.

We would like to specifically thank Jonathan Weedon, the architect of Inprise's EJB server, for providing an excellent CORBA-based EJB container, and the many discussions and thorough review of major parts of the book. We would like to extend our thanks to the EJB, Visibroker, and ITS development teams at Inprise, specifically to George Scott, Patty Grewell, and Suresh Bathini; and to Frederic Desjarlais and Dave Beckedorff for reviewing parts of the document.

We acknowledge the cooperation of the OMG, and in particular Richard Soley, and Sun Microsystems.

We would also like to thank the Inprise customers Andreas has been working with, the participants inthe EJB Design workshop and all the many people who contributed to CORBA and EJB-related mailing lists and news groups. Their feedback has been very helpful and all their questions have improved the content of the book.

Dorit and Meta, I'm sorry for all the weekends I sat in front of the computer working on the book instead of spending them with you. But, now we are done—get the dollies and the trailerbike out!

Radhika, Thank you for supporting me throughout this effort and with out your support this would not have been possible. Special thanks and kisses to my toddler Divya for letting me write during her precious play time.

# About the Authors

**Andreas Vogel** is a Strategic Technology Adviser with Inprise Corporation since January 1997. In this position, he works with customers, mostly Fortune 500 companies, on CORBA and EJB solutions for their distributed computing needs, as well as in Inprise's research and development division. In the more than two years Andreas has been with Visigenic, Borland, and Inprise, he has been involved in more than 40 different projects spanning over almost all industry sectors.

Prior to this appointment he worked as Principal Research Scientist with the Distributed Systems Technology Centre (DSTC) in Brisbane, Australia, and as a Research Scientist for the University of Montreal, Canada. He has worked on various topics in the area of distributed computing including Formal Description Techniques, Distributed Middleware (DCE, CORBA, and EJB), Distributed Multimedia, and Quality of Service.

Andreas regularly publishes and speaks on distributing computing topics. He has co-authored *Java Programming with CORBA*, which is now in its second edition, and *C++ Programming with CORBA*. Andreas holds a PhD and MSc in Computer Science from Humboldt-University in Berlin, Germany. Andreas lives with his wife Dorit Hillmann and daughter Meta Hillmann in San Francisco and enjoys cycling to the office in San Mateo.

**Madhavan Rangarao** is a Senior Architect at TIBCO software who is a pioneer and the leading provider of Enterprise Application Integration and messaging middleware system solutions. Prior to this appointment, he led the core development effort of the Inprise ITS Object Transaction Service. While he was at Sybase Inc., he was one of the key contributors to their distributed transaction management strategy for the SQL Server. Madhavan has been developing distributed transaction management system solutions for the past nine years and specializes in CORBA based distributed object computing.

He holds an M.S. in Computer Science from the University of South Florida, Tampa. He loves to tinker with any electronic gadgets in his sight and enjoys scenic photography.

# Introduction

## How to Read This Book

Today's biggest challenges for Enterprise IT departments are Internet accessibility of services and the integration of heterogeneous applications and systems. A whole new class of products has emerged to address the problem: the *application server*. This book introduces and explains the key technologies on which application servers are built: transactional object middleware. We specifically focus on CORBA and its Object Transaction Service (OTS), its Java incarnation, Java Transaction Service (JTS), and Enterprise JavaBeans (EJB).

The CORBA specification and programming with CORBA is not the main focus of the book. For details on CORBA and programming with CORBA we refer you to the books *Java Programming with CORBA** and *C++ Programming with CORBA***. However, we discuss and explain a number of CORBA design patterns in Chapter 4.

The book has three parts. The first part provides an introduction to the issues addressed and the key technologies used in the book. Chapter 1 investigates the problem in detail and outlines the solution in the large. We also give an introduction of fundamentals of transaction processing, OTS/JTS and EJB. We use a simple example to illustrate the concepts and the programming with OTS/JTS and EJB. Chapter 2 explains the principles of transaction processing.

Part Two is dedicated to OTS and JTS. Chapter 3 introduces the OTS/JTS specification. It explains the specification from an application programmer's perspective. Wherever appropriate, explanations are accompanied by relevant examples. This chapter can be used as a programmer's reference to OTS/JTS specification. Chapter 4 explains the

* *Java Programming with CORBA*, 2nd edition. Andreas Vogel and Keith Duddy. John Wiley and Sons, New York, NY 1998.

** *C++ Programming with CORBA*, Andreas Vogel, et al. John Wiley and Sons, New York, NY 1999.

programming with OTS and JTS. Throughout the chapter, we explain CORBA and OTS/JTS specific design patterns. It provides a comprehensive Flight Booking System example with the step-by-step explanation and design advice.

Part Three is about EJB. Chapter 5 explains the EJB specification from an application programmer's perspective. This chapter can be used as a programmer's reference to EJB specification. Chapter 6 explains the programming with EJB. We use the example from Chapter 4 and show how it can be implemented using EJB technology. We have given detailed explanations on the EJB design patterns that are used.

We recommend the book for self-teaching as well as source material for training and university courses. In any case, it is recommended that readers work through the examples that are provided. The source code can be obtained from the John Wiley & Sons Web site at http://www.wiley.com/compbooks/vogel. The Web site is organized according to chapters, and is easy to navigate.

PART

One

# Overview

CHAPTER

1

# Quick Start to EJB, JTS, and OTS

Distributed transactions are the single most important concept in corporate information technology. This book is about programming distributed transactions with modern object technology, specifically with Enterprise JavaBeans (EJB), CORBA Object Transaction Service (OTS) and its Java incarnation, Java Transaction Service (JTS).

In this chapter, we first explore the problem space in more depth and outline the solution in the large. Then we define and explain the fundamental concepts and explore the state of the art of technology for distributed transactions. We give an overview of the OTS/JTS and the EJB specification. Next, we give you a first feel for the programming with an introductory example. The sample program is implemented for both OTS/JTS and EJB.

## Problem

Today's biggest challenges for Enterprise IT departments are:

**Internet accessibility of services.** Today there is almost no enterprise that can afford to not have an Internet presence. Typically, enterprise Web sites go through three phases. Initial Web presence is mostly concerned with providing advertising and informational material of a static nature. In the second phase, the Web presence is about providing dynamic information services; for example, browsing a catalog or a library, or searching for flight connections. Finally, in the third phase, Web sites provide transactional services. These services are provided by the enterprise's core information systems, which are typically legacy systems. Providing Internet access to those systems creates the additional challenge of system integration. In summary, the third-phase Internet access requires secure and transactional access to one or multiple enterprise systems in a high-performing and reliable manner.

**Integration of heterogeneous applications and systems.** The integration of heterogeneous systems and applications is forced through mergers and acquisitions, and through market requirements specifically caused by the need to provide Internet access. The heterogeneity of the system is multifaceted. There is difference in the operating systems, in the program languages, in the access and network protocol, in the data representation, and so forth. System integration must deal with the bridging between all these differences in a high-performing, secure, and reliant way.

Another important factor is time to market. Specifically, the ubiquitous Internet and the possibility to directly compare different offerings by a click of the mouse puts enormous pressure on the enterprises and their IT departments.

## Solution

A whole new class of products has emerged to address the problem: the *application server*. Different application servers are based on different technology and address different aspects of the wide problem space described earlier. Many application servers are based on distributed object technology. Figure 1.1 illustrates a generic application server.

The most widely used and deployed distributed technology is CORBA (Common Object Request Broker Architecture). CORBA is an open industry standard developed and maintained by the OMG (Object Management Group), providing an object-based middleware spanning over

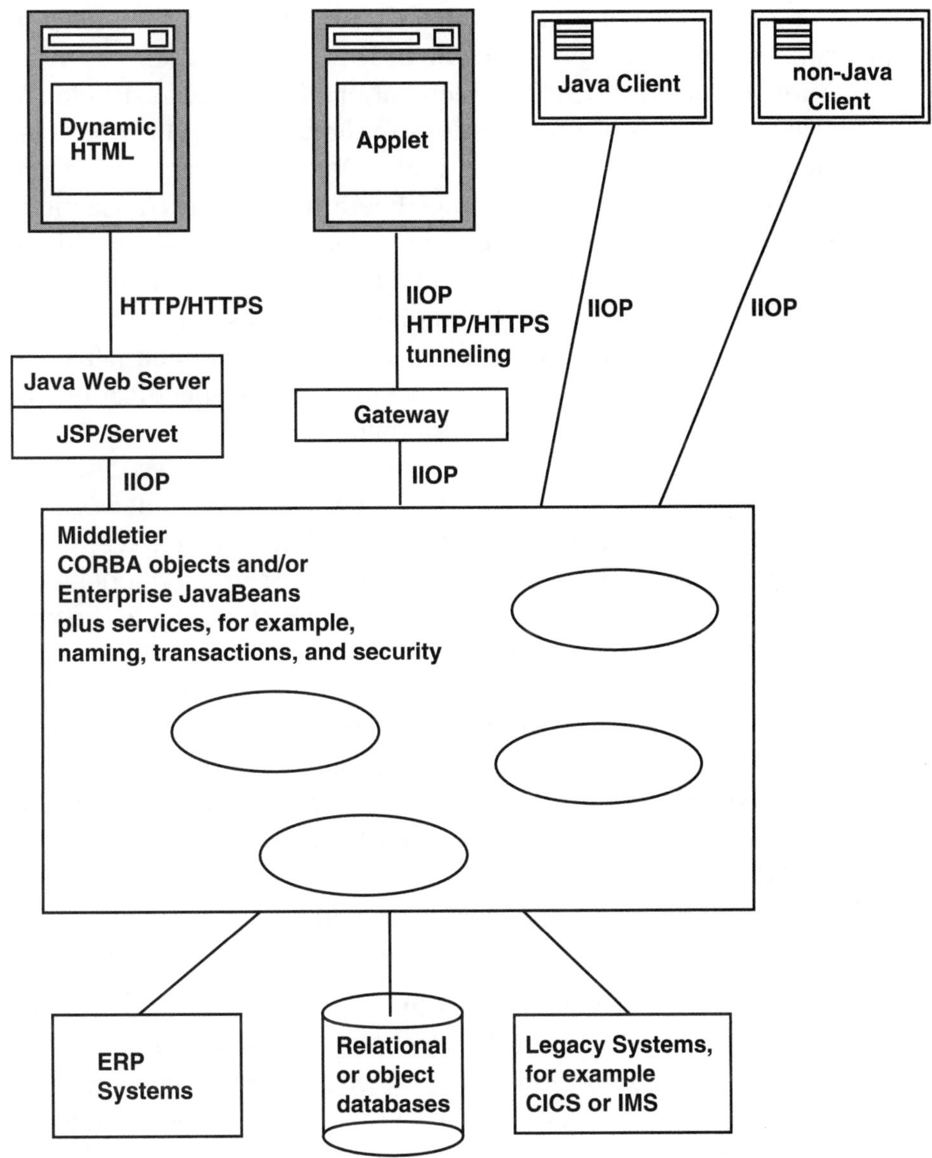


**Figure 1.1** A generic application server.

heterogeneous platforms. Implementations of CORBA, called *ORBs*, are provided by a number of competing vendors. Implementations of CORBA have proven to be an effective mechanism for system integration and for providing Internet access. For details on CORBA and programming with CORBA we refer to the books *Java Programming with*

*CORBA** and *C++ Programming with CORBA***. A large number of today's application servers are based on a CORBA backbone.

In addition, to the core CORBA specification, the OMG has developed and published a number of specifications for horizontal and vertical services. One of the horizontal services is the Object Transaction Service (OTS). This service allows you to coordinate distributed transactions across multiple databases and transactional legacy systems. As with all services, the APIs of OTS are mapped to a number of programming languages. Sun has adopted the Java mapping of OTS as part of the Java platform. The service is known as Java Transaction Service (JTS). In Part Two of this book, "OTS and JTS," we explain the specifications of OTS and JTS and how you program with them.

In 1998, Sun published the first version of its Java EnterpriseBean specification, which is a Java-based component-oriented framework for developing, deploying, and managing distributed, transactional applications. A number of application servers are based on the EJB model. Part Three of this book, "EJB," is devoted to the specification of and the programming with Enterprise JavaBeans.

CORBA and its services, and Enterprise JavaBeans both address the problem space described earlier. Although the two specifications have been developed independently by different groups of people, it turns out that the two technologies are complementary. We explain how an EJB server can be implemented on top of an ORB, the CORBA Naming Service and OTS/JTS.

In either case, Internet access to services can be implemented in different ways:

**Dynamic HTML usually generated by servlets.** The Web browser communicates via HTTP or HTTPS with the Web server, which invokes the servlet determined by the URL. A servlet typically talks IIOP or IIOP over SSL (including RMI over IIOP) to the middle-tier objects/enterprise beans.

**Applets.** An applet can, when it is signed and provided with the appropriate privileges, talk directly to the middle-tier objects via IIOP or IIOP over SSL. In many cases, a gateway is introduced for HTTP/HTTP tunneling or for overcoming (unsigned) applets' communications restrictions.

* *Java Programming with CORBA*, 2nd edition, Andreas Vogel and Keith Duddy. John Wiley and Sons, New York, NY, 1998.

** *C++ Programming with CORBA*, Andreas Vogel, et al. John Wiley and Sons, New York, NY 1999.

**Java and non-Java traditional client applications.** These client applications can be implemented in any programming language for which a mapping from OMG IDL is provided. OMG mapping standards currently exist for C, C++, Smalltalk, Java, COBOL, and Ada. Furthermore, a number of unofficial mappings are provided by various vendors, including ones for Python and Pascal/Delphi.

The middle tier usually encapsulates the business logic and provides the access to various backend systems. Backend systems include relational and object databases, ERP systems, and legacy systems. In this book we focus on the middle-tier part of enterprise applications and, specifically, their transactional aspects. We use simple Java applications to demonstrate the client functionality. The programming of dynamic HTML clients with servlets and of applets is well documented in other books. The kind of client has little influence on the middle-tier components. The relevant aspects, specifically the design of the interface between the client and the middle tier, are explained throughout the book. The access to backend systems, other than relational databases where we have JDBC and XA, is not governed by open standards. The level of integration capabilities differs from vendor to vendor and we refer to the manuals of the various products for details of the integration features and APIs.

## Basic Concepts and Definitions

Before we introduce you to OTS, JTS, and EJB, we define the basic concepts of a transaction and a distributed transaction. For detailed explanation on these concepts we refer you to Chapter 2, "Transaction Processing Basics."

### Transaction

The concept of a transaction is centuries old, yet there is no commonly accepted definition. Here is our definition, as we formulate it from various definitions available:

> A transaction is a unit of work which comprises several operations made on one or more shared system resources that are governed by ACID properties.

The acronym *ACID* stands for Atomicity, Consistency, Isolation, and Durability properties of a transaction. Any unit of work can be transactional only if it satisfies these properties.

**Atomicity.** If a transaction experiences any sort of failure, any changes that were introduced within the scope of the transaction are undone. Example: Database updates.

**Consistency.** If a transaction experiences any sort of failure, the system state is restored to its initial condition as though nothing changed. Example: Database referential integrity constraints.

**Isolation.** The changes made due to a transaction are not visible to other transactions until it completes. Transactions appear to be executed serially, even though they are performed concurrently. Example: A withdraw activity and balance activity performed by two clients on the same account.

**Durability.** The effect of a completed transaction is persistent and can survive a system failure. For example, if a system crashes during a commit operation of a transaction, the changes are correctly applied when the system is brought up again.

A transaction comprises the simple steps *begin transaction, commit transaction,* or *abort transaction.* The transaction is begun using the *begin transaction* control verb and is terminated by a *commit transaction* or *abort transaction* control verbs. When the transaction is committed, the changes that were applied within the scope of the transaction are made persistent. Alternatively, a transaction is aborted, which means that the changes that were applied within the scope of the transaction are undone.

## Distributed Transaction

A distributed transaction is a transaction in which the transactional unit of work spans across multiple nodes in a network. Failure of the transactional work in any node will cause the transaction to abort to preserve ACID properties.

## The Money Transfer Example

A typical example of a distributed transaction is the transfer of money from one account to another. This example involves three entities: the transaction originator, which initiates the transfer operation; and the two accounts (for example, checking and savings), which implement debit and credit operations. The account objects are transactional objects. All three entities can exist in different nodes and run in independent processes.

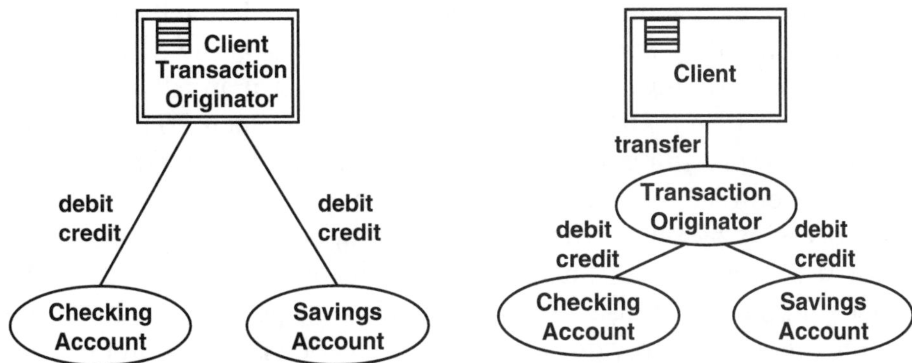


**Figure 1.2** Money transfer transaction.

The debit and credit operations are executed in the same transaction. If the credit operation fails, the money must be redeposited in the account from which it was withdrawn. If the debit operation fails, the credit operation must not be executed. We use this simple scenario for the OTS and EJB programming examples presented later in this chapter.

As shown in Figure 1.2, the client can act as the transaction originator and control the distributed transaction directly. Alternatively, a separate object, typically located in the middle tier, can act as the transaction originator. We discuss the implications of either approach later in the book.

## Distributed Transaction Processing Standards

There are a number of proprietary transaction processing solutions and tools in use today to manage distributed transactions. Many of these products, such as CICS and IMS, pioneered the transaction processing technology and hold a major market share even today. The Unix-based TP monitors introduced in the 1980s advocated the *open* computing model in which the push was toward making heterogeneous systems work together. There have been several attempts to standardize the interaction between various components of transaction processing systems since then. Open Group (X/Open), Open System Interconnection (OSI), and Object Management Group (OMG) standards body organizations have published specifications to address the industry's needs.

An important step toward open and interoperable solutions for distributed transaction processing was made by the Open Group (formerly X/Open and OSF). X/Open specified a Distributed Transaction Processing

Model (DTP) and a number of API specifications to define the primitive functions offered by transaction processing systems. The X/Open DTP model has been widely adopted by several TP monitor and database vendors. OTS, JTS, and EJB specifications use the X/Open DTP model as their basis for providing transactional application frameworks.

The X/Open DTP model, as shown in Figure 1.3, identifies a transaction processing system with three basic components: Application Program (AP), Transaction Manager (TM), and Resource Manager (RM). Inprise's Integrated Transaction Service (ITS) is a good example for the TM component that provides all the functions of a transaction processing system. Sybase's SQL Server is a good example for a Resource Manager, which oversees creation and management of data. An application program interacts with a transaction manager using the TX interface. The transaction manager interacts with resource managers using the XA interface. The application program uses a native interface such as SQL or ISAM to interact with resource managers. X/Open has specified the TX and XA interfaces in great detail.

The X/Open DTP Reference Model has not sufficiently addressed the interoperability issues across different TP domains. X/Open later published another specification by adding another component called the Communications Resource Manager (CRM) to the X/Open DTP Reference Model to specify how the basic DTP components communicate with each other across different TP domains. The details of this model can be found in Chapter 2.

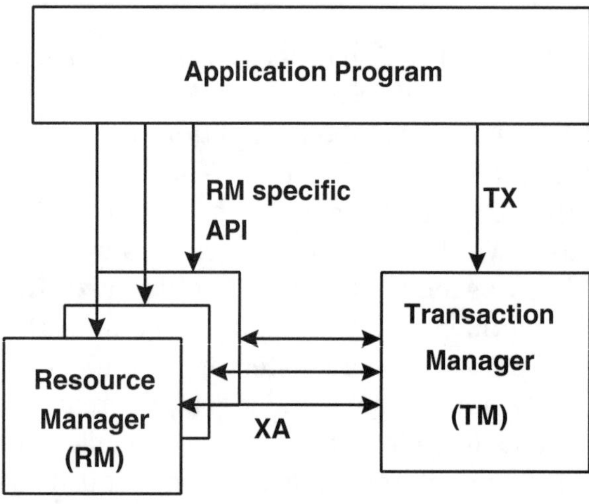


**Figure 1.3** X/Open DTP model.

## Object Transaction Service

The Object Transaction Service provides an object-oriented framework for distributed transaction processing. It defines CORBA IDL interfaces that facilitate multiple distributed objects that are located anywhere on the network to participate in a global transaction. These interfaces specify the transactional primitives to provide the functions that are necessary for any distributed transaction processing system. The specification does not impose any requirements on the language, number of objects in the transaction, the topology of the application, or how the application is distributed across the network. The OTS is a unique piece of middleware that allows objects and their procedural counterparts to coexist in a distributed transaction. OTS conforms to the X/Open DTP Reference Model and defines the integration of transactional subsystems using X/Open APIs. OTS supports both flat and nested transaction models. Detailed explanation of these models can be found in Chapter 2.

### Overview

Figure 1.4 illustrates OMG's representation of a distributed transaction processing model. A client begins a transaction by initiating a request to an object defined by OTS. OTS associates the client thread with the transaction's context. Transaction context uniquely identifies the transaction. Once the transaction context is established, the client issues

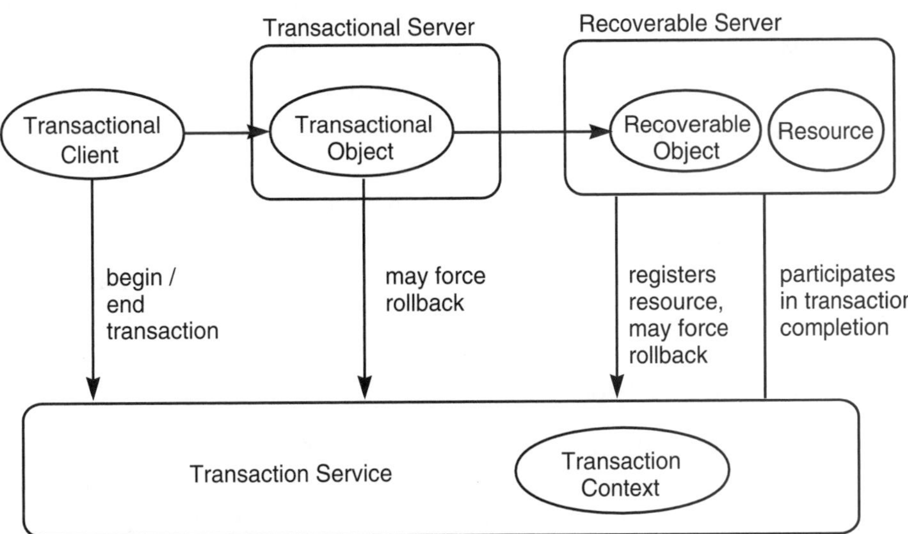


**Figure 1.4** Object Transaction Service entities.

requests to transactional and nontransactional objects that are implicitly associated with the client's transaction. Transactional objects are associated with persistent objects, and any changes applied to these persistent objects will survive failures and conform to ACID properties. The changes that are applied to nontransactional objects may not survive a failure even though they are made within the scope of a transaction. The client ends the transaction by sending another request to the object defined by OTS. The changes that were applied within the scope of this transaction are made permanent if there were no failures. If there were failures, the changes are rolled back.

The scenario just described uses the implicit propagation of the transaction context. This means that along with the client's request, the transaction context is automatically propagated to the recipient object so that any work performed by the object is associated with the same transaction. OTS is flexible and offers a variation of this scheme called *explicit propagation* whereby a client can explicitly pass the transaction context as a parameter in its request.

The following section briefly defines the transaction service entities: transactional client, transactional server, and the recoverable server.

**Transactional client** begins and ends a transaction.

**Transactional server** hosts transactional objects, which are not involved in the completion (e.g., commit request) of a transaction but may force the rollback of a transaction. The changes that were made to these objects within the scope of the transaction are not persistent and hence will not survive a failure. A middle-tier server, which houses the business logic, is an example of the transactional server.

**Recoverable server** hosts recoverable objects and resources, which are involved with the completion of a transaction. A recoverable object is also a transactional object and is directly associated with the recoverable data. A recoverable object implements an object called *Resource* and registers it with the transaction service to participate in the transaction service protocols such as two-phase commit. Typically, you, as an application programmer, would not implement a resource. Resource implementations are typically provided by the OTS vendor.

OTS defines nine key interfaces that help create, execute, and manage distributed CORBA transactions. They are *Current*, *TransactionFactory*, *Control*, *Terminator*, *Coordinator*, *Resource*, *SubtransactionAwareResource*, *RecoveryCoordinator*, *and TransactionalObject*. We have provided a brief description of the most important interfaces that we would need in the following paragraph. For detailed description of all interfaces, please refer to Chapter 3, "Understanding the CORBA Object Transaction Service."

Current is a pseudo CORBA object that provides all the transaction primitives required for an application. Using Current is the easiest way to program CORBA transactions. A client can begin and commit/rollback the transaction using this interface. The transaction context is implicitly propagated by the ORB to all transactional objects during the client's invocation. A client thread's involvement with a transaction can be controlled by a suspend or resume operation. The Control interface represents the transaction and provides handles for the Terminator and Coordinator interfaces, which control the life cycle of the transaction. The Terminator interface provides operations to commit or roll back the transaction. The Coordinator interface is one of the main interfaces and aids the recoverable objects to coordinate their participation in the transaction. It provides operations to get information about the transaction, operations to register themselves with the transaction service, and operations to create subtransactions. The TransactionFactory interface can be used to create new transactions and recreate a transaction from an imported context. Create and recreate operations return the Control object, which represents the newly created transaction. The Resource interface defines operations so that a recoverable object can participate in a two-phase commit protocol orchestrated by the transaction service.

Chapters 3 and 4 have complete descriptions of the OTS specification and comprehensive examples, respectively. We would like to start you up in this chapter with a simple money transfer example to demonstrate the use of the OTS and to introduce the concepts. We define IDL interfaces for the ATM and the account, and implement those interfaces in the client and server programs. Then we run the example and explore how the ACID properties of our transaction could be provided in different scenarios.

## The Money Transfer Example with OTS/JTS

We use the money transfer example to illustrate the use of OTS. We have specified the bank operations as IDL interfaces. The implementation details of both the client and server programs are presented later in this section. We have chosen Java as the implementation language.

### *Interface Specification*

The money transfer example has two major components: accounts and ATM, which are defined with IDL interfaces. In this example implementation, both accounts and ATM are transactional objects. Furthermore, the ATM is the transaction originator and the accounts are the resources. We assume, for simplicity and illustrative purposes, that the object, which implements the interface, acts as a resource, too. Typically, the resources would be provided by another component such as an XA-compliant database. At the time of this writing there was no JDBC-2 driver, which includes XA functionality, available.

We specify the Account interface, which implements two operations: credit() and debit(). Both operations have a float parameter, which determines the amount to be credited and debited. The debit() operation raises the exception InsufficientFunds. (See Figure 1.5.)

The interface Account inherits from CosTransactions::TransactionalObject, which makes it a transactional object. The interface CosTransactions::TransactionalObject does not define any types or operations. It is a marker interface. However, an implementation of the interface adds functionality.

The interface Account also inherits from the interface CosTransactions::Resource, which defines operations for the two-phase-commit protocol such as commit(), rollback(), and so forth.

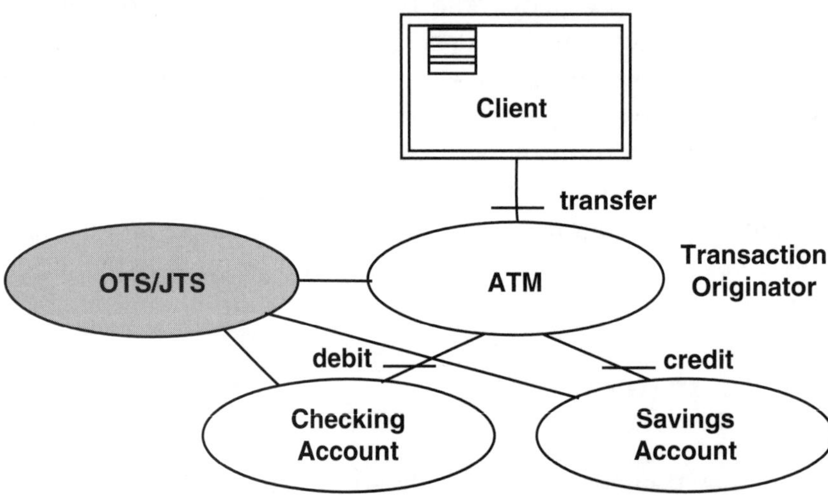


**Figure 1.5** Money transfer with OTS/JTS.

```
#include "CosTransactions.idl"

module transfer {

 exception InsufficientFunds{};

 interface Account :
  ::CosTransactions::Resource,
  ::CosTransactions::TransactionalObject {

  void credit( in float amount );

  void debit( in float amount )
   raises( InsufficientFunds );
 };
```

The interface ATM defines the operation transfer(), which has three parameters. The first two parameters are of the interface type Account, which specifies the source and destination accounts for the money transfer. The third parameter is of type float, which specifies the amount to be transferred between the accounts. The operation raises the exception InsufficientFunds.

```
interface ATM {

  void transfer( in Account source, in Account destination, in float amount )
   raises( InsufficientFunds );
 };
};
```

We assume to have a base directory *base* for all of the examples in the book. The IDL file is in the file *base*/idl/chapter1/transfer-ots.idl. All implementation classes are in the directory *base*/classes. We now compile the IDL interface. We use Visibroker for Java's *idl2java* compiler. Flags for IDL compilers from other vendors may vary.

```
base/classes> idl2java -I../idl -idl2package ::CosTransactions
org.omg.CosTransactions -idl2package ::transfer
vogel.transaction.chapter1.transfer ../idl/chapter1/transfer-ots.idl
```

The flags have the following meanings:

**-I *path*** looks for include files in the directory specified by *path*.

**-idl2package *module package*** maps the IDL module *module* to the Java package *package*.

The idl2java compiler generates Java classes and interfaces as defined by the IDL/Java mapping in the package `vogel.transaction.chapter1.ots.transfer`.

### Implementation

We implement the interfaces and the client and server program in the package `vogel.transaction.chapter1.ots.transferImpl`.

We have simplified the implementation for demonstration purposes. The example demonstrates some simple in-memory rollback. A real implementation of the resource interface is responsible for ensuring the durability of the transaction; that is, persistifying the effects of the transaction. This is typically achieved by a database with a transactional, in most cases XA-compliant, interface. Completely implementing the Resource interface is a non-trivial task, as there are so many failure states to consider from which the application must be able to recover.

In the implementation shown next we just keep the values in memory but ensure most of the other transactional properties. The advantage of doing so is that we can keep the example simple and can also explain the mechanisms of the two-phase commit protocol, which ensures the transaction properties.

In Chapter 3, we explain how to achieve durability through database integration via the XA interface, and in Chapter 4, "Programming with OTS," we demonstrate the usage with a comprehensive example.

#### Implementing the Account Interface

The account interface is implemented in the class `AccountImpl`. We use the inheritance approach; hence, the implementation class extends from the implementation base class `_AccountImplBase`.

```
package vogel.transaction.chapter1.ots.transferImpl;

import vogel.transaction.util.*;
import vogel.transaction.chapter1.ots.transfer.*;

import org.omg.CORBA.*;
import org.omg.CORBA.ORBPackage.*;
import org.omg.CosTransactions.*;

public class AccountImpl extends _AccountImplBase {
```

We define the private variable balance, which determines the state of the object. Additionally, we have private variables for the ORB and the name of the objects. The class `Lock` is a utility class for locking the access to the object during the transactions and is explained later in the chapter.

```
private float balance;
private float newBalance;
private float amount;
private boolean credit;
private ORB orb;
private String name;
private Lock lock;
```

In the constructor we call the superclass constructor with the name as the argument, assign the arguments to the corresponding local variables, and create a new `Lock` instance.

```
public AccountImpl( ORB orb, String name, float deposit ) {

  super( name );
  this.name = name;
  this.orb = orb;

  balance = deposit;
  lock = new Lock();
}
```

In the `credit()` method we first lock the access to the object. Then we memorize what we are doing, so that we can manage a possible rollback of the activity. We usually release the lock in when the transactions terminate; that is in the commit or rollback operation.

```
public synchronized void credit( float amount ) {

  try {

    // lock account
    lock.lock();

    // memorize current activitity
    this.amount = amount;
    credit = true;
```

A resource must be registered with the Transaction Service. Since we have our own resource implementation, we have to take care of the registration of the resource with the Transaction Service. First we obtain the `Current` object using the standard CORBA bootstrap mechanism. From `Current`, we get the `Control` object, and from it the `Coordinator` object. Using the `Coordinator` we register our resource (remember that we inherited the Resource IDL interface in the interface specification).

```
        // obtain current object
        org.omg.CORBA.Object obj =
          orb.resolve_initial_references("TransactionCurrent");
        Current current = CurrentHelper.narrow( obj );
        if( current == null ) {
          System.err.println(
            "Accont::credit: current is not of expected type");
          System.exit( 1 );
        }

        // get control and coordinator
        Control control = current.get_control();
        Coordinator coordinator = control.get_coordinator();

        // register resource
        RecoveryCoordinator recCoordinator =
          coordinator.register_resource( this );
```

Finally, we can implement the business logic; in our case, we credit the amount to the balance of the account.

```
        newBalance = balance + amount;
      }
      catch( Exception ex ) {
        System.err.println(
          "Account " + name + "::credit: exception: " + ex );
      }
    }
```

The implementation of the debit operation follows the same pattern: acquire the lock, memorize activity, register the resource, and implement the business logic.

```
    public synchronized void debit( float amount )
      throws InsufficientFunds {

      try {

        // lock account
        lock.lock();

        // memorize current activitity
        this.amount = amount;
        credit = false;
```

```
        // obtain current object
        org.omg.CORBA.Object obj =
          orb.resolve_initial_references("TransactionCurrent");
        Current current = CurrentHelper.narrow( obj );
        if( current == null ) {
          System.err.println(
            "Accont::debit: current is not of expected type");
          System.exit( 1 );
        }

        Control control = current.get_control();
        Coordinator coordinator = control.get_coordinator();
        RecoveryCoordinator recCoordinator =
          coordinator.register_resource( this );
```

The implementation of the `debit()` method is slightly more complex than the implementation of `credit()`. If the amount to be debited is larger that the current account balance, we unlock the account and throw the exception `InsufficientFunds`.

```
        if( amount > balance ) {
          System.out.println("insufficient funds");
          lock.unlock();
          throw new InsufficientFunds();
        }
        newBalance = balance - amount;
      }
      catch( Exception e ) {
        System.err.println(
          "Account " + name + "::debit: exception: " + e );
      }
    }
```

This implementation delegates the responsibility for the correct transaction termination to the transaction originator. Alternatively, you could mark the transaction for rollback in the previous code segment, just before you throw the exception.

Now we implement the operations defined in the Resource interface. As mentioned earlier, the implementation is usually taken care of by the OTS vendor, which gives you a specialized solution including the integration to a database. We chose to implement the Resource interface manually to demonstrate what usually happens behind the scenes.

All these methods are invoked by the Transaction Service, which is managing the two-phase commit. In the `prepare()` method, we don't have anything to do. We return `Vote.VoteCommit`, which indicates that this resource is prepared to commit the transaction. In the case of an unchanged balance we return `Vote.VoteReadOnly`. Persistent resource implementations write the new state in a temporary data store. If this fails, the resource votes `Vote.VoteRollback`.

```
public Vote prepare() {
  System.out.println("Resource " + name + " : prepare()");
  if( balance == newBalance )
    return Vote.VoteReadOnly;
  return Vote.VoteCommit;
}
```

The `rollback()` method reestablishes the original state of the object. Since we haven't changed the balance state variable, we don't have to do anything. The rollback marks the end of the transaction, so we unlock the object.

```
public void rollback() {
  // remove data from temporary storage
  System.out.println("Resource " + name + " : rollback()");
  System.out.println("Resource " + name +
    " : original balance restored: $" + balance);
  lock.unlock();
  System.out.println("Resource: " + name + " account unlocked");
}
```

During the `commit()` method we actually update the state of the object. We also unlock the objects.

```
public void commit() {
  // move data to final storage
  System.out.println("Resource " + name + " : commit()");
  balance = newBalance;
  lock.unlock();
  System.out.println("Resource: " + name + " account unlocked");
}
```

The method `commit_one_phase()` is called by the Transaction Service if there is only a single resource involved in the transaction; hence, a single-phase commit is sufficient. In our implementation we call `prepare()`, and if successful, immediately `commit()`.

```
public void commit_one_phase() {
  // store data immediately at final destination
  System.out.println("Resource " + name +
    " : commit_one_phase()");
  if(prepare() == Vote.VoteCommit) {
    commit();
```

```
    }
    lock.unlock();
    System.out.println("Resource: " + name + " account unlocked");
  }
```

The `forget()` method is called by the Transaction Service to instruct the resources which have heuristically made a decision to commit or roll back a transaction. We do not use it in our example.

```
  public void forget() {
        System.out.println("Resource " + name + " : forget()");
  }
}
```

### Implementing the Lock

In the account implementation we have used a lock to serialize the access to the object. The lock is implemented in the class `vogel.transaction.util.Lock`. The lock is essentially a `Boolean` variable, which indicates if an object is locked or not.

Here we show a simplified implementation of a lock. It is working fine for our specific example but it prevents you, for example, from invoking the credit() operation more than once within the scope of a transaction. If you have a more complex application, you may need a sophisticated implementation of the lock.

```
package vogel.transaction.util;

public class Lock {

  private boolean locked;

  public Lock() {
    locked = false;
  }
```

The `lock()` method sets the `lock` variable to `true`. If the object is already locked, it waits for a Java event notification, which is caused by the `unlock()` method using `notifyAll()`. The `unlock()` method also sets the lock variable back to false.

```
  synchronized public void lock() {

    while(locked) {
      try {
        this.wait();
      }
```

```
        catch(InterruptedException e) {
        }
      }
      locked = true;
    }

    synchronized public void unlock() {
      locked = false;
      this.notifyAll();
    }
  }
```

#### Implementing the ATM Interface

The ATM object is the transaction originator. It is implemented in the class `ATMImpl`, which inherits from the implementation base class `_ATMImplBase`.

```
  package vogel.transaction.chapter1.ots.transferImpl;

  import vogel.transaction.chapter1.ots.transfer.*;

  import org.omg.CORBA.*;
  import org.omg.CORBA.ORBPackage.*;
  import org.omg.CosTransactions.*;

  public class ATMImpl extends _ATMImplBase {

    private ORB orb;

    public ATMImpl( ORB orb ) {
      this.orb = orb;
    }
```

In the constructor of the ATM object, we just assign the reference to the ORB to a private variable. We only have to implement the transfer method. Since the ATM is acting as the transaction coordinator, we have to obtain a transaction `Current` object, which allows us to begin and terminate the transaction. We obtain the transactional `Current` object via the ORB bootstrap mechanism.

```
    public void transfer(
      Account source, Account destination, float amount )
      throws InsufficientFunds {

   Current current = null;

      try {
        // obtain current object
```

```
    org.omg.CORBA.Object obj =
      orb.resolve_initial_references("TransactionCurrent");
    current = CurrentHelper.narrow( obj );
    if( current == null ) {
      System.err.println("current is not of expected type");
      System.err.println("exiting ...");
      System.exit( 1 );
    }
```

Now we start a new transaction, by invoking `begin()` on the current. Then we invoke the business methods on the source and destination account object. As failures are indicated by exceptions we can go ahead and commit the transaction.

```
    current.begin();

    source.debit( amount );
    destination.credit( amount );

    // commit the transaction
    current.commit( true );
  }
```

There are a number of different exceptions that can be raised and must be handled differently. The exception `InsufficientFunds` is raised by the debit operation and requires to roll back the transaction as there are not sufficient funds available at the source account to complete the transaction.

The exception `InvalidName` can be raised when obtaining the current, that is before the transaction is started. Other exceptions of type `UserException` are raised by the transaction service itself. Finally, in the case of a system exception, we try to roll back the transaction.

```
  catch( InsufficientFunds isf ) {
    try {
      current.rollback();
    }
    catch( NoTransaction nt ) {
      System.err.println("No transaction - give up: " + nt );
      System.exit( 1 );
    }
    throw( isf );
  }
  catch( InvalidName in ) {
    System.err.println("Initialization failure: " + in );
    System.exit( 1 );
  }
  catch( UserException ue ) {
```

```
        System.err.println("transactional failure - give up: " + ue );
        System.exit( 1 );
      }
      catch( SystemException se ) {
        System.err.println(
          "system exception - rollback transaction: " + se );
        try {
          current.rollback();
        }
        catch( Exception e ) {
          System.err.println(
            "Exception during rollback - give up: " + nt );
          System.exit( 1 );
        }
    }
  }
}
```

### Implementing the Server

The server is implemented in the class `Server`. It provides the `main()` method in which we initialize the ORB and the object adapter, create `Account` objects, and eventually wait for invocations. The only important difference from the usual CORBA servers is the initialization of the ORB with the Transaction Service.

```
package vogel.transaction.chapter1.ots.transferImpl;

import vogel.transaction.chapter1.ots.transfer.*;
import java.util.*;
import org.omg.CORBA.*;
import org.omg.CORBA.ORBPackage.*;
import org.omg.CosTransactions.*;

public class Server {

  public static void main(String[] args) {

    if( args.length < 2 ) {
      System.err.println(
        "Usage: vbjvogel.transaction.chapter1.ots.transferImpl.Server "
        + "<account> <account> ... ");
        System.exit( 1 );
      }

    try {
      Properties orbProps = new Properties();
      orbProps.put("ORBservices",
        "com.visigenic.services.CosTransactions");
```

```
      ORB orb = ORB.init( args, orbProps );
      BOA boa = orb.BOA_init();
      Random random = new Random();

       for( int i = 0; i < args.length; i++ ) {
         float deposit = random.nextFloat() * 100;
         AccountImpl accountImpl = new AccountImpl(
           orb, args[i], deposit );
         boa.obj_is_ready( (Account)accountImpl );
       }
       boa.impl_is_ready();
     }
        catch(SystemException se) {
          System.err.println(se);
     }
   }
}
```

### Implementing the Client

The client is implemented in the class `Client`, which acts as the transaction originator. It provides a `main()` method, which is just an execution shell for the ATM object. The ATM object could be wrapped into a servlet or could be implemented as a middle-tier server invoked by an applet and other desktop clients.

```
package vogel.transaction.chapter1.ots.transferImpl;

import vogel.transaction.chapter1.ots.transfer.*;
import java.util.*;
import org.omg.CORBA.*;
import org.omg.CORBA.ORBPackage.*;
import org.omg.CosTransactions.*;

public class Client {

  public static void main(String[] args) {

    if( args.length != 3 ) {
      System.err.println(
        "Usage: vbjvogel.transaction.chapter1.ots.transferImpl.Client "
        + "<source account> <destination account> <ammount>");
        System.exit( 1 );
       }
```

We initialize the ORB and the object adapter, and create an instance of the ATM object, which we register with the object adapter. Then we locate account objects by their name using Visibroker's OSAgent-based directory services. We also convert the command-line argument for the amount to be transferred into a float. Now we can invoke the transfer operation on the ATM object. If an exception is raised, we print out its content.

```
      try {
        Properties orbProps = new Properties();
        orbProps.put("ORBservices",
          "com.visigenic.services.CosTransactions");
           ORB orb = ORB.init( args, orbProps );
           BOA boa = orb.BOA_init();

        ATMImpl atmImpl = new ATMImpl( orb );
        boa.obj_is_ready( (ATM)atmImpl );

        Account source = AccountHelper.bind( orb, args[0] );
        Account destination = AccountHelper.bind( orb, args[1] );
        float amount = Float.valueOf( args[2] ).floatValue();

        atmImpl.transfer( source, destination, amount );
      }
      catch(InsufficientFunds nsf) {
        System.err.println(nsf);
      }
      catch(SystemException se) {
        System.err.println(se);
      }
    }
  }
```

## *Running the Example*

We now run the example in different scenarios to demonstrate the capabilities of the Object Transaction Service. First we start up the infrastructure and a number of account objects in different servers. Then we have clients making successful transfers and a transfer that exceeds the funds available. Finally, we create a situation in which the infrastructure fails (the source account object crashes during the transaction) and see how OTS handles the situation.

### Starting Servers

The starting of services is ORB and OTS product specific. For Visibroker and ITS, the following processes must be started:

- Visibroker OSAgent:
  `Windows> osagent -C`
  `Unix > osagent &`

- Visibroker ITS Transaction Server:
  ```
  Windows> ots
  Unix> ots &
  ```

Now we can start the Server with the Account objects, each command-line argument is the name of an account object to be created. We create a savings, a checking, and a credit card account. The initial balances are randomly created by the server.

```
vbj vogel.transaction.chapter1.ots.transferImpl.Server checking savings
credit

account checking created
initial deposit: $40.15
account savings created
initial deposit: $14.33
account credit created
initial deposit: $96.72
```

#### Normal Transfer—Commit

We start a client and transfer $10 from the checking to the savings account. We can follow the log printed by the client.

```
vbj vogel.transaction.chapter1.ots.transferImpl.Client checking savings
10

resolve transaction current
begin transaction
transaction status: StatusActive
debited
credited
commit transaction
transaction committed
```

At the same time, the server creates the following log:

```
Account::debit: resolve transaction current
Account::debit: status of the transaction: StatusActive
Account checking::debit: get control
Account checking::debit: get coordinator
Account checking::debit: register resource (Account) with ITS
Account checking::debit: resource registered
 debit $10.0
 new balance is $30.15
Account::credit: resolve transaction current
Account::credit: status of the transaction: StatusActive
Account savings::credit: get control
Account savings::credit: get coordinator
Account savings::credit: register resource (Account) with ITS
```

```
 credit $10.0
 new balance is $24.33
Resource checking : prepare()
Resource savings : prepare()
Resource checking : commit()
Resource: checking account unlocked
Resource savings : commit()
Resource: savings account unlocked
```

#### Insufficient Funds—Rollback

Now we try a transaction of $100, which results, as expected, in an exception: insufficient funds. The client is started and produces the following log:

```
vbj vogel.transaction.chapter1.ots.transferImpl.Client checking savings
100

resolve transaction current
begin transaction
transaction status: StatusActive
exception InsufficientFunds{}
```

The server logs looks like this:

```
Account::debit: resolve transaction current
Account::debit: status of the transaction: StatusActive
Account checking::debit: get control
Account checking::debit: get coordinator
Account checking::debit: register resource (Account) with ITS
Account checking::debit: resource registered
insufficient funds
Resource: checking account unlocked
Resource checking : rollback()
Resource checking : original balance restored: $30.15
Resource: checking account unlocked
```

#### Account Crash—Rollback

To demonstrate the crash, we start two servers, one with a checking account and the other with a savings account.

```
vbj vogel.transaction.chapter1.ots.transferImpl.Server checking credit &
vbj vogel.transaction.chapter1.ots.transferImpl.Server savings mortgage &
```

Now we start the client as before. However, we kill the server, which is hosting the checking account during the transaction. As we see in the client log, the ATM object invokes the debit and the credit operation successfully and tries to commit the transaction. During the commit, the checking account disappears and the transaction server rolls back the transaction and raises the system exception `org.omg.CORBA.TRANSACTION_ROLLEDBACK`.

```
vbj vogel.transaction.chapter1.ots.transferImpl.Client checking savings
10
resolve transaction current
begin transaction
transaction status: StatusActive
debited
credited
commit transaction
system exception - rollback transaction:
org.omg.CORBA.TRANSACTION_ROLLEDBACK[completed=NO]
```

The log of the server with checking accounts gets to the point where the debit invocation is completed—then it gets hit by the <Ctrl>C.

```
account checking created
initial deposit: $88.93
account credit created
initial deposit: $17.54
Account::debit: resolve transaction current
Account::debit: status of the transaction: StatusActive
Account checking::debit: get control
Account checking::debit: get coordinator
Account checking::debit: register resource (Account) with ITS
Account checking::debit: resource registered
 debit $10.0
 new balance is $78.93
```

The log of the other server, which is hosting the savings account, shows that the debit operation has also been successfully completed. Then the transaction server invokes `rollback()` at the savings account, which restores the old balance and unlocks the account.

```
account savings created
initial deposit: $15.12
account morgage created
initial deposit: $0.09
Accont::credit: resolve transaction current
Accont::credit: status of the transaction: StatusActive
Account savings::credit: get control
Account savings::credit: get coordinator
Account savings::credit: register resource (Account) with ITS
 credit $10.0
 new balance is $25.12
Resource savings : rollback()
```

```
Resource savings : original balance restored: $15.12
Resource: savings account unlocked
```

## Integrating OTS with Databases and Legacy Transaction Systems

Enterprise systems are rarely implemented from scratch. Typically, existing transaction systems have to be integrated into a new application. Furthermore, a pure implementation of OTS is of limited use as it only deals with the management of distributed transactions and leaves open the implementation of resources. To be successful in the enterprise market, OTS and vendors, who provide OTS implementations, must address both of these issues.

The key to integration is the X/Open DTP Reference Model as introduced earlier in the chapter. It identifies the concepts, roles, and protocols for distributed transaction processing. In fact, most of the commercially relevant databases implement an XA API as defined by the X/Open specification.

The OTS specification acknowledges the importance of DTP specifications and explicitly addresses the model interoperability. In short, OTS allows for importing transactions from the X/Open domain into the OTS domain and vice versa. Figure 1.6 illustrates the integration between OTS and X/Open. The details of the integration are explained in Chapter 3.

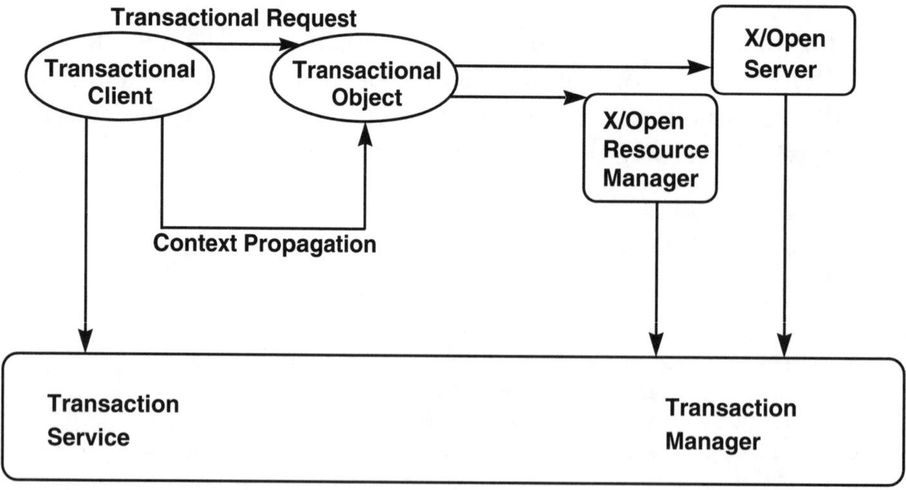


**Figure 1.6** OTS and X/Open DTP.

Additionally, there are transactional subsystems, which do not comply with the X/Open DTP standard. Hence, the integration cannot be addressed on the OTS specification level. However, OTS implementers can extend a pure OTS implementation and support the integration of proprietary transactional interfaces. Possibly the most important proprietary transaction systems are CICS and IMS, which are used for the majority of mainframe-based transaction systems. Since this integration is of a proprietary nature and differs from vendor to vendor, we do not provide details in this book. Instead, you are referred to the manuals of the various product offerings.

## Distributed Transactions and Java

Java is not only a programming language, but also a platform. As a consequence of this approach, Java addresses key features of programming in a wider sense, including distributed transactions. Sun has defined, in conjunction with leading software companies and end users, a number of specifications related to the distributed transaction domain.

**Java Transaction Service.** The Java Transaction Service (JTS) is the IDL/Java mapping applied to OTS. The service is provided in the packages `org.omg.CosTransactions` and `org.omg.CosTSPortability`. We have already covered JTS in the OTS section and have shown the ATM example using OTS/JTS.

**Java Transaction API.** The Java Transaction API (JTA) is a high-level application-oriented and Java-specific transaction API. JTA is provided by the package `javax.transaction`. The package contains an interface definition `UserTransaction` and a number of exception classes, which are thrown by the methods defined in the interface. The interface defines basic transaction primitives:

**void begin()** creates a new transaction and associates it with the current thread.

**void commit()** completes the transaction associated with the current thread.

**int getStatus()** obtains the status of the transaction associated with the current thread.

**void rollback()** rolls back the transaction associated with the current thread.

**void setRollbackOnly( )** modifies the transaction associated with the current thread so that the transaction must be rolled back.

**void setTransactionOut** (in seconds) modifies the time-out value of the transaction associated with the current thread.

**JDBC-2.** JDBC-2 adds, among other features, two-phase commit capabilities based on XA to the JDBC specification.

**Enterprise JavaBeans.** Enterprise JavaBeans defines a Java component model for the server side, which includes distributed transaction processing. Details of the EJB specification and examples are given in this chapter and in Chapters 4 and 6.

## Enterprise JavaBeans

Enterprise JavaBeans is a higher-level component-based architecture for distributed business applications that use the transaction system's lower-level APIs as shown in Figure 1.7. EJB aims to simplify the development process of enterprise systems in Java. Enterprise JavaBeans are defined in a specification developed and edited by Sun Microsystems. This book is based on version 1 of the specification.

### EJB Roles

The approach for simplifying the development of complex business systems is based on dividing the overall development process into different tasks and associating different roles with different tasks. EJB specifies the following six roles, which address the infrastructure, application development, deployment, and operations issues. Since many of these tasks are taken on by infrastructure vendors, the application programmer's job becomes simpler.

#### *Infrastructure*

An **EJB Server Provider** is typically a vendor with expertise in distributed infrastructures and services. The server provider implements a platform, which facilitates the development of distributed applications and provides a runtime environment for them.

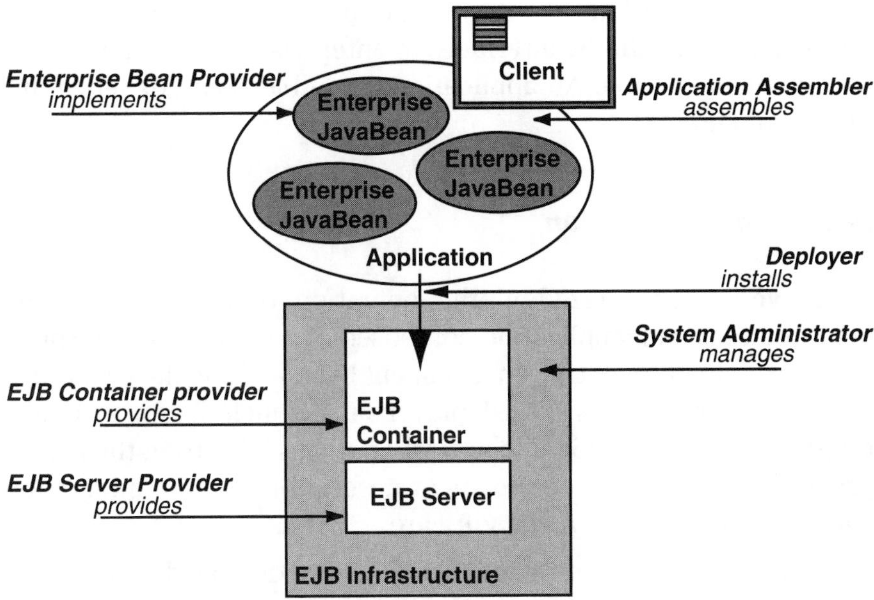


**Figure 1.7** Enterprise JavaBeans.

An **EJB Container Provider** is an expert in distributed systems, transactions, and security. A container is a runtime system for one or multiple enterprise beans. It provides the glue between enterprise beans and the EJB server. A container is both, prefabricated code as well as a tool, which generates code specific for a particular enterprise bean. A container also provides tools for the deployment of an enterprise bean and hooks into the application for monitoring and management.

## *Application*

An **Enterprise Bean Provider** is typically an expert in the application domain; for example, in the financial or telecommunications industry. The bean provider implements the business task without being concerned about the distribution, transaction, security, and other nonbusiness-specific aspects of the application.

An **Application Assembler** composes an application from various prefabricated building blocks (that is, enterprise beans) and adds other components such as GUI clients, applets, and servlets to complete the application. While composing an application, an assembler is only concerned with the interfaces to enterprise beans, but not with their implementation. An application assembler is an expert in his or her domain.

### *Deployment and Operation*

A **Deployer** is specialized in the operation of applications. The deployer adapts an application composed of a number of enterprise beans to a target operation environment by modifying the properties of the enterprise beans. The deployer's tasks include, for example, the setting of transaction and security policies by setting the appropriate properties in the deployment descriptor, and the integration with enterprise management software.

A **System Administrator** is concerned with a deployed application. The administrator monitors the running application and takes appropriate actions in the event of abnormal behavior of the application. Typically, an administrator uses enterprise management tools that are connected to the application by the deployer through the hooks provided by the container.

## EJB Design Patterns and Naming Conventions

There are three major design patterns for building object-based multi-tier distributed systems: *stateless server* approach, *session-oriented* approach, and *persistent object* approach.

The stateless server is an object, which provides certain functionality through its operations without keeping conversational state. That means clients cannot refer to state information provided in previous operations on the same object.

The session-oriented design creates an object in the middle tier, a session, which is acting as an agent for the client. Typically, the lifetime of a session object is determined by the client and the server program that is hosting it. A client can remove the object once it is finished with it. The server can time-out a session object, and when the server terminates, references to the session object may become invalid.

The persistent object design model wraps a certain piece of data (stored in a database) and provides operations to manipulate this data.

Persistent objects are shared among multiple clients. The lifetime of a persistent object is determined by the lifetime of the data storage, which contains its data.

The EJB specification takes these three design patterns and defines them as *stateless session bean*, *stateful session bean*, and *entity bean*. The session bean is modeled after the session-oriented design approach; the entity bean after persistent object design. For each design, it defines a number of interfaces and naming conventions, which we explain in detail later in the chapter.

We use the money transfer example again to illustrate the use of these design patterns, Details about the Enterprise JavaBeans specification and a comprehensive example are given in Chapters 5 and 6, respectively.

## The Money Transfer Example with EJB

We now return to the money transfer example and explain how to implement this example with EJB. To demonstrate session objects as well as entity objects we have decided to implement the ATM as a stateful session bean and the Account as an entity bean as shown in Figure 1.8.

### *Providing an Enterprise JavaBean*

An enterprise bean provider is concerned with the following three components:

- The **Home interface** specifies operations to create, find, and remove enterprise beans. It plays a similar role to a factory object in the common object and CORBA design pattern.
- The **Remote interface** specifies the business methods, which are provided by the enterprise bean.
- The **implementation class** implements the functionality defined in the Home and in the Remote interface.

#### Account as Entity Bean

First we define the Home interface of the Account entity bean. The home is a public Java interface, which extends the `javax.ejb.EJBHome`. We declare a single `create()` method, which returns an Account interface. That is the remote interface of our Account entity bean as we see in the following code. We also define the method `findByPrimaryKey()`, which must be provided by home interfaces for entity beans. As entity beans are usually the runtime representation of a certain data stored in

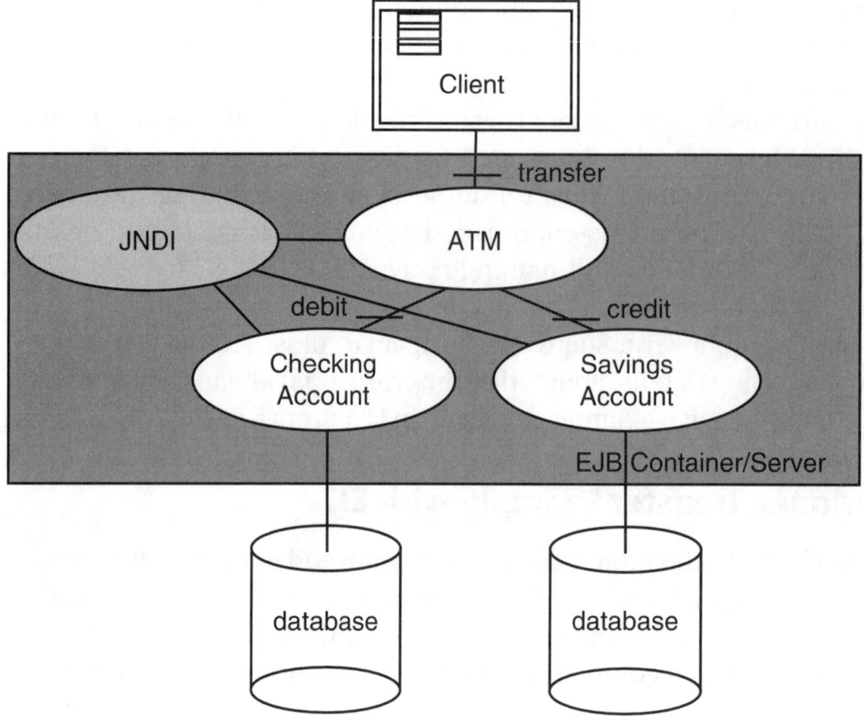


**Figure 1.8** Money transfer with EJB.

a database—for example, a row in a table—this method is the default mechanism to access the data. The Home interface can have many create and find methods, including find methods, which return an enumeration of entity beans.

Create and find methods must throw the exception `java.rmi.RemoteException`, and usually they throw the exceptions `javax.ejb.CreateException`, and `javax.ejb.FinderException`, respectively.

```
package vogel.transaction.chapter1.ejb;

public interface AccountHome extends javax.ejb.EJBHome {

  Account create( String accountId )
    throws java.rmi.RemoteException, javax.ejb.CreateException;

  Account findByPrimaryKey( String key )
    throws java.rmi.RemoteException, javax.ejb.FinderException;

}
```

Then we define the Remote interface of the Account entity bean. The remote interface is a public Java interface, which extends the `javax.ejb.EJBObject`. We declare the business methods `debit()` and `credit()`. The business methods of the remote interface must be declared public and must throw the exception `java.rmi.RemoteException`. Additionally, they can throw application-specific exceptions.

```
package vogel.transaction.chapter1.ejb;

import javax.ejb.*;
import java.rmi.RemoteException;

public interface Account extends EJBObject {

  public void credit( float amount )
    throws RemoteException;

  public void debit( float amount )
    throws RemoteException, InsufficientFundsException;

}
```

Now we can provide the implementation of the Account session bean. It is important to note that the implementation is not in an "implements" or "extends" relationship with the remote and home interface. Instead, there is a whole set of rather complex rules and naming conventions, which provide the mapping between interfaces and implementation. The container glues together the interfaces and the implementation, and enforces these rules and conventions. They are explained in detail in Chapter 4.

Entity beans come in two flavors with respect to handling the persistence of the bean. The persistence can be handled by the bean implementation or by the container. We have chosen for this example the bean-managed persistence. That means we have to implement the code to create, find, remove, load, and store entity beans. Our example uses a relational database and JDBC as the access mechanism. However, other data stores, for example object databases, are also possible.

We implement the Account session bean in the class `AccountBean`, which implements the interface `javax.ejb.EntityBean`. An entity bean must also have an `EntityContext` variable, which provides access to the deployment information (provided by the deployer). We also declare a private variable balance, which holds the state of the Account bean and a private method, which returns the account number, which is the primary key of the entity bean. The primary key is held in the entity context.

```
package vogel.transaction.chapter1.ejb;

import javax.ejb.*;
import java.sql.*;
import java.rmi.RemoteException;

public class AccountBean
  implements EntityBean {

  private EntityContext entityContext;

  private float balance;

  private String accountId() {
    return (String) entityContext.getPrimaryKey();
  }
```

The implementation of the business methods is only concerned with manipulating the state of the bean; in our case, the balance. The implementation is straightforward. The only case where the application logic forces the rollback of a transaction is when the amount to be transferred is larger than the current balance. We leave the transaction control again to the client, the transaction originator. We just threw an application-level exception. Alternatively, we could mark the transaction for rollback by invoking the method `setRollbackOnly()` on the entity context. The client would then see the exception `javax.transaction.TransactionRolledBackException`.

```
  public void credit( float amount ) {

    balance = balance + amount;
    return;
  }

  public void debit( float amount )
    throws InsufficientFundsException {

    if( balance >= amount ) {
      balance = balance - amount;
    }
    else {
      throw new InsufficientFundsException();
    }
    return;
  }
```

The `findbyPrimaryKey()` method declared in the Home interface is implemented by a corresponding `ejbFindByPrimaryKey()` method. The parameter lists of the two methods must match. The implementation method, however, returns a primary key instead of an object reference. The implementation of the method is based on a SQL select query. We make a sanity check of the result set and return the primary key.

```
public String ejbFindByPrimaryKey( String accountId )
    throws RemoteException, FinderException {

    try {
      Connection connection = getConnection();
      Statement statement = connection.createStatement();
      ResultSet resultSet = statement.executeQuery(
        "select balance from accounts where id = '" +
        accountId + "'" );
      if( resultSet.next() ) {
        balance = resultSet.getFloat(1);
        if( resultSet.next() ) {
          statement.close();
          connection.close();
          throw new RemoteException(
            "There is more than one entry for account "
            + accountId() );
        }
        statement.close();
        connection.close();
      }
      else {
        statement.close();
        connection.close();
        throw new FinderException( "Account id doesn't exist" );
      }
    }
    catch( SQLException e ) {
      throw new RemoteException( "DBAccess Error", e );
    }
    return accountId;
  }
```

Similarly, we implement `ejbCreate()`, which corresponds to the Home interface's `create()` method. This time the implementation is based on a SQL insert. Again we return the primary key.

```
public String ejbCreate( String accountId )
    throws RemoteException, CreateException {

    balance = 0;
    try {
```

```
        Connection connection = getConnection();
        Statement statement = connection.createStatement();
        statement.executeUpdate(
          "insert into accounts values( '" + accountId + "', 0.0 )" );
        statement.close();
        connection.close();
      }
      catch( Exception e ) {
        throw new RemoteException( "DBAccess Error", e );
      }
      return accountId;
    }
```

Note that you also have to provide a method `ejbPostCreate()` for each `create()` method declared in the home interface. Here we only provide a trivial implementation. This method gives you access to the object reference for the new entity bean.

```
    public void ejbPostCreate( String accountId ) {

      System.out.println("Account: ejbPostCreate");
      return ;
    }
```

Finally, we have to implement the methods defined in the interface `javax.ejb.EntityBean`. These are the context-related operations, which allow you to set and unset the context of the entity bean.

```
    public void setEntityContext( EntityContext entityContext ) {

      System.out.println("Account: set entity context");
      this.entityContext = entityContext;
    }

    public void unsetEntityContext() {
      System.out.println("Account: unset context");
      entityContext = null;
    }
```

The most significant methods for the bean-managed persistence are `ejbLoad()` and `ejbStore()`. When a transaction starts, the state of the entity bean is loaded from the data storage. That means, in the bean-managed persistence, that the container calls `ejbLoad()` on the entity bean. At the end of the transaction the container calls `ejbStore()`. The methods `ejbLoad()` and `ejbStore()` use SQL select and a SQL update, respectively.

```
public void ejbLoad()
  throws RemoteException {

  try {
    Connection connection = getConnection();
    Statement statement = connection.createStatement();
    ResultSet resultSet = statement.executeQuery(
      "select balance from accounts where id = '" + accountId() + "'"
);

    // expecting only one result back
    if( resultSet.next() ) {
      balance = resultSet.getFloat(1);
      if( resultSet.next() ) {
        statement.close();
        connection.close();
        throw new RemoteException(
          "There is more than one entry for account "
          + accountId() );
      }
      statement.close();
      connection.close();
    }
    else {
      statement.close();
      connection.close();
      throw new RemoteException( "Invalid account id" );
    }
  }
  catch( Exception e ) {
    throw new RemoteException("DBAccess Error", e );
  }
}

public void ejbStore()
  throws RemoteException {

  try {
    Connection connection = getConnection();
    Statement statement = connection.createStatement();
    statement.executeUpdate(
      "update accounts set balance = " + balance +
      " where id = '" + accountId()  + "'");
    statement.close();
    connection.close();
  }
  catch( Exception e ) {
    throw new RemoteException("DBAccess Error", e );
  }
}
```

We also have to provide an implementation of the remove() method, which we do with the ejbRemove() method. The implementation is based on a SQL delete.

```
public void ejbRemove() throws RemoteException {
  try {
    Connection connection = getConnection();
    Statement statement = connection.createStatement();
    ResultSet resultSet = statement.executeQuery(
      "delete from accounts where id = '" + accountId() + "'" );
    statement.close();
    connection.close();
  }
  catch( Exception e ) {
    throw new RemoteException("DBAccess Error", e );
  }
  return;
}
```

There are also the ejbActivate() and ejbPassivate() methods, which are invoked by the container when it deactivates or activates the entity bean.

```
public void ejbActivate(){
  System.out.print("Account: activate");
}

public void ejbPassivate(){
  System.out.println("Account: passivate");
}
```

Finally, we implement a private method to get a connection from the JDBC driver. Note that a JDBC-2 compliant driver would use a connection pool and getConnection() does not necessarily create a new database connection every time, but takes one from the pool instead. We obtain the URL, the username, and password via a Java property object from the entity context. The context in turn has access via the container to the deployment information as shown next.

```
private Connection getConnection() throws SQLException {
  java.util.Properties properties =
    entityContext.getEnvironment();
  String url = properties.getProperty("db-url");
  String username = properties.getProperty("db-username");
  String password = properties.getProperty("db-password");
  return DriverManager.getConnection(url, username, password);
}
```

### ATM as a Session Bean

The basics for a session bean are similar to the entity bean. Again, we first define the Home interface of the ATM session bean. The home is a public Java interface, which extends `javax.ejb.EJBHome`. We declare a single `create()` method, which returns an ATM interface. That is the remote interface of our ATM session bean as we see next. The home interface of a session must at least provide one create method; however, it can have multiple ones with overloaded parameters. Create methods must throw the exception `java.rmi.RemoteException`, and usually they throw the exception `javax.ejb.CreateException`, too.

```
package vogel.transaction.chapter1.ejb;

public interface AtmHome extends javax.ejb.EJBHome {

  Atm create()
    throws java.rmi.RemoteException, javax.ejb.CreateException;
}
```

Then we define the Remote interface of the ATM session bean. The Remote interface is a public Java interface, which extends the `javax.ejb.EJBObject`. We declare a single business method, `transfer()`. The business methods of the remote interface must be declared `public` and must throw the exception `java.rmi.RemoteException`. Additionally, they can throw application-specific exceptions.

```
package vogel.transaction.chapter1.ejb;

public interface Atm extends javax.ejb.EJBObject {

  public void transfer(
    String source, String target, float amount )
    throws java.rmi.RemoteException, InsufficientFundsException;
}
```

Now we can provide the implementation of the ATM session bean in the class `AtmBean`, which implements the interface `javax.ejb.SessionBean` and `Serializable`. A session bean must also have a `SessionContext` variable, which provides access to the deployment information (provided by the deployer).

```
package vogel.transaction.chapter1.ejb;

import javax.ejb.*;
import javax.transaction.*;
```

```
import java.rmi.RemoteException;
import java.io.*;
import java.util.*;

public class AtmBean implements SessionBean, Serializable{

  private SessionContext sessionContext;
```

The implementation has three tasks: the implementation of the business methods, the implementation of the methods defined in the home interface, and the implementation of the methods of the interface `javax.ejb.SessionBean`.

We start with the implementation of the business method `transfer()`. The client identifies the account by account identifier. The ATM bean must obtain the object references to the corresponding Account beans. It can do so by using the `findByPrimaryKey()` method of the Account Home interface. We obtain the Account Home interface via the naming service. The EJB specification prescribes the Java Naming and Directory Interface as the naming service API. This is shown in the following code.

The method `findByPrimaryKey()` either returns the reference to the account or raises an exception. In the case of a `FinderException`, we create a new account. That's not following exactly the common business model, but is appropriate to demonstrate more features of the home interface. If the create operation fails, we give up. Whenever we get a `RemoteException` we just propagate it to the next layer. We do this for the source as well as for the target account.

```
public void transfer(
    String sourceAccountId, String targetAccountId, float amount )
    throws RemoteException, InsufficientFundsException {

    Account sourceAccount = null;
    Account targetAccount = null;

    AccountHome accountHome = getAccountHome();
    try {
      sourceAccount = accountHome.findByPrimaryKey( sourceAccountId );
    }
    catch( javax.ejb.FinderException fe ) {
      System.out.println("ATM: account <" + sourceAccountId +
        "> doesn't exist");
      System.out.println("ATM: Create new account" );
      try {
        sourceAccount = accountHome.create( sourceAccountId );
      }
```

```
        catch( javax.ejb.CreateException ce ) {
          System.out.println("ATM: Could not create account <" +
            sourceAccountId + ">");
          throw new RemoteException();
        }
      }
      try {
        targetAccount = accountHome.findByPrimaryKey( targetAccountId );
      }
      catch( javax.ejb.FinderException fe ) {
        System.out.println("ATM: account <" + targetAccountId +
          "> doesn't exist");
        System.out.println("ATM: Create new account" );
        try {
          targetAccount = accountHome.create( targetAccountId );
        }
        catch( javax.ejb.CreateException ce ) {
          System.out.println("ATM: Could not create account <" +
            targetAccountId + ">");
          throw new RemoteException();
        }
      }
```

Now that we got the accounts we make the transfer: debit the amount from the source account and credit it to the target account. In contrast to the OTS example, we only have to roll back the transaction for an application-level exception. In the case of catching the exception `InsufficientFundsException`, we mark the transaction for rollback by invoking the method `setRollbackOnly()` on the session context. As discussed previously, you could mark the transaction for rollback in the account implementation.

```
  try {
      sourceAccount.debit( amount );
      targetAccount.credit( amount );
      }
      catch( InsufficientFundsException ife ) {
        sessionContext.setRollbackOnly();
        throw ife;
      }
      return;
    }
```

Although one could explicitly code a user transaction using JTA, the transaction management is usually controlled through policies defined in the deployment descriptor, as we explain later in the chapter.

The private method `getAccountHome()` obtains a reference to an Account Home interface from the JNDI. First we have to initialize JNDI with a root context. Therefore, we obtain a class, which implements the context interface via a Java property from the session context. The session context provides access to properties and policies defined in the deployment descriptor. We put the value in a hashtable, which we use to initialize the root context. On the root context `context` we invoke the `lookup()` method to which we pass the name "Account" for our Account Home interface. The `lookup()` method returns an object of type `java.lang.Object`, which we have to cast to the expected type.

```
private AccountHome getAccountHome() {

      AccountHome accountHome = null;

      try {
        javax.naming.Context context;
        // get a JNDI context
        new javax.naming.InitialContext();

        // resolve and narrow account home named "Account"
        accountHome = (AccountHome)
          context.lookup("Account")
    }
    catch( Exception ex ) {
      System.err.println(
        "Could not get home interface for Account EJBs" + ex );
    }
    return accountHome;
  }
```

When we invoke the `create()` method on the Home interface, the container creates a new session bean instance for us. The container triggers the bean implementation class by invoking the `ejbCreate()` method, which allows us to add additional initialization code. The same applies to the `remove()` and the corresponding `ejbRemove()` methods.

```
public void ejbCreate() throws RemoteException {

  System.out.println("ATM: create");

}

public void ejbRemove() {
  System.out.println("ATM: remove");
}
```

There is also a method to set the session context, but none to unset it. The life cycle of a session does not require the unsetting, as explained in detail in Chapter 4.

```
  public void setSessionContext( SessionContext sessionContext ) {
    System.out.println("ATM: set session context");
    this.sessionContext = sessionContext;
  }
```

Session beans can be deactivated. That usually happens according to internal container policies; for example, due to a time-out or to a shortage of memory in the container. The container serializes and stores the state of the session bean during the deactivation. The container recreates the session bean instance and initializes with the saved state during the activation. The methods `ejbActivate()` and `ejbPassivate()` are invoked by the container during these processes and allow the bean provider to add application-specific code; for example, to close/open additional resources.

```
public void ejbActivate() {
    System.out.println("ATM: activate");
  }

  public void ejbPassivate() {
    System.out.println("ATM: passivate");
  }
}
```

### *Deploying a Bean*

EJB deployer is responsible for taking an enterprise bean and deploying it in a certain context. The context determines the policies for executing the bean. These policies determine, for example, the transactional behavior or the access control of an enterprise bean.

EJB deployer would typically use wizard-like tools, provided by the container, to set the deployment descriptor for enterprise beans. The EJB specification version defines serialized Java object of the type `javax.ejb.deployment.SessionDescriptor` or `javax.ejb.deployment.EntityDescriptor`, depending on the type of the enterprise bean. The subsequent versions of the EJB specification will prescribe XML for the definition of deployment descriptors. For both reasons—the change of the specification and the fact that a deployer uses tools—we omit the syntactical representation of the deployment. Instead, we focus on the content of the deployment information.

A deployment descriptor keeps information about the following:

- **Transactional policies**, which govern the transactional behavior of a bean.

- **Access control policies**, which govern the access to an enterprise bean.
- **JNDI names**, which set the name under which the Home interface of the enterprise is registered.
- **Type information**, which defines the types—that is, the name of the classes—for the Home and Remote interfaces and the implementation class.

A complete description of deployment descriptors is given in Chapter 5, "Understanding Enterprise JavaBeans," and the example explained in Chapter 6, "Programming with EJB," makes extensive use of a variety of deployment properties.

#### Access Control Policies

**ATM.** The ATM enterprise bean could be the transaction originator, which requires the policy TX_REQUIRES_NEW. If the client is the transaction originator, the travel agent must have the policy TX_REQUIRED. To support both cases, the ATM would have the policy TX_REQUIRED, which means it uses the client's transaction context or creates a new one when the client makes a nontransactional call. In this example, we set the transaction policy for the whole enterprise bean. However, specifically considering performance, a more fine-grained selection is possible.

**Account.** The booking entity bean is expected to be invoked by another enterprise bean, which already requires a transaction context. Hence, it should have the transaction policy TX_MANDATORY.

#### Access Control Policies

We have not addressed access control in our example for two major reasons. First, the security aspects of the EJB specification are about to change as we write this. Second, what we really need for this example is instance-based access control, such as "only the owner of an account is allowed to access the account," which is neither in the scope of the current EJB specification nor on the EJB road map.

#### Naming

We use a simple, flat naming structure. The ATM home interface is registered as "Atm", and the Account home interface as "Account". More complex, hierarchical naming structures can be applied and are explained in Chapter 6.

#### Miscellaneous Deployment Properties

Miscellaneous deployment properties include the class names for the home and the remote interface, for the bean implementation class, the time-out for stateful and stateless session beans, and the reentrant flag and the primary key class name for entity beans.

#### Deployment Properties for Portability

During the implementation of our enterprise beans we mentioned that we use deployment properties to increase the portability of our components. To abstract from the JNDI initialization class we use a property "context-class-name". To abstract from the database we use properties called "db-url", "db-username", and "db-password" to determine the URL, the username, and the password for database connection, respectively.

### *Assembling an Application*

The role of the application assembler is to build an application by composing a number of beans. For our example, we have to add a client, which interacts with the ATM. We want to build a simple application which allows a customer to make money transfers between accounts.

We omit the GUI code and concentrate on the enterprise bean-specific code. During the initialization of the GUI client we get reference to the ATM Home interface from JNDI and create an ATM session for this client by invoking `create()` on the Home interface.

```
private void ejbInit() throws Exception {

  try {
    // get AtmSessionHome
    atmHome = getAtmHome();

    // get atmSession
    atm = atmHome.create();
  }
  catch( Exception ex ) {
    System.err.println( ex );
  }
}
```

The code to get an ATM Home is very similar to the one shown previously for obtaining an Account Home. We follow the same steps, we just use a different name and a different class for the narrowing.

```
private AtmHome getAtmHome() {

    AtmHome atmHome = null;
```

```
        try {
          javax.naming.Context context;
          // get a JNDI context using the Naming service
          Hashtable env = new Hashtable();
          env.put(javax.naming.Context.INITIAL_CONTEXT_FACTORY,
                "com.inprise.ejb.jndi.Context");
          context = new javax.naming.InitialContext(env);

          atmHome = (AtmHome) context.lookup("Atm");
      }
      catch( Exception ex ) {
        System.err.println(
          "Could not get home interface for ATM EJBs" + ex );
      }
      return atmHome;
    }
```

When the user clicks the Transfer button, the local `transfer()` method is invoked, which in turns invokes the `transfer()` method on the session bean.

```
    private void transfer() {

      Float f = new Float( amountField.getText() );
      float amount = f.floatValue();
      try {
        atm.transfer( fromField.getText(), toField.getText(), amount );
        statusBar.setText("Transaction completed");
      }
      catch( InsufficientFundsException ife ) {
        System.err.println( ife );
        statusBar.setText(
          "Insufficient funds to complete transaction :-(" );
      }
      catch( Exception e ) {
        System.err.println( e );
        statusBar.setText("Error: " + e );
      }

    }
```

This client leaves the transaction control to the session bean. However, another client could run the transfer method in the context of a user transaction as defined in JTA.

CHAPTER

# 2

# Transaction Processing Basics

Transaction processing technology has been the backbone for reliable distributed computing for decades. In the modern age, we cannot live without transactions, since all our day-to-day activities involve some Transaction Processing (TP) system or other. Many industries like banking, communication, transportation, finance, manufacturing, and the stock market totally depend on transaction processing for day-to-day activities. Without transaction processing, these systems would grind to a halt.

Invention of many important technologies like client/server computing, fault tolerant computing, and transactional workflow systems stem from the demanding requirements of TP systems. In the hardware arena, the introduction of powerful new machines pushes the TP systems to their limits in terms of heavy transaction loads. Large-scale transaction processing requirements led us to the TP Monitor (TPM) technology, an all-in-one strategy to create, execute, and manage transactions that specialize in handling heavy transaction loads.

It is very important to understand the nuances of this technology to make good use of it, so we will present the fundamentals of transaction processing in this chapter and explain what a transaction is, and the different transaction models designers employ to achieve their goals. You can find a detailed explanation of the *Two-Phase Commit Protocol*, which is the lifeline of a distributed transaction that glues several participating resources to one global transaction. We give an overview of TP monitors and explain what makes them so special. We also answer the question of why a TP monitor is a superior solution to transaction processing than a database system.

Several transaction processing standards have evolved over the decades and X/Open DTM is one of the widely adopted standards in the TP industry. This is the underlying standard for modern transaction processing systems. TP monitors like Tuxedo, Encina, TopEnd, and their object counterparts like Inprise ITS and Orbix OTM use the X/Open DTM standard to coexist in heterogeneous environments. We will provide an overview of the X/Open DTM model, which is essential for understanding the material, in Chapter 3, "Understanding the CORBA Object Transaction Service."

Finally, we introduce the new mechanism, the Transaction Servers and Object Transaction Monitors, which are a variation from the TP monitors, and explain what value they add to transaction processing.

## What Is a Transaction?

There is no single agreed upon definition in the literature that defines accurately what a transaction really is. The following definition is our version that conveys the essence of work done by many researchers who attempted to define it concisely.

> A transaction is a unit of work comprised of several operations made on one or more shared system resources that are governed by ACID properties.

The acronym ACID stands for Atomicity, Consistency, Isolation, and Durability, and was originally defined by Andreas Reuter.

**Atomicity.** The unit of work performed in the transaction is identified as one atomic entity. In the case of failure, changes that occur due to this unit of work are either made permanent or are reversed to restore to the prior state before the transaction commences. Examples: Database updates, message queue operations.

**Consistency.** When the transaction execution is completed, the system is left in a stable condition. If the system is left in an inconsistent state, the unit of work done as part of this transaction should be reversed to restore the system to its initial state. Example: Database referential integrity constraints.

**Isolation.** The correctness of the unit of work performed within a transaction is not compromised when another concurrent transaction accesses the same set of resources as the current transaction. The changes that were made to the shared resources as part of the current transaction will not be visible to other transactions that are accessing the shared resources concurrently. Example: A withdraw activity from the same account by two concurrent transactions. Only the first transaction that gets access to the data will succeed, and the update to the account is not visible to others until the transaction commits.

**Durability.** The changes that are made as part of the transaction is made persistent once it is committed. This requires that the behavior should be repeatable in the case of a system failure. Example: Let us assume the withdraw operation from a bank account has been performed and the system crashes during the commit of the transaction. If the information about this transaction is not made persistent to disk, the changes that were made as part of this transaction could be lost. This would result in a data integrity situation. The databases and TP monitors typically solve this problem by logging the "commit" operation. In the case of a failure, the information is retrieved from the system log during recovery and the operation is replayed to produce the correct results.

In a nutshell, the work done within the auspices of a transaction is either all completed as one entity or no work is done at all in the case of a failure, with complete data integrity.

A TP application is a collection of such transactions put together to execute the business transaction requirements in a reliable way. The famous example for a TP application is the SABRE (Semi-Automated Business Research Environment) airline reservation system, which was a joint venture between IBM and American Airlines. This online TP application has been widely used for the past several decades and is one of the major TP applications in the world even today.

A TP system is the backbone for running a TP application that provides the transactional services. A TP system is often referred to as a TP monitor (TPM) and is usually comprised of the following functionality:

- Efficient connection handling so that large number of clients can be serviced

- Presentation layer to handle the client's requests, the results of which are presented to the client
- Workflow control to route the client's requests to the appropriate server
- Transactional integrity and global transaction coordination for the programs that are run under the control of the monitor
- Optimized use of the data resources by utilizing fewer connections
- Heterogeneous connectivity for disparate data resources

Applications using the TPM framework are often multitiered. The application logic (also called the *business rules*) typically resides in the middle tier as an application server, which fulfills the requests from clients. The servers access the shared data located in data resources like databases, to modify the data as per the client's request. TP systems are designed to connect a large number of clients to multiple servers that typically access multiple data resources. They are optimized to use operating system resources and the network resources efficiently. You can find a detailed explanation of TP monitors' architecture and features in the section "TP Monitors."

## Different Transaction Models

A simple transaction is comprised of the simple steps *begin transaction, commit transaction/abort transaction*. Real-life business applications are often so sophisticated that the simple transaction model may not be enough in certain situations. The requirements for transaction processing systems can be categorized:

- Ability to commit or abort all the changes
- Ability to abort part of the changes, yet commit the transaction
- Ability to incrementally commit part of the changes in the transaction

Various models have evolved to address these needs. They are:

- Flat transactions
- Chained transactions
- Nested transactions

## Flat Transaction

The simple transaction model described next is called a *flat transaction*. The transaction is *flat* because the units of work done as part of the transaction are at the same hierarchy. The transaction is commenced with the *begin transaction* command and concluded with the *commit transaction* or *abort transaction* command. The changes that are done as part of this transaction are either committed or aborted.

Let us take a look at a simple loan-processing example in Figure 2.1. A bank is processing an applicant's loan, and the minimal requirement for processing the loan is that the applicant have a good credit history. If the applicant does not qualify, the transaction is aborted. If the applicant qualifies for the loan, the bank proceeds with processing the loan.

One may think, in real life, that it would be difficult to address the whole gamut of business problems with this simple model. But surprisingly, most commercial OLTP (On Line Transaction Processing) systems use flat transactions to solve their complex problems.

Even though the simple model of flat transactions is versatile in many business applications, it suffers from a few limitations that fail to address some of the business requirements. We present a couple of situations in which the flat transaction model does not fit. In these situations, we need a flexible alternate approach to handle transactions.

**TP applications that require an abort of a selective unit of work.** A common example that fits into this category is a travel agent application. A reservation might typically include the purchase of airline tickets, hotel accommodations, and rental car arrangements. If we use a flat transaction to handle this reservation, what will happen if there is no availability of a rental car at this time? The entire transaction will have to be aborted. We will have to cancel the airline

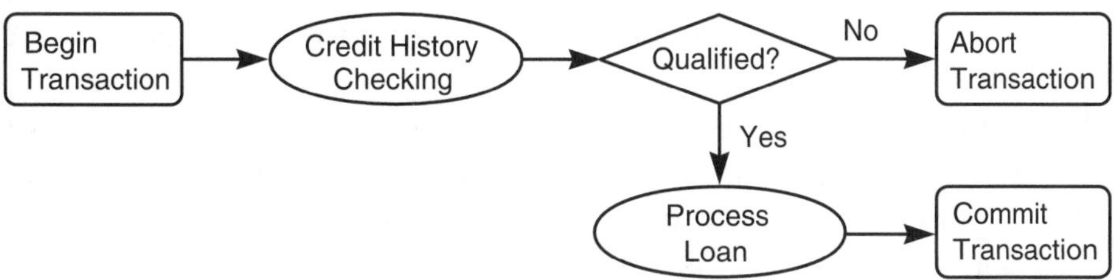


**Figure 2.1** Flat transaction example.

reservation as well as the hotel accommodations since we cannot get the rental car. This application could use a nested transaction model to achieve the desired effect, but the flat transaction model purist might argue that this compound transaction can be split into three different transactions to better handle this situation.

**Mass update problem.** A common example that fits into this category is a banking application where the bank has to credit daily interest on thousands of accounts at the end of the day. If this operation uses a flat transaction on 100,000 accounts, what happens when there is a failure after processing 99,000 accounts? We have to abort the transaction to preserve data integrity. Imagine a rerun of this time-consuming operation. This application could use save points or chained transactions to better handle this situation. Again, the flat transaction model purists might argue that this transaction could be broken into manageable chunks to handle the failure scenario in an optimal way.

## Chained Transactions

The inability of the *flat transaction* model to control parts of the work done in a transaction led to the evolution of the *chained transactions* model. It gives us the ability to roll back part of the work done within a transaction without aborting the entire transaction. There are several techniques applied to achieve this effect. *Save point* is one of the basic techniques used to achieve the chaining behavior. It is a marker within a *flat transaction* that is defined by the application at specific intervals. The Transaction Manager saves the accumulated work at save points. The difference between the *save point* and the actual commit operation is that an application will be able to selectively roll back the work to a *save point* while keeping the transaction active. One thing to note is that the *save point* operation is not persistent; in other words, it cannot survive a system crash.

Another technique is called *chained transactions*, which is a variation of the *save point*. *Chained transactions* allow you to persistify a portion of the work done within a transaction. This means that the work is committed but the transaction is still active. While committing, the system does not have to release the locks on shared resources. The important thing to note is that we cannot roll back all the work done to the beginning of the chained transaction.

Another technique is called *saga*, which is a refined *chained transactions* model. It allows you to roll back all of the work done to the beginning of the chained transaction. This effect is achieved by maintaining compensating actions, which represent the work done in the chain. In the case of a failure, the compensating actions are applied to the rollback of the chained transaction.

## Nested Transactions

As the name suggests, a *nested transaction* is simply a transaction nested within another transaction, as illustrated in Figure 2.2. This model allows a main transaction to have its own subtransactions. The unit of work done in a subtransaction can be individually committed or aborted. Only the parent transaction of a subtransaction can access the results of this subtransaction. The commit operation done in the subtransaction is persistified only when all the ancestor transactions commit.

Nested transactions are generally used to simplify a complex transaction whose logic can be divided into manageable subtransactions, and

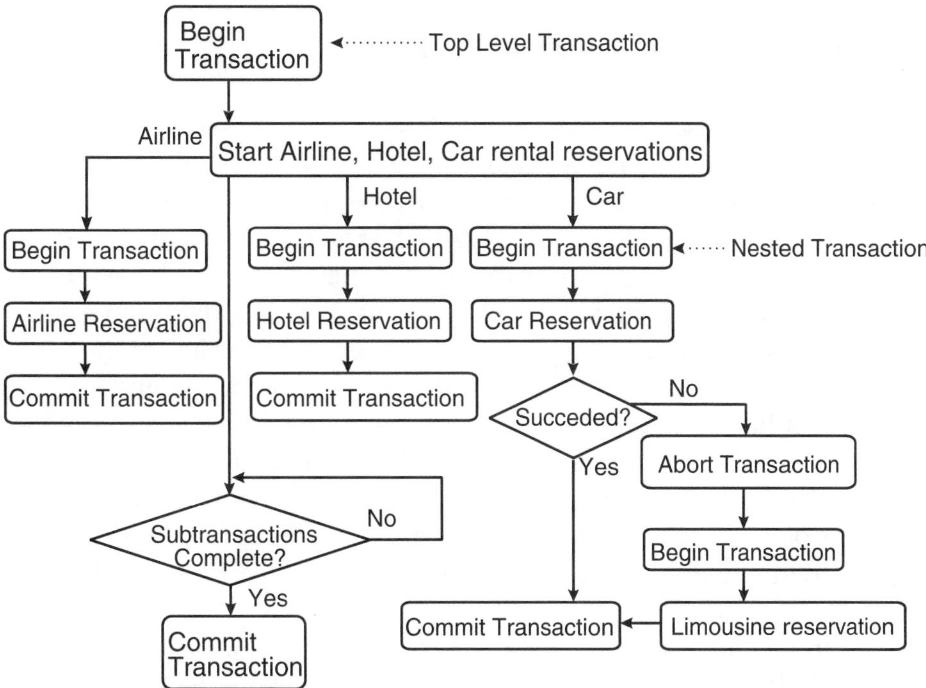


**Figure 2.2** Nested transaction example.

all of these do not have to succeed in order for the transaction to finish successfully. This means that a failure in a subtransaction can be isolated and a different logic can be executed if the application wishes to continue with the transaction. This model allows flexibility and greater control for programs to manage complex transactions.

The travel agent application is a perfect example that could employ the nested transaction model. If a client wishes to book his trip to Paris and wants all his travel arrangements such as airline tickets, accommodation, and transportation to be taken care of, the travel agent application will employ a nested transaction to take care of this complex reservation. Airline reservations, hotel reservations, and car rental reservations are handled as subtransactions and are executed in parallel. The travel agent is able to obtain an airline reservation and hotel accommodation successfully, but he cannot get the car rental reservation confirmed. If the program were to use a flat transaction model, we would be forced to abort the entire transaction, even though we held reservations for airline and hotel accommodation. Here the travel agent can do an alternative arrangement for transportation through a limousine service.

## Two-Phase Commit Protocol

A distributed transaction typically updates data that is located in multiple systems. The resource managers that manage the data (for example, Sybase and Oracle databases) are usually located in different geographical areas that are connected by LAN/WAN. The updates made in a single transaction in this case have to be synchronized across all systems to preserve the *atomicity* property. This means that all updates done in different resource managers have to commit together in order for the transaction to succeed. If there is any failure during one of the updates, the transaction has to be aborted. This coordination can be really complex since any system involved in the transaction can crash and recover, and this can occur at any time during the execution of the transaction. A Transaction Manager handles this coordination, and the protocol that is applied to implement it is called a *Two-Phase Commit Protocol.* It is usually referred to as 2PC.

To help us understand how a 2PC protocol works, let us first analyze the life cycle of a distributed transaction and its components. A Transaction Manager (also referred to here as the *Transaction Coordinator*) coordinates the distributed transaction across two or more resources.

The anatomy of a distributed transaction that involves updates in two resources (A & B) is given next.

1. Application requests the Transaction Manager to begin a transaction.
2. Application performs updates in resource A.
3. Application performs updates in resource B.
4. Application requests the Transaction Manager to commit the transaction.
5. Transaction Manager executes the 2PC protocol.

Since the Transaction Manager has to coordinate the transaction across the multiple resources involved, it has to keep track of the resources involved in the transaction. This application disseminates the information by registering a resource with the Transaction Manager before it begins an update operation. This is an important piece of information because the Transaction Manager uses this list to coordinate updates to the resource managers during the execution of the 2PC protocol. The coordination is done in two phases, namely *prepare* and *commit*. Figure 2.3 illustrates the 2PC protocol.

## First Phase

At the commit request, the transaction coordinator sends a *prepare to commit* message to all resource managers involved in the transaction. When the resource managers get this message, they write the information about the updates to disk to make it durable (this information will be used to recover this transaction should there be a failure before the actual commit operation). When the transaction coordinator receives *prepared to commit* acknowledgments from all the resource managers, it makes its own decision to commit durable. This concludes phase one.

## Second Phase

The transaction coordinator sends a *commit* message to all resource managers involved in the transaction. When the resource managers get this message, the work that is done as part of this transaction is made durable. Resource managers advise the transaction coordinator that they have committed their portions of the transactional work. When the transaction coordinator receives the confirmation from all the resource managers involved in the transaction, it commits the transaction and notifies the client of the outcome of this transaction. Second phase is concluded.

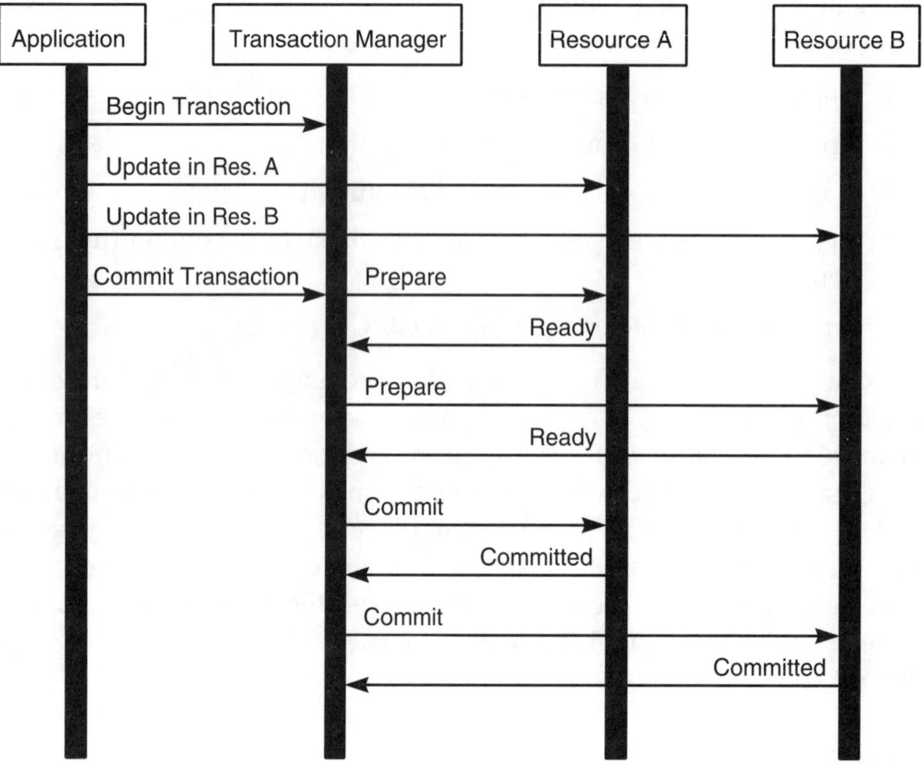


**Figure 2.3** Two-phase commit protocol interactions.

The explanation just given explains a simple case of a 2PC. The 2PC protocol is designed to handle all possible failure scenarios that could happen either in the transaction coordinator node or in the resource manager nodes during the execution of 2PC. We present a few different failure scenarios to give the reader a better understanding of the protocol.

### *Scenario 1*

Let us assume that the resource manager B could not prepare the local transaction due to an internal resource manager error. The transaction coordinator will decide to abort the transaction in this case. An abort message will be sent to both resources. Scenario 1 is shown in Figure 2.4.

### *Scenario 2*

Now, what happens when the resource manager B crashes during the commit phase (indicated by an X in Figure 2.5)? The resource manager

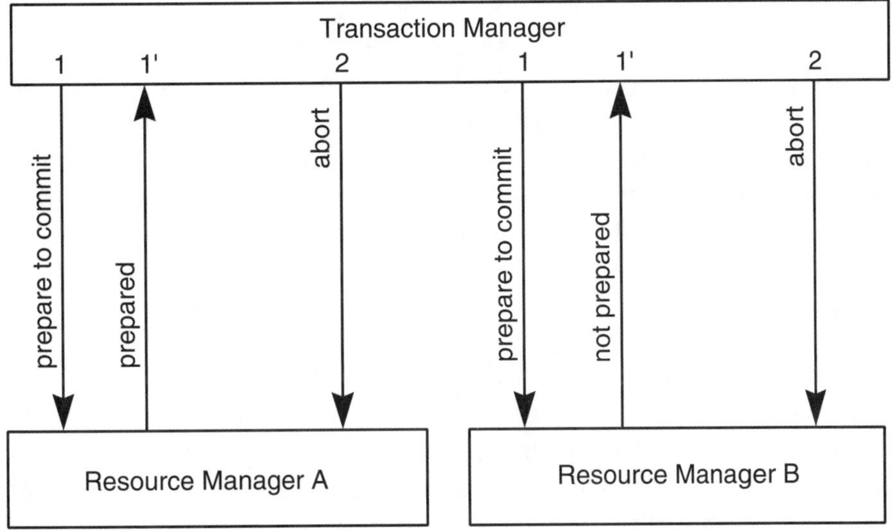


**Figure 2.4** Resource failure in prepare phase.

A has already committed the updates. In this case, resource manager B must commit its updates to preserve ACID properties. There are several possibilities to make this happen. The transaction coordinator can periodically check to see whether the resource manager B is available to

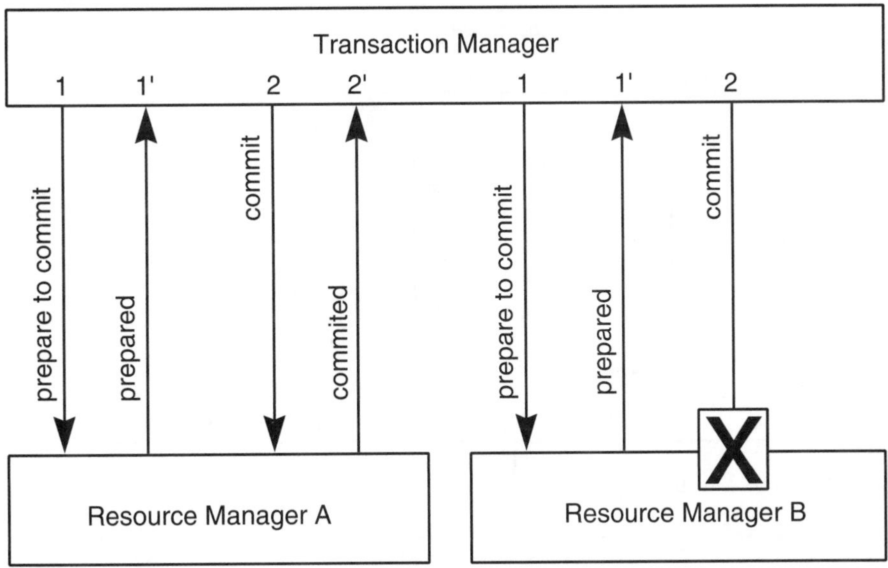


**Figure 2.5** Resource failure in commit phase.

complete the transaction. Alternately, a resource manager can establish a conversation with the transaction manager and obtain the status of completion for this transaction. The mechanism is implementation-dependent. If the resource manager B cannot recover from its failure, usually a system administrator has to intervene and heuristically commit or roll back the transaction. The transaction manager will be notified by the resource manager of such an outcome.

### *Scenario 3*

Let us consider a case in which the transaction manager itself crashes during a commit phase. This situation can be easily resolved. As shown in Figure 2.6, when phase one completes, it receives an acknowledgment from each of the participating resources that it is prepared to commit. The transaction coordinator decides to commit the transaction. Before it starts the second phase, it writes the information about this decision to disk, which usually contains information about the decision and the participants. If the crash occurs at this point, the transaction manager goes through a recovery phase in which it finds this incomplete transaction and initiates a completion procedure for this transaction again. The commit request is then sent to the participating resources to complete the transaction.

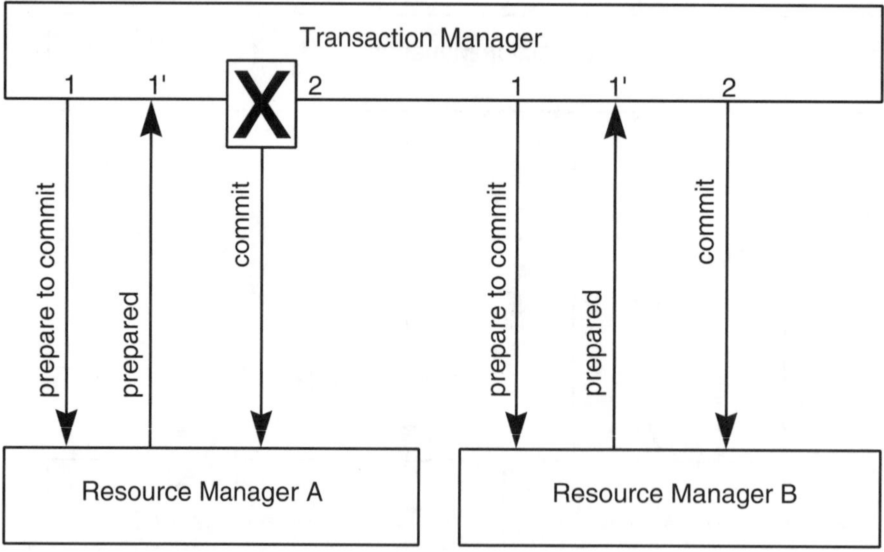


**Figure 2.6** Transaction manager failure during commit.

## TP Monitors

There is no single definition of a TP monitor that is widely used in the industry. Various literature attempts to describe the TP monitor as:

> An operating system that specializes in creation, execution, and management of transaction processing applications.

We think this is the simplest definition for a TP monitor, and yet it conveys the idea of what a TP monitor is, in a nutshell.

Distributed Transaction Processing (DTP) applications are usually complex in nature and typically service large numbers of client requests. When users submit a transactional request to a TP system, they wish to get a reply to their request immediately. When there are thousands of requests that need to be serviced, the underlying application has to handle them concurrently so that the requests can be replied to within a reasonable time (this is referred to as the *latency*). To make this happen, the application has to make efficient use of the operating system, network, and database resources so that the user requests can be satisfied within the required time limit. If every application to be developed has to worry about the complexities of mundane system-level programming, the time it takes to develop such applications would be unacceptable. The TP monitor comes to the rescue by providing a framework for the transaction processing application and hides the complexities of connection handling, network routing, and efficient use of the OS resources. Application programmers do not have to bother about checking availability of resources, synchronization of the resources, connection management, process management, and load balancing. TP monitors are adept at scaling an application for thousands of transactional requests without making a heavy demand on operating system resources.

### TP Monitor Architecture

Figure 2.7 shows the components of a typical TP monitor system. Transaction processing applications that use a TP monitor usually fit in a three-tier client/server architecture. The clients form the first tier. Client programs collect the data that are required for a specific transactional request and submit it to the TP monitor. When the results are available for the request, the client program presents it to the user. Modern applications use a fancy GUI front end, which is developed using 4GL builder tools like Inprise JBuilder. An OLTP application such as the

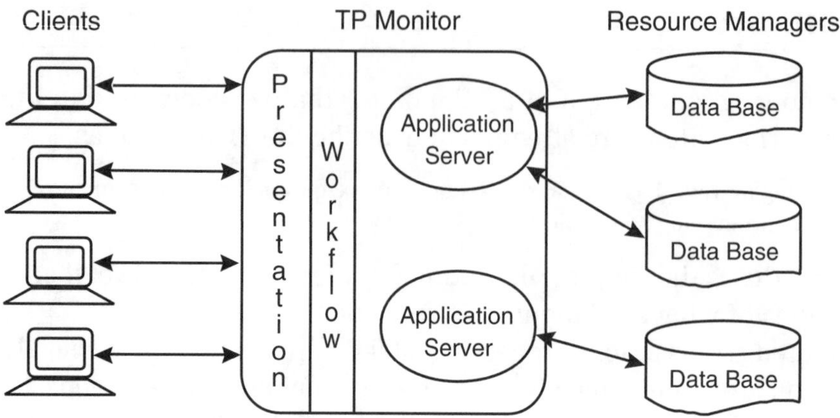


**Figure 2.7** TP monitor components.

SABRE system can have thousands of clients connected to the TP monitor at any one time. The second tier is comprised of the TP monitor itself as well as the application servers that implement the business logic as services. Application servers are included in the TP monitor domain here, but they usually have separate process boundaries. The TP monitor manages the connection-handling chore by efficiently multiplexing a huge number of client connections to a manageable set of connections to the actual resources. Also, the TP monitor routes the requests to the proper servers by providing some sort of naming or routing facilities. A commercial TP monitor is loaded with features, and we explain most of them in the following sections.

### Connection Multiplexing

Typically, a user application needs a network connection to communicate with the application server to get its work done. In a commercial application, thousands of client requests are active at the same time, waiting for an immediate response. If each of these clients needs operating system resources like network connections, processes, and so forth, the system could grind to a halt. TP monitors typically provide one process responsible for handling the communication with the clients. Client connections are multiplexed efficiently by the TP monitor connection handler, and the client's connection request to an application server is handled transparently by the TP monitor. This *fan in* act enormously reduces the operating system resource requirements, helping the Transaction Processing applications to scale more effectively.

### Naming Services

In a simple client/server application, the client is responsible for sending the request to an appropriate server that implements the services required by the client. This means that the client has to know the physical location on the network so that the request can be routed appropriately. Naming Services provide a map of the symbolic names of the application servers to their actual location on the network. The client's request to execute a service is transparently routed by the TP monitor by resolving the request from the Naming Services mapping.

### Data-Dependent Routing

The simple routing provided by the Naming Services may not be sophisticated enough for certain kinds of TP applications for which the proximity of the application servers to the locality of the data is critical. For example, a stock trading application implements two trading servers that provide identical services. But these servers are strategically located in San Francisco and New York to serve the Pacific and Atlantic regions. If the databases that maintain the customer's account are partitioned in such a way that a range of account numbers is maintained in one database, then the TP monitor has to take into account the account_id information in addition to the server naming mapping to route to the appropriate server. The data-dependent routing helps to reduce the extra network calls in some cases, as shown in Figure 2.8.

A client with an account number S2300 wishes to purchase 100 shares of XYZ stock. The TP monitor routes the request to the server dedicated

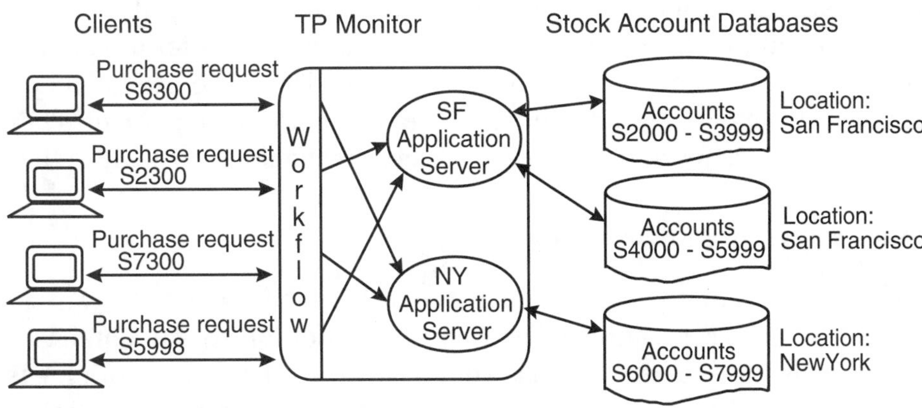


**Figure 2.8** Data-dependent routing example.

to the San Francisco database where the account is held. If the workflow router is not sensitive to the data dependency, the client's request could have been sent to the New York server because of lighter load conditions. However, the New York server has to access the database from the San Francisco location to access the account. This adds extra remote calls that can be avoided by data-dependent routing. Routing criterion can be usually provided as a configuration information before a TP monitor is activated.

### *Heterogeneous Access to Resource Managers*

TP monitors work with a variety of application tools and disparate data resources. Often, in a distributed application, the data in different geographical locations are maintained by heterogeneous resource managers. In the stock trading application described earlier, the New York location is managed by a Sybase system and the San Francisco location is managed by an Oracle system. TP monitors employ the X/Open XA interface to achieve heterogeneous access to disparate data resources. A detailed explanation of this interface can be found in the next section.

### *High Availability*

Many mission-critical applications have been built with TP monitors as the underlying system, which glues all of the clients and servers together. Obviously, downtime due to any kind of failure is not an option for these applications. TP monitors provide facilities for handling failover conditions due to hardware or software failure. If there is a software failure in the server and the server is brought down, the TP monitor can automatically restart another instance of the server. If there is a hardware failure, the TP monitor can automatically transfer the coordination to another process in a different node. There are products that can provide very high availability in the range of above 99 percent. They employ hot backups and very fast recovery mechanisms to achieve this.

### *Low Cost, High Performance*

How can a TP monitor solution save money? Don't we have to pay extra money for the TP monitor infrastructure in addition to any databases that we may have to use? The answer lies in how the database pricing is done. The cost of ownership of the database is directly proportional to the number of active client connection licenses required to run a specific application. Without a TP monitor, the number of connections an application would make to a database is much higher; hence, the cost of a database-centric solution is much higher. A TP monitor, on the other hand, handles all the complexities associated with the client-side connection, multiplexes them, and initiates very few connections compared to the number of client connections requested.

Another main benefit of using reduced system resources on the database is boosted application performance, since the database is more responsive due to fewer required database resources. Further, the TP monitor has built-in libraries to provide the framework for client/server development, cutting down the development cost. TP monitors have been traditionally used for benchmarking databases since they help achieve good price performance ratio for transactions. Tuxedo is a popular example, which is used by many relational databases for benchmarking purposes.

### *Load Balancing*

TP monitors are adept at distributing the workload across several application servers by replicating the servers on the same or on a different node. The decision for starting another server to handle the excess load can either be done at startup time or it can be decided on the fly. Modern TP monitors provide both static and dynamic load-balancing features. Static load balancing is usually decided at the startup time and the amount of replication of server instances is decided based on some statistical data of prior application runs. Dynamic load balancing kicks in on the fly and, depending on the load of the system detected by the TP monitor, it starts up the server processes on the nodes where the load is comparatively low. Tuxedo and Encina products provide both static and dynamic load-balancing features.

## Distributed Transaction Management Standards: X/Open, OSI, OMG

A sophisticated middleware application like a TP monitor glues disparate data sources, which typically are managed by proprietary database applications and often have a need to interoperate with other TP monitors of a dissimilar kind. Things could get unmanageable without standard protocols to glue all these dissimilar systems together. These requirements led to the evolution of standardizing the interfaces between TP monitors, resource managers, and applications. The widely used standards were specified by X/Open, OSI, and OMG organizations.

## X/Open

X/Open is a standards organization whose goal is to standardize several interfaces between components in a distributed transaction processing framework. The X/Open consortium was initially formed to promote the *Open Systems Computing* paradigm and application portability. X/Open specified the most popular Distributed Transaction Processing Model (DTP) in 1991. This standard has been implemented by most of the TP monitor and database vendors.

The DTP model defines the three basic modules: Application Program (AP), Transaction Manager (TM), and Resource Manager (RM). AP is just a client program, which uses the libraries provided by TM and RM to interact with them (e.g., a stockbroker application). TM is responsible for transaction coordination and control of execution of transactions (e.g., Inprise ITS). RM is responsible for managing the access to the shared resources like databases, files, message queues, print spooler, and so forth (e.g., Oracle, Sybase databases). Figure 2.9 denotes the interfaces between these components.

The various interfaces are defined next.

### *TX Interface*

This interface defines the interaction between the AP and the TM modules. The interface APIs are prefixed with tx_, which specify the transaction bracketing, transaction status, and transaction control operations. The table given below lists few commonly used *tx_* calls.

| CALLS | PURPOSE |
|---|---|
| tx_begin | Starts a transaction. |
| tx_commit | Commits a transaction. |
| tx_rollback | Aborts a transaction. |
| tx_info | Gets the status of the transaction. |

### *XA Interface*

The XA interface defines the interaction between the TM and the RM modules. The interface APIs are prefixed with *xa_* or *ax_*. The transac-

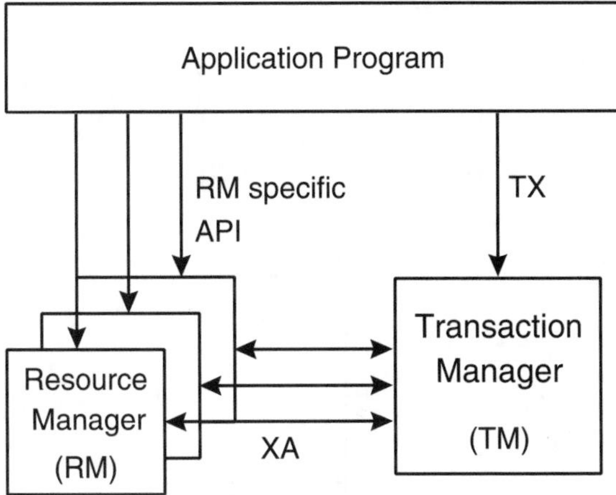


**Figure 2.9** X/Open DTM model.

tion manager issues *xa_* calls to interface with the resource manager, and the resource manager issues *ax_* calls to interface with the transaction manager. Note that both the transaction manager and the resource manager modules have to implement this bidirectional interface, which allows a transaction manager to interact with any resource manager.

| CALLS | PURPOSE |
|---|---|
| xa_start | Starts a transaction. |
| xa_prepare | Prepares a transaction in the 2PC. |
| xa_end | Ends the association of the transaction. |
| xa_commit | Commits the transaction. |
| ax_reg | Resource uses this operation to dynamically register it with a TM. |

The application program communicates with the resource manager by using its native interface APIs. Example: SQL.

The initial model specified by X/Open defined the components within a single domain. It did not specify how these components communicate with each other from across different domains. X/Open addressed this shortcoming and proposed another specification in 1994. The new model includes another component in the DTP model called Communication Resource Managers (CRM), as illustrated in Figure 2.10. CRM controls communications between distributed applications across the domains. X/Open has specified new interfaces—XA+, TxRPC, XATMI,

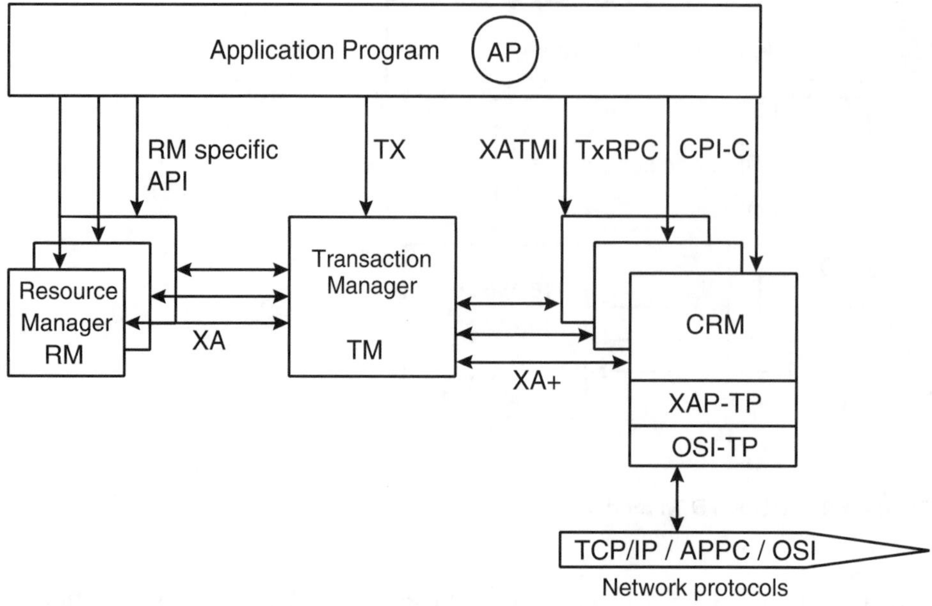


**Figure 2.10** X/Open DTM model with CRM.

and CPI-C—to define the interactions with CRM. It is interesting to note that an application program communicates with the CRM with three standard interfaces (instead of one). Applications from different domains can communicate with each other using only one of these CRM interfaces, and they are not interoperable. For example, if an application uses TxRPC in one domain, it has to use TxRPC on the other domain to which it is communicating.

### XA+ Interface

This interface defines the interaction between a transaction manager and the CRM components. The global transaction information is communicated between different TM domains using this interface. XA+ interface uses *xa_*()* calls to CRM to request suspending or completing transaction branches and to propagate global transaction information to other transaction branches. CRMs use *ax_*()* function calls to request TM to save and retrieve recovery information, to create subordinate transaction branches, and to communicate the start and the end of blocking conditions. This is an extension to the XA interface and is a superset.

### *TxRPC Interface*

An application program uses this interface to communicate with the CRM that uses transactional Remote Procedure Calls (RPC). This interface is based on the DCE RPC technology.

### *XATMI Interface*

This interface is based on Tuxedo's Application Transaction Management Interface (ATMI). You can use *tpcall* to synchronously request for a service to be executed remotely, or use *tpconnect*, *tpsend*, and *tprecv* calls to work in the conversational mode.

### *CPI-C Interface*

Common Programming Interface for Communications (CPI-C) is used by an application program to communicate with the CRM. This interface is used by applications that run on various systems that require communication between them in a consistent manner. This conversational interface is based on IBM's CICS API and LU6.2.

## OSI

The OSI-TP specification gives guidelines in terms of how a two-phase commit protocol should work. However, this is not as widely deployed as the X/Open specification since the X/Open specification includes the two-phase commit protocol.

## OMG

The Object Management Group (OMG) is a consortium which specified the Common Object Request Broker Architecture (CORBA). CORBA is widely accepted in the enterprise community to provide the next-generation middleware solutions. CORBA specifies the way in which distributed objects can exist anywhere on the network, where clients can invoke the methods on the remote objects transparently without regard to the location or the execution environment. Further, it provides a distributed objects framework with an elaborate set of object services such as Naming Service, Transaction Service, Concurrency Service, and Security Service, to name a few. Designing a distributed application is easily achieved by using the required services provided by the ORB. For example, a distributed transaction processing application can use the transaction service for transaction coordination, and ORB is used as the backbone for communication.

One of the most important services specified by CORBA is the Object Transaction Service (OTS), which adds the distributed transaction processing capabilities to the distributed object's framework. This specification is based on X/Open DTP model, and they are interoperable. OTS defines a set of CORBA IDL interfaces for the TX and XA interfaces of the DTP model. The method invocations on the OTS interfaces are equivalent to the procedural invocation of TX and XA calls. The OTS specification requires that an application uses either the TX interface or an OTS interface for transaction bracketing since they are interoperable. We present the OTS specification in greater detail in Chapter 3.

## Why Use a TP Monitor Instead of a Database Server?

This is a classic dilemma faced by the designers of a transaction processing application in the past couple of decades. Most of the current database servers in the market such as Sybase, Oracle, and Informix, offer advanced transaction processing capabilities that are sometimes equivalent to their TP monitor counterparts. If that is the case, why would anyone want to buy a TP monitor that adds extra complexity and expense to their solutions? To find an answer, a comparison of these two technologies is in order.

Before we delve into the comparisons of these two competing technologies, we would like to introduce two terms that are often used: *TP-Lite* and *TP-Heavy*.

A transaction processing application could be implemented by a database server solution, which uses the concept of stored procedures. This approach is much akin to a two-tier TP monitor solution and is often referred to as *TP-Lite*. The main characteristics of a TP-Lite solution are that they use similar database resources, and applications written using this paradigm use proprietary technology and are not portable.

On the contrary, a TP monitor-based solution can be characterized by the use of global transactions that can involve heterogeneous resources and are usually designed to fit in a three-tier model. This approach is called *TP-Heavy*.

A few decades ago there was a clear distinction in the products offered by database companies and TP monitor companies since each of them excelled in different areas. Databases specialized in the management and access to data, while TP monitors specialized in the management and execution of transactions. Now, the database vendors are incorporating more and more of the TP monitor features into their products to make it more compelling to use a database-centric solution for their transaction processing applications. Even though a database-centric solution might serve a low-end TP monitor-based solution, we still believe there is enough distinction between these two models and that the TP monitor-based approach is the right way to go for most of the transaction processing applications. The following paragraphs present the issues surrounding the TP-Lite or TP-Heavy debate. You can conclude for yourselves which is the best way to go!

### Application Model

TP-Lite solutions are mostly based on a traditional two-tier client/server model. The applications written using this model often support a large number of clients and a few database servers of the same kind. A distributed application typically uses the native interfaces for the database to communicate with the server; for example, a distributed application written using CT-Lib, stored procedures, and the Sybase SQL Server. Here the business logic is collocated in the second tier. As we discussed in earlier sections, this model suffers from the fact that a large number of connections to the database are required and therefore increases the cost per transaction. TP-Heavy solutions purport the three-tier client/server model in which the middle tiers handle the complexities of the business logic, and the databases handle the mundane chores of managing data. The connection multiplexing is again handled in the middle tier by a TP monitor. Modern Internet client/server applications often involve $n$-tier components and a TP-Heavy solution seems to be a better fit.

### Features

The TP-Lite solution is a weak competitor when we compare it in terms of the feature sets offered by the TP-Heavy solution. Many of the features offered by TP monitors (e.g., load balancing, priorities for transactions, data-dependent routing, high availability, connection multiplexing, etc.) are not offered by many of the database servers. Even though the database vendors are catching up in some of the areas like load balancing and high availability, they still have a long way to go in terms of matching the feature sets offered by their TP-Heavy counterparts.

### Performance

A TP-Lite framework may not be suitable for large-scale enterprise-wide applications since it could cause performance bottlenecks in an uneven server load scenario. For example, consider a case in which a database is partitioned across different nodes. In this scenario, one of the Database Servers handling high-volume requests could cause a hotspot in the access to the partitioned data. Load balancing at the Database Server level will not come to the rescue in this case. TP-Heavy frameworks typically address this problem by their load-balancing and data-dependent routing capabilities in the middle tier. These features help the system to scale well since the available system resource can be effectively utilized to improve transaction throughput. Connection multiplexing performed by TP monitors inherently improves the price performance for transactions by reducing the connections to the database and by reducing the system resource requirements such as network connections, number of processes, and so forth.

### Open Computing

A distributed transaction processing application that involves several resources (databases) can be written using the TP-Lite framework. However, these solutions often require the use of the resources provided by the same vendor. For example, a distributed application using Sybase SQL Server product can access multiple servers of the same kind within the same transaction. An Oracle Database Server cannot participate in this global transaction. A TP monitor-based application can access heterogeneous resources within the same global transaction; for example, a distributed application that uses Inprise ITS can access data from an Oracle database, a Sybase database, and a CICS database within the same global transaction. Further, most of the TP monitors conform to the X/Open DTP standards, which allow the application designers to write portable applications.

## Transaction Servers

TP monitors provide the robust, scalable infrastructure for writing mission-critical applications that require transactional integrity. They have been instrumental in incorporating heterogeneous resources in a global transaction. They have been serving the IT community for a few decades and pioneered the concept of application servers to improve performance and scalability. TP monitors have served the departmental and branch office systems category of computing very well. Typically, application servers provided by the TP monitors and other client/server products have catered to the specialized requirements of the distributed transaction processing applications. Enterprise systems push the envelope on modern computing, and the solution provided by a single product is often not sufficient to address the complex technical requirements mandated by them. Further, Internet and intranet applications introduce new challenges to the distributed computing methodologies. These result in a proliferation of specialized application servers and Web-based products that address the needs of the enterprise-wide systems.

Enterprise-wide systems typically have the following technical requirements:

- Ease of use and shorter development life cycles
- Interoperability with existing client/server technologies
- Support for object-oriented component-based computing
- High transaction throughput with minimal latency
- High availability and reliability
- Distributed management of the application
- Scalable system from few users to thousands of users

It would be a tremendous effort and impracticable for any single product to meet these tall-order requirements. TP monitors are the only products that can satisfy most of the requirements just listed. Hence, in order to satisfy all the enterprise-wide system requirements, we are forced to choose several products that can meet the individual requirements through TP monitors, operating systems, network servers, and Web servers.

A new class of products called Transaction Servers has emerged to address the enterprise-wide computing needs. Transaction servers belong to the TP monitor family that provide a robust development and deployment environment. Transaction servers provide a variety of programming languages to implement applications using 4GL RAD tools, and generally make the deployment of the application easier by providing good system administration tools. They provide infrastructure to interoperate with existing application servers. Transaction servers seamlessly integrate with heterogeneous data resources and let a transaction span through various data resources transparently across a LAN/WAN.

Several transaction servers have recently been announced in the industry and they meet the expectations of enterprise-wide client/server computing. Some prominent examples are Microsoft Transaction Server (MTS), IBM Transaction Server, and Sybase Jaguar Transaction Server.

## Object Transaction Monitors

Enterprise-wide mission-critical applications are more demanding than ever in terms of the feature requirements. Internet or intranet-based computing is one of the main ingredients for successful business applications. These classes of applications require distributed object frameworks to provide rapid development, easy deployment, and a scalable architecture. Distributed transaction processing capability is a requirement to create mission-critical business applications. Existing enterprise applications often carry a baggage of legacy technology, and when they are upgraded to use the newer technologies, the main business requirement is complete interoperability with existing application infrastructure. These requirements catch the essence of a modern enterprise application.

Now, the crux is to find a product that can satisfy all these requirements (well, at least most of them). A new trend has emerged in enterprise computing and many companies offer a product that promises to provide all these requirements in one package. The product is fondly referred to as *Object Transaction Monitor* (OTM), which is the next generation of TP monitors. These products offer most of the features required by modern enterprise applications. They offer a flexible object-oriented development environment, distributed object computing and management using Object Request Broker (ORB) infrastructure, and distributed transaction processing capability using Object Transaction Service (OTS). Inprise ITS (Integrated Transaction Service), Orbix OTM, and BEA M3 are a few examples of products in this category.

Chapter 3 describes some of the features and specifications for an OTM.

# PART Two

# OTS and JTS

CHAPTER

3

# Understanding the CORBA Object Transaction Service

Transaction processing systems have become ubiquitous and are the basis for all facets of commercial applications that rely on concurrent access to shared data. The transaction paradigm has been an integral part of the strategy in designing reliable distributed applications. The object computing paradigm has been proven to increase productivity and improve quality in the application development that purports the reuse of components and distributed computing. Amalgamation of these paradigms successfully addresses the business requirements of the commercial transaction processing systems.

OMG's CORBA Object Transaction Service (OTS) provides transactional semantics to the distributed objects world. It enables multiple distributed objects located over the Internet and intranets to participate in a single global transaction. A distributed application can use the IDL interfaces provided by OTS to perform transactional work involving these distributed objects. While ORB handles the complexities in locating and communicating with the objects, OTS provides a good framework to implement mission-critical applications in distributed environments by providing transactional integrity.

We have explained the OTS specification in this chapter from an application programmer's point of view. Detailed explanations are given wherever appropriate and we have added examples using the IDL/C++ mapping to illustrate the concepts introduced in the specification. We have omitted some intricate details of the specification that are relevant only to the implementors of the OTS specification.

## What Does OTS Offer?

OTS specification was put together by industry leading experts from various companies. It offers a rich set of functionality to simplify the task of designing a distributed application. Integration with existing transaction processing standards and the coexistence with the legacy enterprise applications have been well thought through to make this a viable standard for distributed transaction processing applications.

We present a set of salient features that an OTS implementation should provide to comply with the specification. This would give you an idea of what to expect from an implementation of the transaction service presented by different vendors.

**Support for multiple transaction models.** All transaction processing systems support the *Flat Transactions* model. Hence, any OTS implementation must provide the support for the *Flat Transactions* model. Support for the *Nested Transactions* model is an optional feature. Many resource manager vendors such as Sybase or Oracle do not provide *Nested Transactions* support as of now.

**Support for legacy applications.** Object-oriented technology is used to wrap existing legacy business applications and encapsulate them for reuse in the object-oriented frameworks. This would allow customers to migrate to the object world without having to reimplement their legacy code. There is a wealth of data managed by the legacy applications that still comprises most parts of the enterprise information industry. For example, applications written using CICS do not have to be redesigned. They can be wrapped in transactional objects and can be deployed in the new object-oriented business application.

**Model interoperability.** Any new software model or implementation has to always coexist with the legacy applications, which introduces new challenges. We meet with the challenge of marrying existing procedural applications and the object implementations in this case. This mandates an environment in which a single transaction should be able to share both object and procedural code. Many of the existing Transaction Managers comply with the X/Open DTP model, and hence, OTS must interoperate with these Transaction Managers that execute procedural applications.

**Network interoperability.** Modern applications require the interoperability between systems offered by different vendors. This is one of the challenging parts of the specification where it brings dissimilar systems together. There are various combinations of ORB and transaction service implementations that are possible in an enterprise environment. OTS requires that various implementations of the transaction service be able to interoperate in a single ORB or multiple ORB environments and specifies the interaction between these entities.

**Flexible transaction propagation control.** Transaction service allows both client and object implementations to specify whether a transaction context should be propagated with any of the transactional operations. Further, it allows an object to specify transactional behavior for its interfaces. This means that operations on objects with and without transactional behaviors can coexist within the scope of a single transaction. The transaction context is propagated in two different ways, implicitly or explicitly. Implicit propagation is automatically managed by the system; therefore, a transactional operation does not have to specify the transactional behavior in its signature. Explicit propagation is managed by the application by specifying the transactional behavior in its signature explicitly.

**Portability.** Applications that are written for one OTS implementation should be able to run on a different OTS implementation. OTS specification defines an interface between the ORB and the transaction service to enable the portability of the transaction service implementations across different ORB implementations.

## Components of an OTS System

Let us take a look at the basic building blocks of a distributed transaction processing CORBA application. For illustration purposes, Figure 3.1 shows all possible components that are applicable to an *n*-tier model of distributed computing. It is possible to have fewer components in an application. For example, a transaction client could directly communicate to the recoverable server. The application consists of the following entities:

- Transactional client
- Transactional object
- Recoverable and resource objects
- Transactional server
- Recoverable server
- Transaction context

Figure 3.1 depicts the role of each entity and the interactions between them.

### *Transactional Client*

Transactional client is a program that initiates requests to the transactional objects under the umbrella of a transaction. The whole operation is done under the auspices of the transaction service, which guarantees the ACID properties. A transactional client is often referred to as the transaction originator.

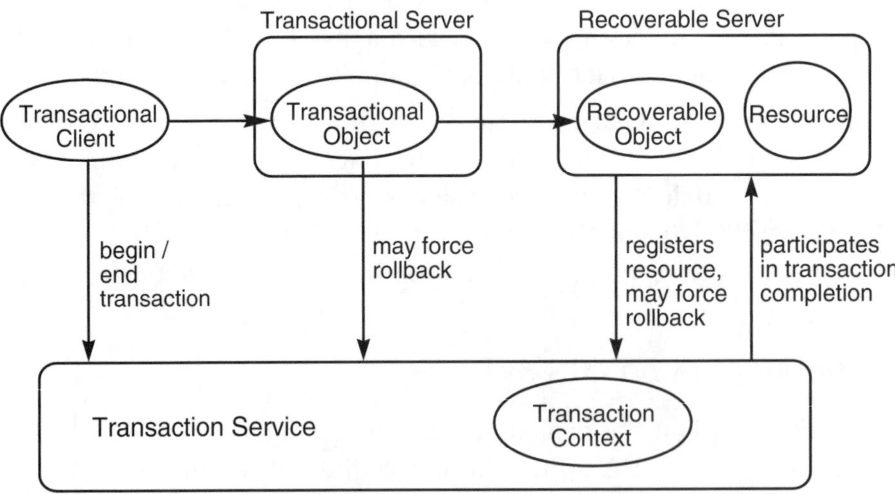


**Figure 3.1** A distributed client/server application.

### *Transactional Object*

A transactional object is an object that can take part in a distributed transaction. Optionally it contains persistent data or has some reference to the persistent data stored elsewhere that can be modified by requests from clients. These requests do not have to be transactional even when issued within the scope of the transaction. A transactional object has the option of supporting transactional behavior at its own discretion. In the case of a client request made to a nontransactional object that does not support the transactional behavior, the work done as part of the request may not survive a failure and it cannot be rolled back if the transaction associated with this work is rolled back. Recoverable object and resource object inherit from the transactional object to obtain the transactional behavior.

### *Recoverable Object and Resource Object*

A recoverable object is basically a transactional object that has the additional responsibility of interfacing with the actual recoverable data. In other words, if the data represented by the object is changed by the act of committing or rolling back a transaction, then it is called a *recoverable object*. Since a recoverable object is directly associated with the recoverable data, it must participate in the transaction service protocols. The participation is done via registering a special object called *resource* with the transaction service. The transaction service coordinates the appropriate transaction completion protocol by invoking requests to the respective resources that are registered in the transaction. Recoverable objects are also required to keep some key runtime information in a persistent storage. This information is critical when a recoverable object restarts after a failure, which aids in the recovery process orchestrated by the transaction service.

### *Transactional Server*

A transactional server is a collection of one or more objects that participate in the transaction that are not directly associated with recoverable data. This means that it does not have any recoverable state of its own. The work done within the transactional server influences the outcome of the transaction only for rollback operations, and it does not directly participate in the completion of the transaction. A good example is an application server. The application server generally houses the business logic in the middle tier of a DTP application. The recoverable data is typically managed by a database, such as Sybase SQL Server. In the case of a failure, application server does not have to go through a recovery process since it does not contain any recoverable data.

### Recoverable Server

A recoverable server is a collection of one or more objects of which at least one of them is recoverable. A recoverable server registers all the resource objects with the transaction service. This vital information is needed by the transaction service to coordinate the transaction completion protocol during a commit operation. The transaction service issues prepare and commit requests to these resources; for example, any server that manages recoverable data and supports a Resource interface. The traditional RDBMS products such as Sybase or Oracle databasE servers are recoverable servers but they do not implement the resource object that OTS requires. They are mainly implemented using procedural interfaces to access the resources. To alleviate this, vendors who offer CORBA OTS service usually provide the resource implementation for these database servers. With this offering in place, a distributed application that uses OTS should seamlessly integrate with the existing database servers. For example, Inprise ITS provides a resource director for Oracle and SybAse databases that implements the resource interface.

### Transaction Context

The transaction context is like the blood running through the transaction's veins. It feeds some metainformation like transaction identifier, timeout values, and some information about its parent transaction (if exists) to all transactional objects. The transaction context associated with an executing thread determines that whether the work done by this thread is transactional or not. If the transaction context is set, it implies that there is a transaction associated with it; otherwise, none. Multiple threads can be simultaneously associated with the same transaction. In the case of a Flat Transaction model, the transaction context has to contain the information about only this transaction. Nested semantics require that the transaction context has to contain the information about the whole transaction, including subtransactions. The transaction context is implicitly propagated to the transactional objects when the client requests a transactional operation on a transactional object. Alternately, the client can explicitly pass the transaction context programmatically. We will talk about the details of how these things work in a later section.

## Basic Concepts

Before we proceed with the explanation of the detailed architecture, let us understand some basic concepts: transaction termination, checked behavior, synchronization, and heuristic completion.

### Transaction Termination

Transaction termination is an act of committing or rolling back the work done within the scope of a transaction. This action is initiated from the client by issuing a request to commit or roll back a transaction. A transaction originator typically initiates transaction termination and, optionally, a transaction service client other than the originator can initiate it. At the client's request to commit the transaction, transaction service starts a two-phase commit protocol with the participants involved. A participant may request to roll back the transaction after a failure condition occurs. In such a case, the transaction will be rolled back by the transaction service and all other participants will roll back their changes. We also use the term *transaction completion* in this book to refer to transaction termination in certain contexts.

### Checked and Unchecked Behavior

X/Open DTP model imposes restriction of premature commitment of a transaction before the work done in a transaction is marked as done. This rule helps to preserve the ACID properties of a transaction and the transactional integrity. This is called a *checked behavior*. For example, the commit operation is not allowed before the credit and debit operations are complete in a credit-debit transaction. The transaction service extends the same concept to provide transactional integrity, but it is totally implementation specific. Some implementations will enforce the checked behavior by providing measures to ensure that all transactional requests issued by the application have completed their execution prior to an attempt to commit the transaction. Some implementations impart this responsibility to the application to provide transactional integrity, which is called *unchecked transaction behavior*.

## Synchron)zation

For some applications it would be desirable to know when the traNsaction service begins to coordinate the transaction termination and ends it. The advantage of this information is that an application can perform a few integrity checks before and after the termination of the transaction is performed. Transaction service allows objects to be notified before and after the transaction termination if they are registered as synchronization objects with the transaction service. For example, before the transaction termination commences, a synchronization object could trigger a background credit check before a loan request is processed. More information on the synchronization objects is presented when we describe the Synchronization interface in detail later in the chapter.

## Heuristic Completion

A resource participating in a global transaction may decide to commit or roll back a transaction independent of the direct orders from the coordinator based on some heuristic decision. A transaction is said to have heuristically completed when one or more of its participating resources made a heuristic decision. Heuristic decisions are made during unusual circumstances that prevent normal processing of a transaction; for example, due to a network failure or a transaction service failure, the resource did not get a request to commit or roll back in a timely manner. The resource may decide to heuristically roll back the work done in the transaction.

By heuristically completing a transaction, a resource (for example, Sybase database) may release all the machine resources that are held (locks, memory, etc.) once the heuristic decision is made. Please note that there is an inherent risk involved here that the final decision by the coordinator might differ from the heuristic decision made by the resource, resulting in a loss of data integrity. Further, if the heuristic decision is not made persistent we may lose the information during a resource failure. Hence, a resource must record its decision in a persistent storage. When the coordinator is able to contact the resource again regarding this transaction, the resource must present the heuristic decision that was made earlier. When the coordinator completes the transaction, it sends a request to the resource to forget about this heuristic outcome.

A resource may return one of the following heuristic outcomes: Heuristic Rollback, Heuristic Commit, HeuristicMixed, and HeuristicHazard.

These exceptions are explained in detail later in the section "Datatypes, Structures, and Exceptions."

## Transaction Service Architecture

The following sections explain the inner workings of the transaction service and the interface details. In Figure 3.2, transaction originator is an arbitrary program that initiates the transaction. A recoverable server hosts the resource objects. The transaction originator either directly or indirectly invokes the objects in the recoverable server by using transactional objects. There are two approaches to deal with the transaction control, *implicit* and *explicit*.

The implicit approach is based on the Current interface that provides operations to create and terminate a transaction. This is a pseudo-interface. When a transaction is begun using the Current interface, the transaction is implicitly associated with the originator's thread. Then the originator issues requests to either transactional or nontransactional objects. When the request is made to a transactional object, the transaction context is automatically propagated by the ORB to the thread executing the method on the transactional object. The Current interface can

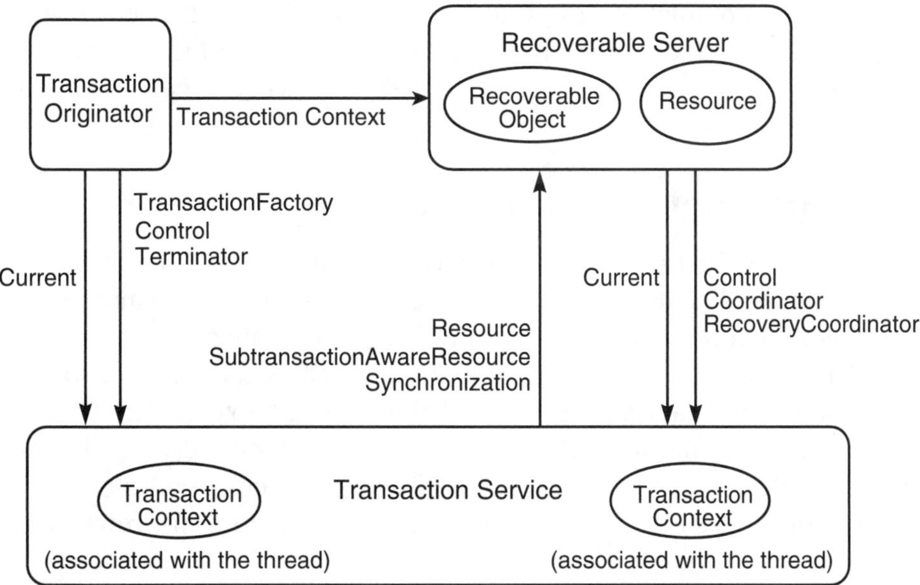


**Figure 3.2** Transaction service architecture.

be used to terminate the transaction by invoking commit or rollback operations. There are few other operations that are exposed by the Current interface, which makes the client's programming easier. Many applications use the Current interface for transaction control since it is simple to use. You can find the detailed explanation on these methods in the section, "Current Interface."

The explicit approach uses more than one interface to control the transaction. In this approach, the transaction originator uses the TransactionFactory interface to create a transaction, which returns a Control object. The Control interface contains methods that expose the Terminator and Coordinator interfaces. The transaction originator can obtain the Terminator or Coordinator objects through the Control object. The transaction originator uses Terminator to commit or roll back the transaction. The Coordinator is either implicitly propagated to the recoverable server through the propagation context or explicitly propagated by the originator. The resource implemented by the recoverable server has to register itself with the transaction service to participate in the two-phase commit protocol. It uses the Coordinator interface to register. The recoverable server optionally registers a synchronization object with the transaction service to get notifications before it begins the two-phase commit protocol and after it completes it. A recoverable server optionally registers a SubtransactionAwareResource object with the transaction service to control the completion of subtransactions. The Resource uses a RecoveryCoordinator object to estimate the outcome of the transaction in failure situations and to coordinate the recovery process with the transaction service.

## Data Types, Structures, and Exceptions

The OTS specification defines the interfaces in an IDL file called CosTransactions.idl. This file defines the CosTransactions module and its interfaces. Before we plunge into the detailed explanation of interfaces that arE offered by the transaction service, let us take a brief look at some important data structures and the relevant exceptions that are explained in the module. This will help you understand the following sections better, when we walk through the interfaces. A complete list of the IDL interfaces is presented at the end of this chapter for reference.

### *Data Types*

The CosTransactions module defines two data types, Status and Vote. Status enumerates all possible states that a transaction can go through.

Vote is an enumeration for all the possible replies from the resource during the prepare phase of the two-phase commit protocol.

```
enum Status {
   StatusActive,
   StatusMarkedRollback,
   StatusPrepared,
   StatusCommitted,
   StatusRolledBack,
   StatusUnknown,
   StatusNoTransaction,
   StatusPreparing,
   StatusCommitting,
   StatusRollingBack
};
enum Vote {
   VoteCommit,
   VoteRollback,
   VoteReadOnly
};
```

VoteCommit indicates that the resource has already prepared the transaction and the decision to commit the transaction has already been written to a stable storage (to assist recovery during a failuRe). VoteRollback indicates that the resource wishes to roll back the transaction. VoteReadOnly is used to indicate that there were no modifications done to the persistent data represented by the resource during this transaction.

## *Data Structures*

CosTransactions module defines three basic data structures: otid_t, TransIDentity, and PropagationContext.

### otid_t

otid_t is an IDLized version of the X/Open specified transaction identifier *XID*. This is a unique global identifier that represents a transaction. Since otid_t is based on *XID*, given an otid_t, it can be easily converted to an *XID*.

```
struct otid_t {
   long formatID; /*format identifier. 0 is OSI TP */
   long bqual_length;
   sequence <octet> tid;
};
```

#### TransIdentity

TransIdentity structure contains information about a transaction. It holds coordinator, terminator, and the otid information. Setting the value for the terminator is optional. Both coordinator and terminator information set by an exporting transaction service can be used by another transaction service to recreate the transaction in its domain. If a transaction service does not allow entities other than the transaction originator to terminate a transaction, the terminator should be set to NULL.

```
struct TransIdentity {
   Coordinator coordinator;
   Terminator terminator;
   otid_t otid;
};
```

#### PropagationContext Structure

The main ingredients of the PropagationContext structure are the TransIdentity and timeout value. In addition, it includes a sequence of TransIdentity structures for an implementation of the transaction service that supports nested transactions. The sequence contains information about the parent and all the ancestors of this transaction. It is flexible enough to include implementation-specific data that could be used for propagating data of a proprietary nature.

```
struct PropagationContext {
   unsigned long timeout;
   TransIdentity current;
   sequence <TransIdentity> parents;
   any implementation_specific_data;
};
```

### *Exceptions*

We can categorize the exceptions into three groups: *standard*, *heuristic*, and *module specific*.

#### Standard Exceptions

There are three Transaction Service specific exceptions that have been added to the CORBA specification under the standard exceptions category. These exceptions can be raised by any ORB request.

```
exception TRANSACTION_REQUIRED {};
exception TRANSACTION_ROLLEDBACK {};
exception INVALID_TRANSACTION {};
```

The TRANSACTION_REQUIRED exception can be raised to indicate that a valid transaction context is required for this request.

The TRANSACTION_ROLLEDBACK exception can be raised to indicate that the transaction associated with the request has already been rolled back or has been destined to roll back eventually.

The INVALID_TRANSACTION exception can be raised to indicate that an invalid transaction context was used associated with the request.

In addition to this, transaction service adds another exception called WRONG_TRANSACTION to the CORBA specification to cater to the needs of the deferred synchronous request. This exception is thrown to indicate that the transaction context associated with the requesting thread is not the same as the thread that is executing the deferred synchronous requests.

### Heuristic Exceptions

Heuristic exceptions are used as a vehicle to convey the independent decision made by a resource to commit or roll back the transaction without the specific instructions from the transaction service about the outcome of the transaction. There are several scenarios in which a heuristic decision can be made. The following exceptions represent each one of those scenarios. These exceptions should be treated with special care due to the fact that there may be a possible loss of data integrity.

```
exception HeuristicRollback {};
exception HeuristicCommit {};
exception HeuristicMixed {};
exception HeuristicHazard {};
```

A resource throws HeuristicRollback exception for a commit request to indicate that all relevant updates have been rolled back.

A resource throws HeuristicCommit exception for a rollback request to indicate that all relevant updates have been committed.

A resource throws HeuristicMixed exception to indicate that some relevant updates have been committed and others have been rolled back.

A resource throws HeuristicHazard exception to report that either the relevant updates are committed or rolled back. It is possible that we may not know whether all updates are complete.

Out of these exceptions, the HeuristicMixed scenario seems to have suffered the worst and it takes priority over HeuristicHazard exception.

### Module-Specific Exceptions

The following exceptions are thrown from the operations that are defined by the interfaces from the CosTransactions module. Explanations for these exceptions can be found in the following sections where we describe each interface in detail.

```
exception SubtransactionsUnavailable {};
exception NotSubtransaction {};
exception Inactive {};
exception NotPrepared {};
exception NoTransaction {};
exception InvalidControl {};
exception Unavailable {};
exception SynchronizationUnavailable {};
```

## Transaction Service Interfaces

OTS specification defines several interfaces in the CosTransactions module that are responsible for the key functions that constitute the life cycle of a CORBA transaction. These interfaces are:

- Current
- TransactionFactory
- Control
- Terminator
- Coordinator
- RecoveryCoordinator
- Resource
- Synchronization
- SubtransactionAwareResource
- TransactionalObject

The following sections explain these interfaces in detail and we have illustrated their use with simple examples.

## Current Interface

Current is one of the most important interfaces and is designed to make application programming easier by providing all the necessary operations that are required to write CORBA transactions in one interface. It provides operations to simplify transaction management that are required by CORBA transactional applications. For example, the Current interface:

- Allows the client to begin and end a CORBA transaction.
- Allows implicit propagation of transaction context to the transaction service and other transactional objects.
- Allows operations to obtain information about the current transaction.

The Current interface is implemented as a CORBA pseudo-object. Depending on the invoking thread, it may alter the transaction context associated with it. Since this is not a true CORBA object, it cannot be accessed remotely.

```
interface Current {

   void begin()
      raises(SubtransactionsUnavailable);
   void commit(in boolean report_heuristics)
      raises(
         NoTransaction,
         HeuristicMixed,
         HeuristicHazard
      );
   void rollback()
      raises(NoTransaction);
   void rollback_only()
      raises(NoTransaction);
   Status get_status();
   string get_transaction_name();
   void set_timeout(in unsigned long seconds);
   Control get_control();
   Control suspend();
   void resume(in Control which)
      raises(InvalidControl);
};
```

**begin()** creates a new transaction. The transaction context associated with the client thread is set to this new transaction. If a top-level transaction already exists, subsequent begin operations start subtransactions. Nested transaction is not a required feature for the transaction service; hence, a SubtransactionsUnavailable exception is raised if an implementation does not support Nested Transactions.

**commit()** terminates the transaction that is associated with the current thread. The transaction context associated with this thread is restored to its prior state of the begin request. The exception NoTransaction is raised if there was no transaction associated with the client thread. The exception NO_PERMISSION is raised if the client does not have permission to commit the transaction. This operation is equivalent to issuing a commit on a terminator object. To find out if there were any heuristic decisions made by the resources, set report_heuristics to true.

**rollback()** ends the transaction that is associated with the current thread and it is rolled back. The transaction context associated with this thread is restored to its prior state of the begin request. The exception NoTransaction is raised if there was no transaction associated with the client thread. The exception NO_PERMISSION is raised if the client does not have permission to roll back the transaction. This operation is equivalent to issuing a rollback on a terminator object.

**rollback_only()** modifies the transaction associated with the current thread so that the final outcome of the transaction when it completes is to roll back the transaction. The exception NoTransaction is raised if there was no transaction associated with the client thread. This operation is equivalent to issuing a rollback_only() on a coordinator object.

**get_status()** returns the status of the transaction that is associated with the client thread. The exception NoTransaction is raised if there was no transaction associated with the client thread. It is equivalent to issuing a get_status() operation on a coordinator object.

**get_transaction_name()** is used mainly for debugging or diagnostic purposes. It returns a printable string that is indicative of a transaction. It is equivalent to issuing a get_transaction_name() on a coordinator object.

**get_control()** returns a control object that represents the transaction context currently associated with the client thread. If there is no transaction context associated with this transaction, a nil value is returned. Since control object represents a transaction, this object can be passed around if explicit control of the transaction propagation is desired.

**set_timeout()** sets a timeout value for a transaction. The transaction service will attempt to roll back the transaction if the transaction does not complete before the timeout expires. If the timeout value is set to 0, it signifies that there will not be any application-specific timeout values.

**suspend()** disassociates the transaction from the current thread and returns a control object that represents the transaction context of the suspended thread. If the client thread is not associated with a transaction, a nil object reference is returned. This is a powerful operation that allows the sharing of transactions by multiple threads. The control object returned by suspend operation can be given to a resume operation to reestablish the transaction context in the same thread or a different thread. After a suspend operation, an attempt to use the current interface other than resume will raise a TRANSACTION_REQUIRED exception.

**resume()** associates the client thread with the specified transaction. If an invalid control object is passed, it raises an InvalidControl exception. This is a very useful operation that allows sharing of the transaction by multiple threads. Implicit propagation is achieved by associating the thread with the specified transaction context. If the client thread was previously associated with another transaction, it switches to the specified context and the old transaction context is forgotten.

## *How to Use the Current Interface*

We provide a few C++ code samples to illustrate the usage of the Current interface in the following sections.

### Obtaining Current Interface

The following code sample shows how a reference to a Current object is obtained using resolve_initial_references() operation provided by the ORB.

```
int main() {
  try {
    // ORB releated initialization procedures
    CORBA::ORB_var orb = CORBA::ORB_init(argc, argv);
```

```
        // Get Current.
        CORBA::Object_var curObject =
          orb->resolove_initial_references("TransactionCurrent");
        CosTransactions::Current_var current =
          CosTransactions::Current::_narrow(curObject);

      }
      catch(...) {

        // Handle the exception.
      }
    }
```

### Transaction Bracketing

This code sample demonstrates the use of transaction delineation operations like begin, commit, and rollback.

```
...
// Begin a transaction.
current->begin();
// Place an order to sell Microsoft shares at a limit price of $130.
retStatus = stock->sell("Microsoft", 130);
if (retStatus == SOLD) {

  // Commit the transaction and if a heuristic decision was
  // made, handle the exception.
  try {

    current->commit(1);
  }
  catch(...) {

    // handle heuristic exception here.
  }
}
else {

  // Rollback the transaction.
  current->rollback();
}
...
```

### Managing Transaction

We have shown how to use different operations to control or get information about a transaction.

```
...
// Print the transaction's name and status.
```

```
  cout << "Transaction name = " << current->get_transaction_name() <<
endl;
  cout << "Transaction status = " << current->get_status() << endl;

  // Set the transaction timeout value to be 15 seconds from now on.
  current->set_timeout(15);

  // Save the control object for tracking purposes.
  CosTransactions::Control_var oldControl = current->get_control();
```

### Sharing Transactions from the Same Thread

The following code sample shows how a thread can work on different transactions by switching the transaction context.

```
// Assume transaction A is in progress now.
// Suspend to get the control object.
CosTransactions::Control_var controlObjA = current->suspend();
try {

  // Start a new transaction B.
  current->begin();
  // Do work.
  Current->commit(1); //End of transaction B.
}
catch(...) {

  // Continue with Transaction A.
  current->resume(controlObjA);
  // Carry out your planned action.
}
```

## TransactionFactory Interface

In the previous section, the Current interface was used to create a transaction. Another way to create a transaction is to use the Transaction-Factory interface. It defines two operations, create and recreate, that initiate top-level transactions. Unlike Current, this is a CORBA object; therefore, a location facility like the FactoryFinder interface of the life cycle service can be used to obtain a reference. Then a client can invoke create or recreate operations to get a Control object for a transaction.

```
interface TransactionFactory {

  Control create(in unsigned long time_out);
  Control recreate(in PropagationContext ctx);
};
```

**create().** A new top-level transaction is created with the specified time_out value. This operation returns a Control object that can be used by the originator to complete the transaction or can be passed explicitly to another program for controlling the transaction. This mechanism allows a nonoriginator to conclude the transaction if the transaction service implementation provides this facility. The transaction expires after the specified time_out value and the transaction service will attempt to roll back the transaction. If the time_out value is set to 0, there is no application-specific timeout established.

**recreate().** It does the magic of reincarnating an existing transaction in an arbitrary thread. The PropagationContext of the existing transaction is passed in as a parameter to this operation. A control object is returned that is a new representation of the transaction. This operation serves an interesting purpose when we import transactions from another transaction service domain or during *interpositioning*. Interpositioning is a technique used to create a surrogate coordinator in the importing domain to collocate the coordinating function close to the resources to avoid extra network traffic.

### *How to Use the TransactionFactory Interface*

Next we illustrate the use of the TransactionFactory interface with a C++ sample code.

```
// Create a new transaction with 15 seconds timeout value.
CosTransactions::TransactionFactory_var tFactory;
CosTransactions::Control_var control = tFactory->create(15);

// Obtain the propagation context from the control object.
CosTransactions::PropagationContext_var propContext;
propContext = control->get_coordinator()->get_txcontext();

// Let us recreate the transaction from this propagation context.
CosTransactions::Control_var recreatedControl =
                  tFactory->recreate(propContext);

// Both control objects returned by create and recreate operations
     // must be the same.
if (control != recreatedControl) {

  // transaction service internal error. //
       cout << "Fatal transaction service internal error." << "\n";
}
```

## Control Interface

A transaction context can be explicitly managed by using this interface. Further, this object can be propagated to other programs programmatically for controlling the participation in the transaction. It provides two operations, get_terminator() and get_coordinator(). The operation get_terminator() provides facilities to either commit or roll back the transaction. The operation get_coordinator() provides facilities that are required by resources to participate in a transaction.

```
interface Control {

    Terminator get_terminator()
        raises(Unavailable);
    Coordinator get_coordinator()
        raises(Unavailable);
};
```

**get_terminator()** returns a terminator object that can be used to commit or roll back the transaction. This operation raises an Unavailable exception if control cannot provide the request. In some OTS implementations, you may not be allowed to pass the terminator explicitly to other programs with the intent of terminating the transaction. This is to prevent a nonoriginator from terminating the transaction.

**get_coordinator()** returns a coordinator object that can be used to register resources and for other utility functions. This operation raises an Unavailable exception if control cannot provide the request. In some OTS implementations, you may not be allowed to pass the Coordinator explicitly to other programs with the intent of terminating the transaction. This is to prevent a nonoriginator from terminating the transaction.

## Terminator Interface

This interface provides two operations that are required to conclude a transaction, commit and rollback. Typically, a transaction originator uses it. A transaction service implementation decides the scope of availability of this object (i.e., whether a nonoriginator can use Terminator object to conclude a transaction).

```
interface Terminator
{
    void commit(in boolean report_heuristics)
        raises(
            HeuristicMixed,
            HeuristicHazard
        );
    void rollback();
};
```

**commit( ).** A number of conditions have to be met before a transaction can be committed. A transaction can successfully commit only if it has not been marked for rollback and the participants involved in the transaction all vote affirmatively to commit the transaction. The transaction is rolled back if any of these conditions are not met. If report_heuristics flag is set to TRUE, the transaction service will report any heuristic decisions that were reported by resources during the completion of the transaction. In case of an inconsistent outcome, the terminator raises either HeuristicMixed exception or HeuristicHazard exception.

After a top-level transaction commits, the changes that were made to the recoverable objects within the scope of this transaction are made persistent. The changes are visible to other clients only after committing. However, when a subtransaction is committed, the visibility of the changes to other clients is dictated by the isolation policies enforced by the resources.

**rollback( ).** This operation rolls back the transaction and the changes that were made to the recoverable objects within the scope of this transaction. In the case of nested transactions, all changes made by subordinate transactions are rolled back along with the top-level transaction. Resource-level locks for this transaction are released depending on the isolation policies enforced by the resources.

### *How to Use the Terminator Interface*

The following code sample shows how to use the Terminator object to terminate a transaction.

```
// Create a new transaction with 15 seconds timeout value.
  CosTransactions::TransactionFactory_var tFactory;
  CosTransactions::Control_var control = tFactory->create(15);
  CosTransactions::Terminator_var terminator =
```

```
    control->get_terminator();
  retStatus = stock->buy("Microsoft", 70);
  if (retStatus == BOUGHT) {

    // Commit the transaction and inform if there was any heuristic
    // decision.
    terminator->commit(1);
  }
  else {

    // Rollback the transaction.
    terminator->rollback();
  }
  ...
```

## Coordinator Interface

This is one of the heavily used interfaces that provides several operations required for transaction coordination. We have categorized these operations into five groups for easy comprehension. They are:

- Creation and control of transactions
- get_ operations for transaction status, name, and context
- is_ operations for comparing two transactions
- Register operations to register the participants or synchronization objects with the transaction service
- Hash operations for quick retrieval of transactions

```
interface Coordinator {

  Status get_status();
  Status get_parent_status();
  Status get_top_level_status();
  boolean is_same_transaction(in Coordinator tc);
  boolean is_related_transaction(in Coordinator tc);
  boolean is_ancestor_transaction(in Coordinator tc);
  boolean is_descendant_transaction(in Coordinator tc);
  boolean is_top_level_transaction();
  unsigned long hash_transaction();
  unsigned long hash_top_level_tran();
  RecoverYCoordinator register_resource(in Resource r)
    raises(Inactive);
  void register_synchronization (in Synchronization sync)
    raises(Inactive, SynchronizationUnavailable);
  void register_subtran_aware(in SubtransactionAwareResource r)
```

```
        raises(Inactive, NotSubtransaction);
    void rollback_only()
        raises(Inactive);
    string get_transaction_name();
    Control create_subtransaction()
        raises(SubtransactionsUnavailable, Inactive);
    PropagationContext get_txcontext ()
        raises(Unavailable);
};
```

### *Creation and Control of Transactions*

**create_subtransaction()** is used to create a new subOrdinate transaction. The transaction associated with the current object is the parent of this subtransaction. Inactive exception will be raised if the transaction has already been prepared. In the case where the transaction service does not support nested transactions, SubtransactionsUnavailable exception will be raised. Like the TransactionFactory create operation, this operation returns the Control object that can be used to terminate the subordinate transaction.

**rollback_only()** is used to indicate to the transaction service that the object wishes to roll back the entire transaction. Once the transaction service responds affirmatively to this request, the only possible outcome is to roll back the transaction. Inactive exception will be raised if the transaction has already been prepared.

### *get_ Operations*

These operations allow the target object to obtain the transaction's name, status, or context. This information is required for the participants to explicitly control the transaction.

**get_status().** Returns status of the transaction associated with this object. Example: StatusPrepared.

**get_parent_status().** Returns the status of the parent transaction. If the transaction associated with the object is top-level, the behavior is equivalent to get_status() operation.

**get_top_level_status().** Returns the status of the top-level ancestor transaction. If the transaction associated with the object is top-level, the behavior is equivalent to get_status() operation.

**get_transaction_name().** For debugging purposes, one can obtain a printable string of the transaction's name.

**get_tx_context().** Obtains the propagation context information that is very useful during importing from or exporting to different transaction service implementations. Transaction service raises the Unavailable exception if it chooses to restrict the availability of the propagation context.

### *is_ Operations*

These operations are used to compare the transaction associated with the target object to the transaction that is being compared. The Coordinator object is passed as an argument for comparison.

**is_same_transaction().** Compares the transaction associated with the target object to the transaction represented by the Coordinator object that is passed in. Returns true if they are the same.

**is_ancestor_transaction().** Returns true if the transaction associated with the target object is the ancestor of the transaction represented by the Coordinator object.

**is_descendant_transaction().** Returns true if the transaction associated with the Coordinator object is the ancestor of the transaction represented by the target object.

**is_related_transaction().** This operation allows us to find out whether the transaction associated with the target object and the transaction represented by the Coordinator object have a common ancestor.

**is_top_level_transaction().** This operation is used to find out whether the transaction associated with the target object has a parent or not.

### *register_ Operations*

Resource objects have to register with the transaction service to include themselves as participants in a global transaction, and synchronization objects have to register with the transaction service to get notifications.

**register_resource().** Register a resource as a participant in the transaction associated with this object. This is required so that when the transaction terminates, the transaction service can send requests to prepare, commit, or roll back the work done as part of this transaction. If the current transaction is a subtransaction, the resources will not get these requests until the top-level transaction terminates.

**register_synchronization( ).** This operation registers a synchronization object in the transaction. This enables the transaction service to send notification to the synchronization object before and after the completion of the transaction.

**register_subtran_aware( ).** This operation registers a subtransaction aware resource so that it can receive notification when the subtransaction commits or rolls back.

### Hash Operations

These operations return the hash code for the transactions associated with the target object. Each instance of the transaction service maintains a single hash code for a transaction. Given the coordinator objects, we can use hash codes to efficiently compare whether the coordinators belong to the same transaction. Note that it is possible to have the same hash code but still they could represent two different transactions if the coordinators belong to different instances of the transaction service. In this case, to make sure we are referring to the same transaction, is_same_transaction() operation can be used.

**hash_transaction( ).** Returns the hash code for the transaction associated with this object.

**hash_top_level_tran( ).** Returns the hash code for the top-level transaction associated with this object.

### How to Use Coordinator Interface

Coordinator is a rich interface that offers many operations to the client to manage the current transaction. The following code sample is intended to show how some of these operations can be used in different situations.

```
// Get the coordinator object.
  CosTransactions::Coordinator_var coord = control->get_coordinator();
  // Register a resource object with the transaction service.
  CosTransactions::RecoveryCoordinator_var rcoord =
    coord->register_resource(resource);
  // Create a sub transaction.
  CosTransactions::Control_var subTran =
    coord->create_subtransaction();
  retStatus = doWork();
```

```
if (retStatus == FAILED) {

  // Work done under the subtransaction failed. Rollback the
  // entire transaction.
  cout << "The transaction " << coord->get_transaction_name() <<
    " is being rolled back due to subtransaction failure";
  cout << "Current Status of the transaction is " <<
    coordinator->get_status();
  coordinator->rollback_only();
}
...
```

## RecoveryCoordinator Interface

When a resource is registered, a RecoveryCoordinator object is returned. This could be used to handle certain recovery situations; for example, a resource could use its own timeout mechanism for a transaction to complete. If the timeout expires and if the resource did not receive any requests to commit or roll back the transaction, it can send a hint to the transaction service to initiate completion by sending a replay_completion() request. The RecoveryCoordinator object is implicitly associated with the resource, and only that resource can use it.

```
interface RecoveryCoordinator {

  Status replay_completion(in Resource r)
     raises(NotPrepared);
};
```

The resource can send this request only after it has prepared itself for a commit. This operation sends a hint to the Coordinator that the resource has not received any requests to commit or roll back the transaction. This is a nonblocking operation and it returns the current status of the transaction.

## Resource Interface

Recoverable objects implement this interface. When these objects are registered with the transaction service, the transaction service can orchestrate the completion of the transaction using the two-phase commit protocol on each resource. Resource interfaCe defines operations that are invoked by the transaction service during the two-phase commit processing; for example, prepare(), commit(), rollback(), commit_one_phase(), and forget().

```
interface Resource {

    Vote prepare()
        raiSes(
            HeuristicMixed,
            HeuRisticHazard
        );
    void rollback()
        raises(
            HeuristicCommit,
            HeuristicMixed,
            HeuristicHazard
        );
    void commit()
        raises(
            NotPrepared,
            HeuristicRollback,
            HeuristicMixed,
            HeuristicHazard
        );
    void cOmmit_one_phase()
        raises(
            HeuristicHazard
        );
    void forget();
};
```

**prepare().** This initiates the first phase of the two-phase commit protocol in the resource. Resource reports the result of the prepare operation using a vote token. It returns VoteReadOnly to indicate that there were no modifications done to the persistent data in this transaction. It returns VoteCommit to indicate that it is prepared to commit the transaction since it has already written its decision to a persistent resource storage. It returns VoteRollback to indicate that either the resource does not know anything about this transaction (happens after a crash), or a failure occurred while preparing. If this response is received, the transaction must be rolled back and the resource can be forgotten. If the resource happened to conclude the transaction based on heuristics, it has to throw HeuristicMixed or HeuristicHazard exception, depending on the situation. Once the transaction service receives affirmative responses (VoteCommit) from all the resources, it decides to commit the transaction.

**rollback().** This operation instructs the resource to roll back all the work done on behalf of the transaction with which it is associated. If the resource happened to conclude the transaction based on heuristics, it has to throw HeuristicCommit, HeuristicMixed, or HeuristicHazard exception, depending on the situation.

**commit().** This operation instructs the resource to commit all the work done on behalf of the transaction with which it is associated. If the resource happened to conclude the transaction based on heuristics, it has to throw HeuristicRollback, HeuristicMixed, or HeuristicHazard exception, depending on the situation. NotPrepared exception can be raised if the commit request arrived before the transaction is prepared.

**commit_one_phase().** This is an optimization to cover a case in which there is only a single resource that is involved in the transaction. Resource can directly commit the transaction without performing the prepare phase. In the case of a failure to commit, resource raises a TRANSACTION_ROLLEDBACK exception. If the resource happened to conclude the transaction based on heuristics, it has to raise HeuristicHazard exception.

**forget().** If a resource raised a heuristic exception for rollback(), commit(), or commit_one_phase() operations, the coordinator of the transaction has to send a forget request to the resource. When a resource raises a heuristic exception it is supposed to store this decision in a persistent storage to survive failures and is not allowed to throw away this information until the coordinator explicitly asks the resource to forget this information.

### *How to Use Resource Interface*

Typically, an application programmer is not concerned with the implementation of the resource interface. Exceptions are special resource objects that do not use resource managers associated with databases. We have already shown a model implementation of a resource interface in Chapter 1, "Quick Start to EJB, JTS, and OTS."

## Synchronization Interface

Synchronization is a vehicle for the Transaction Service to notify a transactional object before the commencement of the one-phase or two-phase commit protocol and after completing it. Figure 3.3 illustrates the organization of the synchronization objects and how it fits in the overall architecture. The synchronization interface provides two operations, before_completion() and after_completion(), to synchronize the application events. Since these operations are user-defined, it allows the users to customize these operations to fit their application needs. Note that the synchronization objects are not recoverable and hence in the case of transaction service failures, the synchronization objects will not be notified.

```
interface Synchronization : TransactionalObject {

    void before_completion();
    void after_completion(in Status status);
};
```

**before_completion().** Before the transaction completion procedure commences, either Through one-phase or two-phase commit protocols, the transaction service invokes this operation to synchronize the events. In a two-phase commit scenario, this operation is called prior to the commencement of the prepare phase. A synchronization object can make sure that any transient data that needs to be made persistent is provided to the resource.

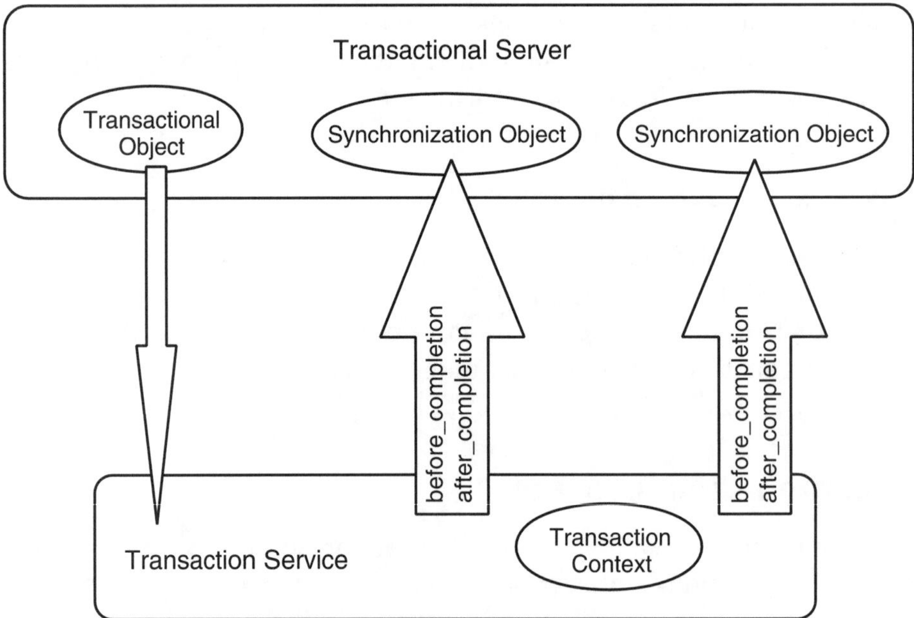


**Figure 3.3** Synchronization interface.

**after_completion( ).** After the transaction completion procedure completes (i.e., after the transaction coordinator receives all the commit or rollback responses), this operation is invoked to synchronize the events. The synchronization objects are notified with the current status of the transaction.

### *How to Use Synchronization Objects*

Synchronization is a powerful tool that can be used in a transactional application for various purposes, such as reducing the use of system resources, use helper services that aid in the check of transactional integrity, mail notification when transaction completes, and others. The following are a few examples of how a synchronization object can be used.

#### Using before_completion()

This operation is called before the transaction service issues a prepare() or commit_one_phase() operation to a resource. You can implement these by before_completion():

**Optimize the use of system resources.** The state changes and transient data that belongs to transactional object can be cached, and just before the transaction commences completion, we may want to flush these changes to a permanent storage managed by a database. We can also register a resource from a Synchronization object to delay the use of one until we need it. The justification here is that we do not need a resource until we start accessing it and we do not have to keep a connection open until we need one to flush the changes to disk.

**Implementing qualifications to commit.** Before allowing a credit purchase, a credit history check can be performed. If the account holder has a bad credit history, the purchase can be denied.

#### Using after_completion()

This operation is called after the transaction service issues a commit(), commit_one_phase(), or rollback() operation to a resource. You can implement these by after_completion():

**Notification to other processes.** When the stock purchase transaction is complete you may want to notify the customer via e-mail.

The after_completion() operation can send an e-mail explaining the status of the transaction depending on the status provided (StatusCommitted or StatusRolledback).

**Cleaning up resources.** A Transactional object can clean up the memory resources that it acquired.

### *Scope of the Synchronization Operations*

Figure 3.4 depicts the scope of the before_completion() and after_completion() operations during commit(), commit_one_phase(), or rollback() invocations. It also explains when these operations occur.

### *Synchronization Object Failure Scenarios*

If any of the synchronization objects is not available when before_completion() is invoked on them, the transaction will be rolled back and the before_completion() will not be invoked for the remaining synchronization objects. If any of the synchronization objects are not available when after_completion() is invoked, it is simply ignored. In the case of a transaction service failure, on recovery, the synchronization objects will not receive before_completion() or after_completion() notifications.

## SubtransactionAwareResource Interface

This specialized resource interface is used for the resources that use the nested transaction model. If a recoverable object wishes to receive a notification when a subtransaction completes, it has to register a specialized resource object that offers a SubtransactionAwareResource interface with the transaction service. To register, either register_resource() or register_subtran_aware() operations of the current ***Coordinator*** object can be used. This resource interface offers commit_subtransaction() and rollback_transaction() operations to instruct the resource to commit and roll back the subtransaction, respectively.

```
interface SubtransactionAwareResource : Resource {

    void commit_subtransaction(in Coordinator parent);
    void rollback_subtransaction();
};
```

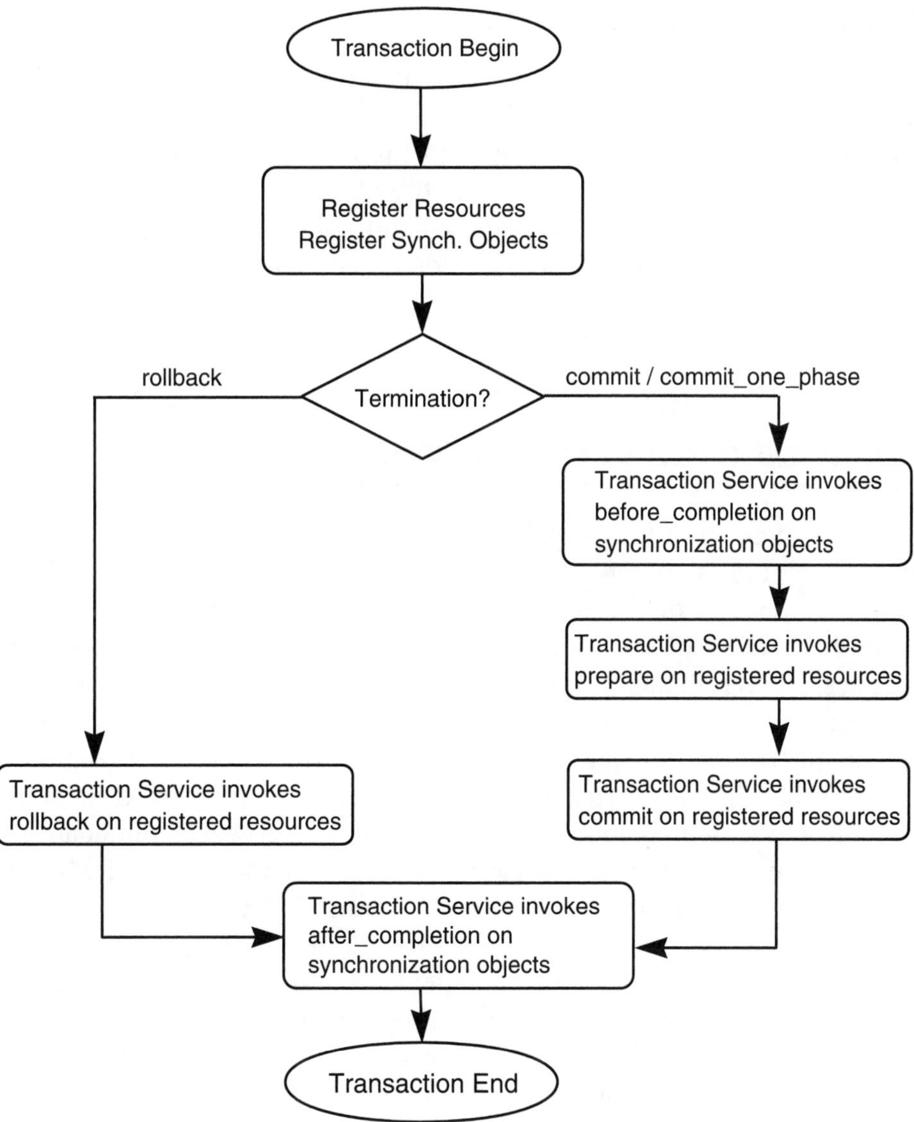


**Figure 3.4** Scope of synchronization operations.

**commit_subtransaction( ).** Transaction service invokes this operation only if the resource has been registered with a subtransaction and the subtransaction has been committed. It takes the parent Coordinator object as the argument.

**rollback_subtransaction( ).** Transaction service invokes this operation only if the resource has been registered with a subtransaction and the subtransaction has been rolled back.

### TransactionalObject Interface

This is a very important interface that controls the transactional behavior of an object. This abstract interface has no operations. To qualify your object as a transactional object, just inherit your object from TransactionalObject. If an object is transactional, ORB will implicitly propagate the transaction context associated with the client thread during any of the client invocations of the methods implemented by the object.

```
interface TransactionalObject { };
```

## Application Programming Models

OTS specification is very flexible and supports several application programming models to cater to modern enterprise business applications. The complexities of these applications vary tremendously depending upon the number of resources, number of application servers, and who initiates and terminates a transaction. For simple applications, transaction service provides a model that is simple to use, has fewer knobs to control the transaction, and the propagation of the transaction context is implicitly handled by the transaction service. This model requires very little effort from the application designer to implement powerful applications. For complex applications, transaction service provides a model wherein the application designer has the complete control of the transaction origination, termination, and propagation of the transaction context.

The transaction service allows a client program to manage a transaction indirectly or directly. Indirect context management implies that the application program uses current object to associate the transaction context with the application thread of control. Direct context management implies that the application program uses control object to manipulate the transaction context and other objects associated with the transaction. With these two models in place for managing the transaction, propagating the transaction context can happen in two different ways, *implicitly* or *explicitly*. With implicit propagation, the transaction context associated with the client thread is passed on to the transactional objects without the client's intervention. With explicit propagation, the application passes the transaction context to the objects as explicit parameters in the method invocation. A client may use either form of context management and may control the propagation of the transaction context by using either method of transaction propagation. This provides us with four application models that a client can use to communicate with the transactional objects.

**Indirect Context Management with Implicit Propagation.** Creation and control of the transaction is done using the operations provided by the current object. When a client invokes methods implemented by a transactional object, the ORB automatically propagates the transaction context associated with the client's thread to the object.

**Direct Context Management with Explicit Propagation.** Control, coordinator, or terminator objects have the transaction context information. A client application can send the transaction's context by passing these objects in the method invocation of the object. The object can use this information to control the transaction.

**Indirect Context Management with Explicit Propagation.** Some applications that use current object may require transaction service objects such as control to enable the termination of the transaction by a nonoriginator. In this case, the get_control() operation of the current interface can be used to obtain the control object. The control object can be passed in the method invocation of the object.

**Direct Context Management with Implicit Propagation.** A client can use the resume operation on the current interface to set the implicit transaction context associated with its thread. Subsequent method invocations on the transactional object cause the transaction context to be propagated automatically.

Even though all of the four models are useful for various applications, the first two models are most widely used due to their simplicity. The following examples show how to use these two models. The interfaces given next define various objects that are transactional and nontransactional.

Note that the IDL specifications are different when using implicit or explicit propagation.

```
interface Bank {

    ...
    Account getAccount(in string account_name);
    ...
};

interface Account : CosTransactions::TransationalObject {
```

```
    ...
    void withdraw(in int account_number, in float amount);
    ...
};
```

Bank interface implements getAccount() operation that returns the Account object matching the account holder's name. Once the Account object is obtained, money can be withdrawn from the account holder's account using withdraw() operation. Bank object is nontransactional and Account object is transactional.

### *Indirect Context Management with Implicit Propagation*

In this example, the transaction originator uses indirect context management and implicit propagation. The client uses Current interface and invokes the begin operation to start a transaction. get_account() operation is invoked on the Bank object to get the account holder's Account and, subsequently, withdraw() operation is issued. Since the Account object is transactional, the ORB implicitly propagates the transaction context to the transactional object. Figure 3.5 illustrates the implicit context propagation.

```
main() {

    ...
    current->begin();
    // Obtain bank IOR.
    Account_var account = bank->get_account("Donald Duck");
    // Transaction context is implicitly propagated here.
    account->withdraw(account->account_number, 100);      current-
>commit(1);
    ...
  }
```

### *Direct Context Management with Explicit Propagation*

In this example, the transaction originator uses direct context management and explicit transaction propagation. The TransactionFactory interface is used to create the transaction. When the transaction is created, a Control object is returned. The Control object is used to obtain the Terminator and Coordinator objects. Client program uses the terminator object to commit or roll back the transaction. Alternately, the

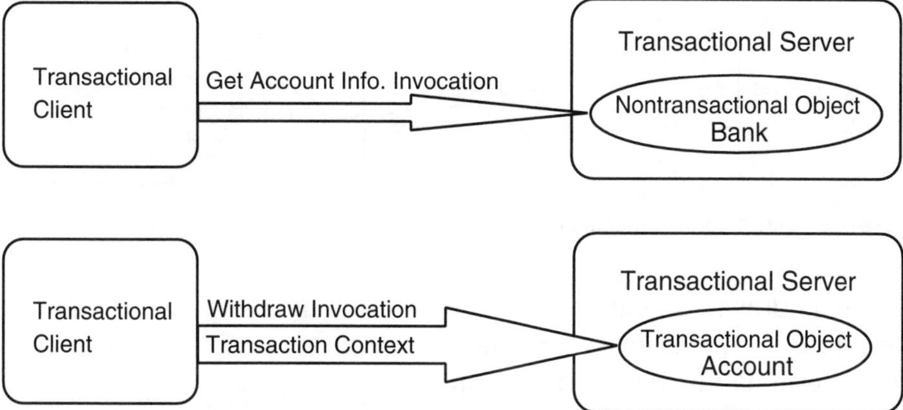


**Figure 3.5** Indirect context management.

client can pass the transaction context explicitly to the operation that it is invoking. In this case, a nonoriginator will be able to terminate the transaction. Figure 3.6 illustrates the explicit context propagation.

The Account interface has to be redefined to accommodate explicit propagation of the transaction context. The Control object is passed in as an argument to the withdraw operation.

```
interface Account : CosTransactions::TransationalObject {

  ...
  void withdraw(
    in int account_number,
    in float amount,
    in CosTransactions::Control control );
  ...
};


 main() {

   ...
   // Obtain the Transaction Factory IOR.
   // Create a new transaction with 15 seconds timeout value.
   control = tFactory->create(15);
   // Obtain bank object by binding to it.
   Account_var account = bank->get_account("Donald Duck");
   // Transaction context is explicitly propagated here.
   account->withdraw(account_number, 100, control);
   ...
 }
```

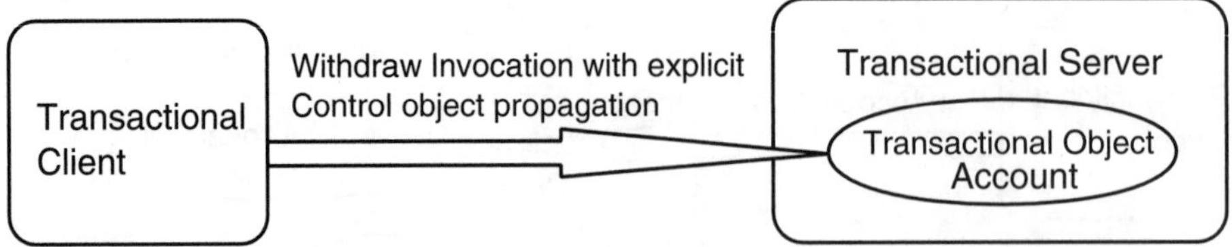


**Figure 3.6** Direct context management.

The withdraw() operation gets the transaction context through the Control object that is passed in. The implementation of withdraw() operation is terminating the transaction in this case.

```
// withdraw implementation code.
...
CosTransactions::Terminator_var terminator =
  control->get_terminator();
// Do actual work involved with the withdraw operation from the
//account.
// Set retStatus to SUCCESS if successful.
if( retStatus == SUCCESS ) {

  try {
     terminator->commit(1);
  }
  catch(...) {

    // handle heuristic exceptions here.
  }
}
else {

  terminator->rollback();
}
```

## Interpositioning

Transaction context is propagated automatically if implicit propagation is used for transactional invocations. Another transaction service implementation can import this transaction by recreating the transaction to represent a new Control object that in turn refers to a new coordinator with the local domain scope. This technique is called *interpositioning*. Now, this local subcoordinator takes charge and handles the function of the main coordinator in the imported domain. Hence, when interpositioning occurs, multiple Coordinator objects represent a global transaction.

In a distributed enterprise environment, the transaction service, transactional servers, and recoverable servers often are located on different nodes. If a single coordinator has to orchestrate the two-phase commit protocol to all different nodes, then the number of network messages that we incur is quite high. Interposing a local coordinator and making it responsible for the completion of the transaction can optimize this overhead. Since the interposed coordinator is collocated with the resources on the same domain, the extra network messages can be avoided.

The relationship between the main coordinator and the interposed coordinators can be represented by a tree structure. The root coordinator is responsible for completing the transaction. To create the local coordinator, the importing transaction service derives the control object from the PropagationContext associated with the thread by using the recreate operation of the TransactionFactory interface.

Figure 3.7 explains how interpositioning can help reduce the network overhead in certain situations. When the client requests the transaction service to commit the transaction, the transaction service commences the two-phase commit protocol. Since the registered resources are located in Node B, the Transaction Service has to make at least four remote calls to issue two prepares and two commits. Interposing another Coordinator in Node B can reduce the remote calls.

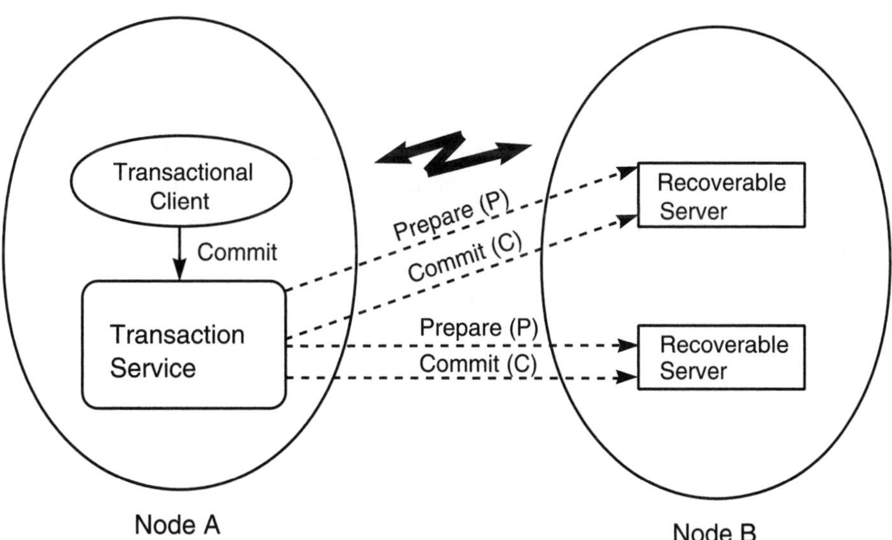


**Figure 3.7** 2PC without interpositioning.

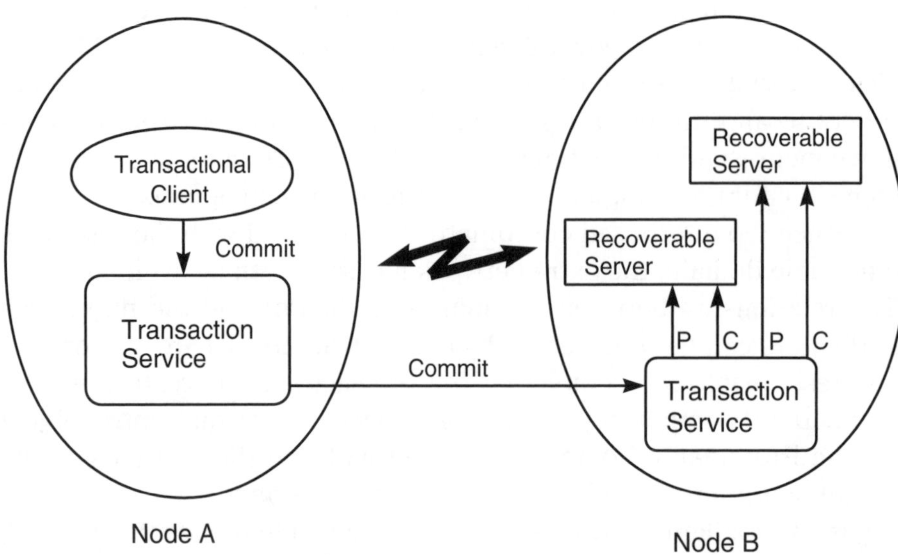


**Figure 3.8** 2PC with interpositioning.

Figure 3.8 shows how the interposed coordinator comes to the rescue to reduce the remote calls. The root coordinator in node A issues just one remote call to node B to commit the transaction. The subcoordinator in node B handles the prepares and commits locally.

## Failure Protocol

Failures are inevitable in any kind of application. It is more critical when it happens in a transaction processing application. Transaction service guarantees ACID properties and provides atomic outcomes for the transactions even when an application, system, or communication failure occurs. In the case of a failure, the application is responsible for handling the error situations caused by itself or the transaction service. Similarly, the transaction service is responsible for handling the error situations caused by itself or the application.

In this section we have described how an application should handle the failure situations. We have omitted failure protocol details that are relevant only to OTS implementations. If you want more details on how a transaction service handles various failure situations, please refer to the OTS specification.

An application can be affected by two types of failure, local or external. Local failure can be caused by the program itself at runtime. External failure can be caused by the entities that are external to the application; for example, a user application receiving exceptions from the transaction service during a commit request. We have presented the failure protocol for the expected behavior of transaction originator, transactional server, and recoverable server from the programmer's perspective.

### Transaction Originator

If there is a local failure in the transaction originator before issuing a commit request, the transaction will be rolled back. If the originator fails after issuing commit but before receiving the reply, the transaction will either be committed or rolled back depending on the state of the transaction.

If there is an external failure that caused the transaction to fail before a commit request, the transaction will be rolled back and the TRANSACTION_ROLLEDBACK exception will be raised in the originator when it issues a commit request. External failure that occurred after commit request was issued but before it received any reply, indicates that the originator may not be informed of the outcome. An example scenario for this situation is a communication failure between the originator and the transaction service. In this case, an originator may use get_status() on the Coordinator interface to determine the transaction outcome; however, the result of this finding is ambiguous. NoTransaction can mean that the transaction committed and has been forgotten, or the transaction rolled back and has been forgotten. If the originator has to know the transaction outcome, then the originator's implementation must use a resource object so that it can include itself in a two-phase commit protocol.

### Transactional Server

If a transactional server suffers through a local failure, the transaction service may roll back the transaction if the transaction follows checked behavior. If unchecked behavior is desired, a transactional server failure may trigger a rollback only if the commit decision has not yet been made.

The transaction will be rolled back if there is an external failure at runtime of the transactional server. If the external failure occurs during the execution of a method call, the method may terminate normally, returning a status to its client. TRANSACTION_ROLLEDBACK exception will be thrown by the external entity in this case.

### *Recoverable Server*

The failure scenarios in this case are governed by the rules of the two-phase commit protocol performed between the resource (recoverable) objects and the coordinator. Please refer to the OTS specification for the complete protocol specification.

## Transaction Integrity

Transaction integrity is usually provided at the resource level. To provide an extra level of transaction integrity, transaction service may also enforce checked behavior for the transactions. The checked behavior guarantees that a commit operation will not succeed unless the processing of all the transactional requests involved in the transaction is complete prior to a commit. Imagine the consequences of issuing a commit operation before the updates are complete in a money transfer application—a debit operation is performed in a transfer application and the transaction is committed before a subsequent credit operation can occur. This would lead to inconsistencies in the account balances and make several customers unhappy.

Checked behavior can be implemented in the transaction service in many ways. One of the popular models for checking the transactional integrity is X/Open's request/response interprocess communication model. This model is widely used in the TP Monitor world and is best suited for OTS.

The basis of the X/Open model of checking is that a request is complete only when the method invocation on the object has completed execution and has replied to the request. Checked behavior is available only when using the implicit propagation. If explicit propagation is used, the transaction service cannot track the objects that are involved in the transaction. A synchronous request made from an application automatically exhibits the checked behavior. If a deferred synchronous request is made, the transaction service can enforce checked behavior by applying reply and commit checks. Resume check is applied to make sure that the transaction context was associated with this thread earlier.

**Reply check.** For a transactional request, a reply is sent only after making sure that the object has received replies to all deferred synchronous requests it has made. If it is not so, the transaction cannot be committed successfully.

**Commit check.** To commit a transaction, the commit request must be issued from the same execution environment as the originator, and the client must receive replies to all the deferred synchronous requests that involved the propagation of the transaction.

**Resume check.** This check ensures that the same transaction context was associated with this thread in earlier operations. This is possible if the thread is the originator or if it obtained the transaction context from a transactional operation.

## Portability Issues

The OTS specification addresses both application portability and the transaction service portability. Application portability issues are relevant to the programmers and we have explained them in this section. Details of the transaction service portability issues are beyond the scope of this book and are relevant only to the implementors of the OTS specification. We refer to the specification directly if you need more implementation details on transaction service portability.

The OTS specification purports the adherence of flat transaction models and X/Open checked transactions for an application to be portable.

Flat transaction model is a mandated requirement of the specification and all transaction service implementations are required to provide it. Nested transaction model is optional. Some OTS implementations do provide the Nested semantics for a transaction. If you want to write a portable application, it is advisable to use the flat transaction model since that is the only model guaranteed to be supported by all transaction service implementations.

The availability of the checked behavior in OTS implementations varies. Some implementations provide checked behavior and some provide unchecked behavior. It is not a mandatory requirement for a transaction service to implement the X/Open checked behavior, but many transaction service implementations already adhere to the X/Open model of interprocess communications. Hence, applications that are written to check for the transactional integrity constraints as provided by X/Open will be portable across other implementations that follow the same protocol.

For an enterprise application that uses disparate transaction service implementations and ORB implementations, the application should be portable across all these systems. The OTS specification addresses the transaction service portability issues and provides the way in which the ORB and the transaction service interoperate. The specification defines how the PropagationContext should be passed and how to enforce X/Open-style checking to be done on transactional requests. For a transaction service to interact with multiple ORB implementations, contract interfaces have been specified for both identification purposes and for callback facility purposes. TSIdentification interface is specified for a transaction service to identify itself to the ORB located in the same domain and sets callback hooks for transactional requests and replies. CosTSPortability module defines sender and receiver interfaces to manage the callbacks that are invoked by the ORB during sending or receiving the transactional requests. These interfaces are defined in pseudo-IDL to facilitate procedural implementation of these operations.

## Interoperability with Existing Transaction Managers

The architecture of the transaction service is compatible with the X/Open DTP model. The indirect context management programming model is compatible with the X/Open DTP model and is implemented by most of the existing TP monitors. To be completely interoperable, the transaction service can provide the TX and XA interfaces of X/Open DTP in addition to the interfaces provided by the service itself. This makes the transaction service an X/Open transaction manager. Figure 3.9 explains how an OTS application can fit into the X/Open DTP model.

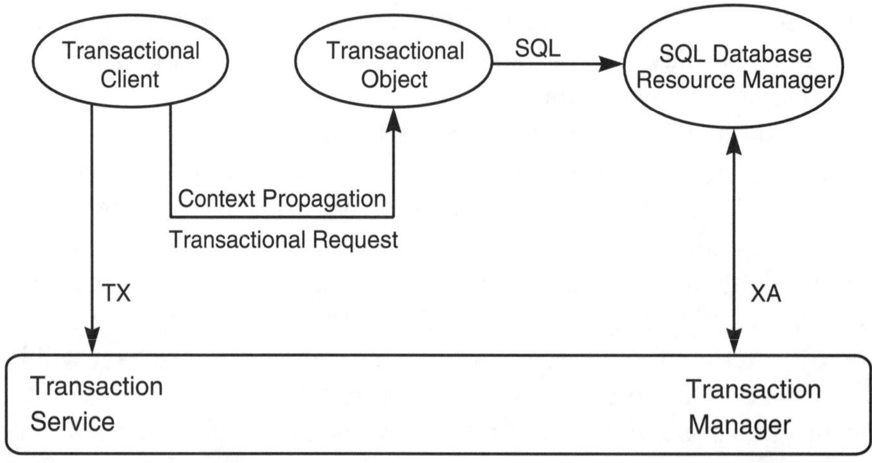


**Figure 3.9** Compatibility with X/Open DTP model.

Transaction originator is issuing begin and commit commands to delineate the transaction. This can be done either through the TX interface calls or through the Current, TransactionFactory, and Terminator interfaces. The transactional object communicates with the resource manager through its native programming interfaces; in this case, via SQL. The coordinator of the transaction service orchestrates the two-phase commit protocol and it uses the XA interface to communicate to the resource manager.

Since the transaction service is versatile, it can allow importing a transaction from the X/Open domain to its domain and exporting a transaction from its domain to the X/Open domain.

## Importing a Transaction from an X/Open Domain

An existing client or server application written using X/Open interfaces can invoke transactional operations in the transaction service domain. This allows a client application to either use the TX interface or the transaction service interfaces to create and terminate a transaction. The transaction service uses the *recreate* operation on the TransactionFactory interface to import the transaction.

Figures 3.10 and 3.11 show conceptually how importing is done for a client and a server application.

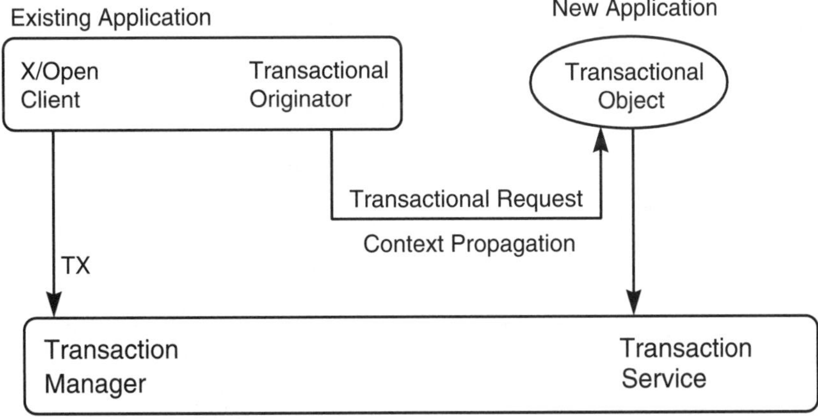


**Figure 3.10** Importing transaction from X/Open client.

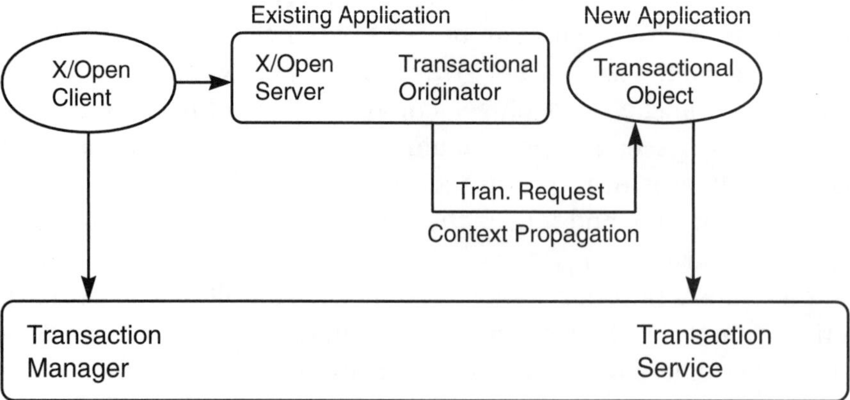


**Figure 3.11** Importing transaction from X/Open server.

## Exporting a Transaction to the X/Open Domain

An OTS application can use X/Open interfaces and resource manager interfaces to include the resources as participants in a global transaction. Figure 3.12 depicts the scenario of exporting the transaction to the X/Open domain.

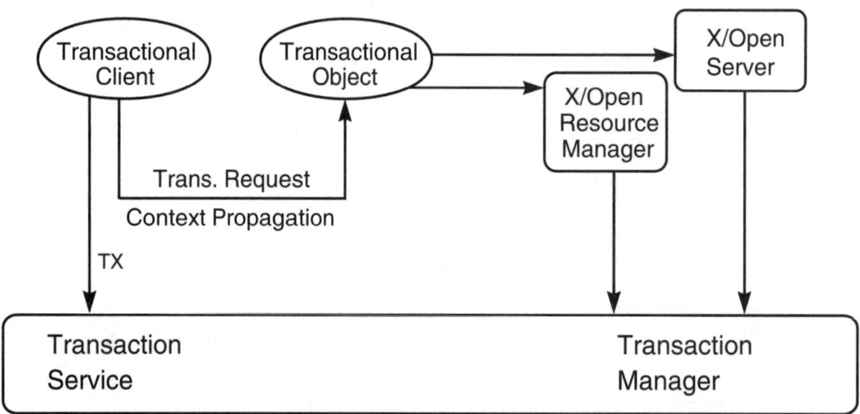


**Figure 3.12** Exporting a transaction to X/Open domain.

## Coexistence with Other TP Standards

One of the main functional goals of the OTS architecture is to reuse the existing legacy applications by object wrapping and to leverage their existing business infrastructure by tapping into this new technology. This is a challenging process, but luckily, each of these domains is already standardized in its own microcosm. Hence, the challenge is to suitably interface all these standards so that they can happily coexist. OTS specification explains some of the possible interactions with the existing standards:

- X/Open TX interface
- X/Open XA interface
- OSI TP protocol
- LU 6.2 protocol
- ODMG standard

### X/Open TX Interface Mappings

The Transaction Service and the X/Open DTP model are interoperable, and therefore the transaction delineation operation can be mapped between these interfaces. Table 3.1 gives the OTS equivalent of the TX interface primitives.

### X/Open XA Interface Mappings

These mappings allow OTS to execute the two-phase commit protocol via the X/Open XA interface to all participating XA-compliant resource managers. Many RDBMS vendors offer XA-compliant resource managers, and some Object Data Base Management System (ODBMS) vendors do support XA. Table 3.2 gives the Transaction Service equivalent of the XA interface primitives.

The interaction between the transaction service and the resource manager (RM) can happen in two ways, either through *static registration* or *dynamic registration*. In static registration, the transaction service involves an RM during the execution of the transaction (uses xa_* calls). In dynamic registration, the RM notifies the transaction service that it has been asked to perform some transactional work and requests the global transaction identifier of the current transaction (uses ax_* calls).

**Table 3.1** X/Open TX Interface Mappings

| TX INTERFACE | OTS CURRENT INTERFACE |
|---|---|
| tx_open()<br>tx_close() | No equivalent operations. |
| tx_begin()<br>tx_rollback() | Current::begin()<br>Current::rollback() / Current::rollback_only() |
| tx_commit()<br>tx_set_commit_return() | Current::commit()<br>report_heuristic parameter of Current::commit() |
| tx_set_transaction_control() | No support for chained transactions. |
| tx_set_transaction_timeout() | Current::set_timeout() |
| tx_info() - XID<br><br>tx_info() - COMMIT_RETURN | Coordinator::get_txcontext()<br>Current::get_transaction_name()<br>No equivalent operation. |
| tx_info() - TRANSACTION_TIME_OUT<br>tx_info() - TRANSACTION_TIMEOUT | No equivalent operation.<br>Current::get_status() |

The OTS specification explains how to interact with an XA-compliant RM, rules, and how to handle failure scenarios in greater detail. We have chosen not to explain the details here since it is irrelevant to the application programmer. Many OTS products like Inprise ITS, Orbix OTM, and BEA M3 support XA-compliant resource managers.

**Table 3.2** X/Open XA Interface Mappings

| XA INTERFACE | OTS INTERFACE |
|---|---|
| xa_start()<br>ax_reg()<br>xa_end() | Receiver::received_request()<br>Current::resume()<br>Receiver::sending_reply()<br>Current::suspend() |
| ax_unreg()<br>xa_prepare() | No equivalent interface.<br>Resource::prepare() |
| xa_commit()<br>xa_rollback() | Resource::commit()<br>Resource::rollback() |
| xa_recover()<br>No equivalent interface | No equivalent interface.<br>RecoveryCoordinator::replay_completion() |
| xa_forget() | Resource::forget() |

## Support for Other Transaction Protocols

Applications written using the CORBA/OTS framework may often have to coexist with their legacy counterparts. This means that we need a way of interacting with the existing standard protocols; for example, OSI TP and SNA LU 6.2. The requirement here is that these applications be able to import or export transactions that are governed by these *de facto* standard protocols. Since OTS uses X/Open and OSI TP model, interacting with OSI TP is trivial. OSI TP is a superset of SNA LU 6.2; therefore, a mapping to SNA communication protocol can also be easily accomplished. OSI TP and LU 6.2 protocols do not support nested transactions. OTS specification defines the mapping for the two-phase commit protocol, rollback, and recovery mechanisms and for the transaction identifiers. We skip the details here since it is irrelevant to the application programmer.

## Support for ODMG Standard

A portable interface to access ODBMS has been defined by the ODMG-93 standard created by ODMG (Object Database Management Group). Even though ODBMS solutions are not popular, in the future, objects involved in a transaction may be handled by an ODBMS. ODMG-93 does not define ways in which external transaction managers can coordinate a transaction in an ODBMS system; hence, it is difficult for the transaction service to import or export transactions into the ODBMS domain. This problem can be solved if ODBMS can act as an XA-compliant resource. Efforts are underway to make ODBMS a recoverable server so that it can participate in a global transaction managed by external transaction managers.

# IDL Reference

The transaction service is defined through CosTransactions.idl. We have given the complete definition here for your reference.

```
#ifndef _costransactions_idl_
#define _costransactions_idl_

#pragma prefix "omg.org"

module CosTransactions
{
    // Forward references for interfaces defined later in module
```

```
// In Java we will generate pseudo classes for Current
interface Current;

interface TransactionFactory;
interface Control;
interface Terminator;
interface Coordinator;
interface RecoveryCoordinator;
interface Resource;
interface Synchronization;
interface SubtransactionAwareResource;
interface TransactionalObject;

// DATATYPES
enum Status
{
    StatusActive,
    StatusMarkedRollback,
    StatusPrepared,
    StatusCommitted,
    StatusRolledBack,
    StatusUnknown,
    StatusNoTransaction,
    StatusPreparing,        StatusCommitting,
    StatusRollingBack
};
enum Vote
{
    VoteCommit,
    VoteRollback,
    VoteReadOnly
};

// Structure definitions
struct otid_t
{
    long formatID; /*format identifier. 0 is OSI TP */
    long bqual_length;
    sequence <octet> tid;
};
struct TransIdentity
{
    Coordinator coordinator;
    Terminator terminator;
    otid_t otid;
};
struct PropagationContext
{
    unsigned long timeout;
    TransIdentity current;
```

```
        sequence <TransIdentity> parents;
        any implementation_specific_data;
    };

    // Heuristic exceptions
    exception HeuristicRollback {};
    exception HeuristicCommit {};
    exception HeuristicMixed {};
    exception HeuristicHazard {};

    // Other transaction-specific exceptions
    exception SubtransactionsUnavailable {};
    exception NotSubtransaction {};
    exception Inactive {};
    exception NotPrepared {};
    exception NoTransaction {};
    exception InvalidControl {};
    exception Unavailable {};
    exception SynchronizationUnavailable {};


    // Current transaction
    interface Current
    {
        void begin()
                raises(SubtransactionsUnavailable);
        void commit(in boolean report_heuristics)
            raises(
                NoTransaction,
                HeuristicMixed,
                HeuristicHazard
            );
        void rollback()
             raises(NoTransaction);
        void rollback_only()
            raises(NoTransaction);
        Status get_status();
        string get_transaction_name();
        void set_timeout(in unsigned long seconds);
        Control get_control();
        Control suspend();
        void resume(in Control which)
            raises(InvalidControl);
    };

    interface TransactionFactory
    {
        Control create(in unsigned long time_out);
        Control recreate(in PropagationContext ctx);
    };
```

```
interface Control
{
    Terminator get_terminator()
        raises(Unavailable);
    Coordinator get_coordinator()
        raises(Unavailable);
};

interface Terminator
{
    void commit(in boolean report_heuristics)
        raises(
            HeuristicMixed,
            HeuristicHazard
        );
    void rollback();
};

interface Coordinator
{
    Status get_status();
    Status get_parent_status();
    Status get_top_level_status();
    boolean is_same_transaction(in Coordinator tc);
    boolean is_related_transaction(in Coordinator tc);
    boolean is_ancestor_transaction(in Coordinator tc);
    boolean is_descendant_transaction(in Coordinator tc);
    boolean is_top_level_transaction();
    unsigned long hash_transaction();
    unsigned long hash_top_level_tran();
    RecoveryCoordinator register_resource(in Resource r)
        raises(Inactive);
    void register_synchronization (in Synchronization sync)
        raises(Inactive, SynchronizationUnavailable);
    void register_subtran_aware(in SubtransactionAwareResource r)
        raises(Inactive, NotSubtransaction);
    void rollback_only()
        raises(Inactive);
    string get_transaction_name();
    Control create_subtransaction()
        raises(SubtransactionsUnavailable, Inactive);
    PropagationContext get_txcontext ()
        raises(Unavailable);
};

interface RecoveryCoordinator
{
    Status replay_completion(in Resource r)
        raises(NotPrepared);
```

```
    };

    interface Resource
    {
        Vote prepare()
            raises(
                HeuristicMixed,
                HeuristicHazard
            );
        void rollback()
            raises(
                HeuristicCommit,
                HeuristicMixed,
                HeuristicHazard
            );
        void commit()
            raises(
                NotPrepared,
                HeuristicRollback,
                HeuristicMixed,
                HeuristicHazard
            );
        void commit_one_phase()
            raises(
                HeuristicHazard
            );
       void forget();
    };

    interface TransactionalObject
    {
    };

    interface Synchronization : TransactionalObject
    {
        void before_completion();
        void after_completion(in Status status);
    };

    interface SubtransactionAwareResource : Resource
    {
        void commit_subtransaction(in Coordinator parent);
        void rollback_subtransaction();
    };

}; // End of CosTransactions Module

#pragma prefix ""
#endif
```

CHAPTER

4

# Programming with OTS

In this chapter we illustrate the use of OTS by building a comprehensive application. We implement a flight-booking system with CORBA and OTS and also identify a number of design patterns during this process.

First we define the requirements for our application. Then we work on the architecture by defining the IDL interfaces of the main objects. We employ a number of design patterns and explain each one. We specifically address different approaches of transaction management and security issues. For each of the interfaces that follow a certain design pattern, we explain the implications of the pattern on thread synchronization, garbage collection, and load balancing.

We give detailed explanation on the design of the implementation objects. We have implementations in Java as well as in C++. The main reason for the C++ implementation is the unavailability of XA Java APIs to relational databases at the time of writing.

We explain various configuration options. We also explain failover strategies in this context, as they are configuration dependent. We then show how to run the application. Finally, we outline possible extensions of the application.

## Application Requirements

Our application is a flight-booking system. We simplify the application due to the time and space constraints of the book and for clarity. Our main goal is to identify common design patterns in the context of a real-world application and to provide sample implementations. From an application point of view, the principal objective is to make inquiries about available flights and to book flights.

The application is comprised of the following components:

- **Client Program.** A graphical user interface that allows a customer to make, view, and modify bookings.
- **Travel Agent.** The client's point of contact.
- **Central Flight Repository.** Provides information about scheduled flights of all airlines.
- **Airline Booking Servers.** Books a flight with a particular airline.

A flight, from a customer's perspective, can involve different legs, which can be booked with various airlines. Booking a flight is a distributed transaction, and ACID properties must be ensured. The communication channel between clients and travel agents must be protected and access control must be enforced—only the owner of a booking and the travel agent are allowed to access a booking.

## Application Architecture and Design Patterns

According to the requirements we must define three major server-side components: central flight booking, airline, and travel agent. As shown in Figure 4.1, the travel agent is a single point of access for the client.

The CORBA Naming Service is used to locate instances of the application objects. Clients find a travel agent via the naming service, and travel agents locate flight query and various airline objects via the naming service. An alternative design approach would be to use the CORBA Object Trading Service (trader). As you will see later in the chapter, we must define conventions for determining the relationship between names and types of objects to use the naming service successfully. The trader already provides a yellow-page style type system.

A typical configuration involves a number of different travel agent objects representing different agencies, a number of replicated query

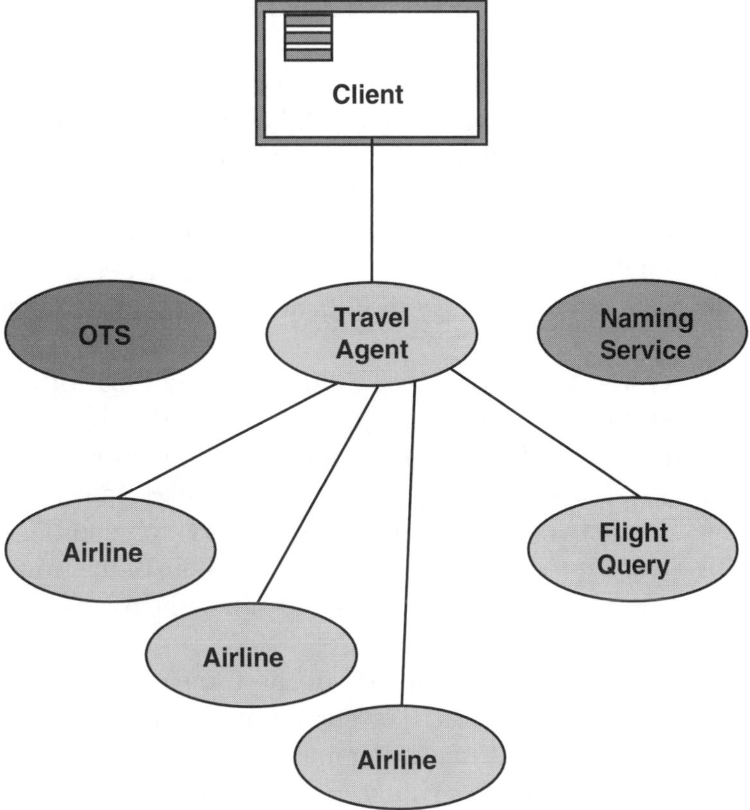


**Figure 4.1** Application architecture.

objects (replicated for load balancing and fault tolerance), and one or more airline objects for each airline.

We have chosen to use and demonstrate the most common design patterns for CORBA objects within this application. These patterns and their application to our example are explained in the following sections. It is not a surprise that these design patterns resemble those which have been formalized by the Enterprise JavaBeans specification as they are proven design patterns for building distributed object systems. When we revisit the EJB version of this application later in the book, we will, however, notice a number of subtle differences in the details of these design patterns.

## Transactions

A client can be directly involved in a distributed transaction, as a transaction originator. Alternatively, a client can delegate the transaction management to a server-side object. Figures 4.2 and 4.3 illustrate the two cases, respectively.

The client, which is also the transaction originator, is directly involved in a distributed transaction as shown in Figure 4.2. This implies that the client not only communicates with the various transactional resources but also with the transaction manager provided by OTS.

Figure 4.3 shows a client that requests a middle-tier object to start a transaction on its behalf. The transaction originator object begins the transaction in this case and interacts with OTS and other transactional resources.

The choice between the two approaches influences the design of the application. In the first approach, the client is directly involved in the transaction and hence is directly notified about the outcome of the transaction. In the second approach, this is not the case. For example, it could happen that the communication between the client and the transaction coordinator breaks and the client would be unsure about the outcome of the transaction. Then the client needs a lookup mechanism to obtain the transaction result.

The first approach provides a high quality of the transaction execution; however, this isn't coming for free. The client must make additional calls for the transaction coordination, which may create a performance problem specifically on low-bandwidth links. Furthermore, transactions may be forced to roll back due to communication failures in the client-middle tier link, which may not be a desired behavior.

If the client communicates with the server-side objects via a slow communication link (for example, an applet client via a modem connection),

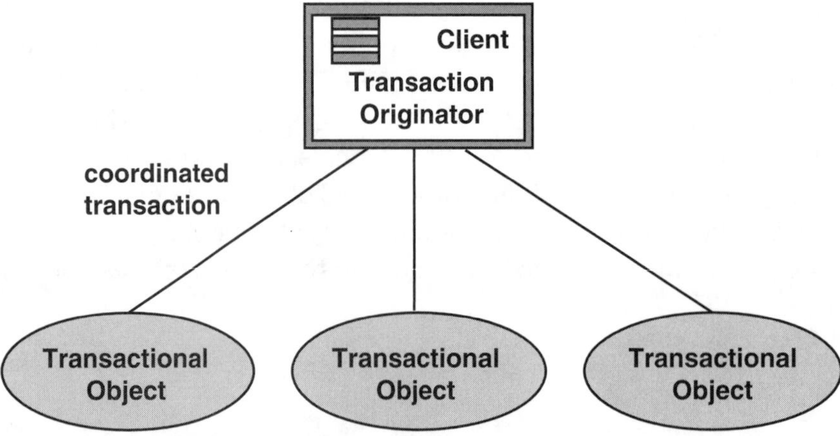


**Figure 4.2** Client involved transaction management.

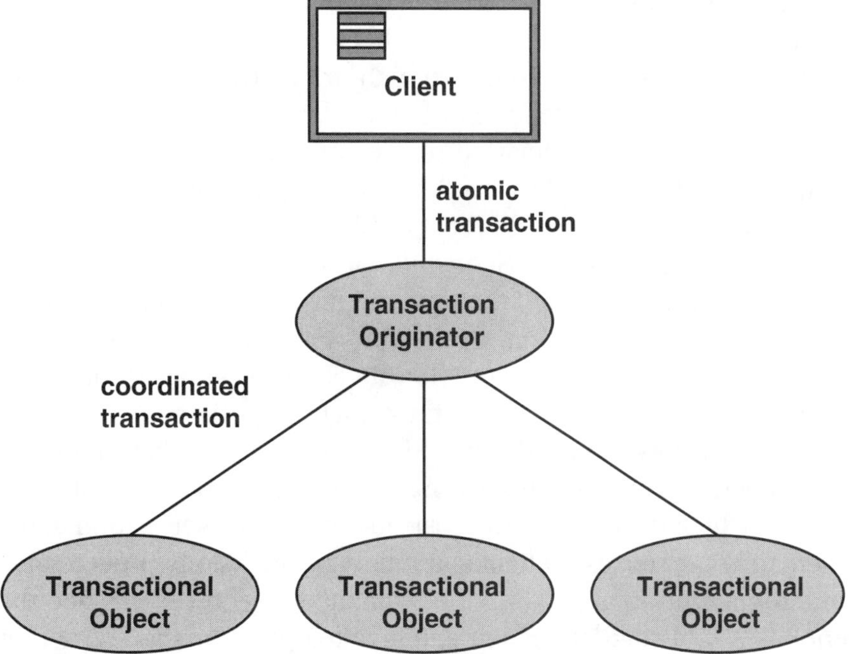


**Figure 4.3** Client decoupled transaction management.

the first approach introduces a heavy performance penalty. The inclusion of the client in a transaction can also have an impact on the performance and scalability on the backend application components. If, for example, clients get frequently disconnected or abnormally terminate, OTS tries to terminate the transactions, which freezes resources in OTS and the transactional objects involved in the transaction.

As a rule of thumb, transactional applications, which involve clients using the Internet to access the backend components, should be designed using the second approach.

## Security

The example implementation focuses mainly on transactional aspects and hence we have omitted the details on implementing a security solution. However, we briefly address the main security concerns: securing the communication channel, access control, and auditing. Implementations of this approach are presented in the book *Java Programming with CORBA**.

* *Java Programming with CORBA*, 2nd edition, by Andreas Vogel and Keith Duddy. New York: John Wiley and Sons, 1998.

The CORBA Security Service's IIOP-over-SSL specification addresses some of the security concerns. SSL has been specifically designed for securing Internet communication. Although originally needed to secure HTTP traffic, the design is generic enough to support any transport or higher-layer protocol that otherwise resides on top of TCP/IP. SSL provides equivalent networking APIs to TCP sockets plus additional APIs to control security features. The IIOP-over-SSL specification defines how IIOP is implemented on top of SSL instead of plain TCP/IP.

SSL provides authentication of the server. Transmitted data is encrypted and protected against corruption. Optionally, SSL offers the capability to authenticate a client. The authentication mechanism is based on X.509 certificates. Various encryption algorithms can be negotiated.

Figure 4.4 illustrates the IIOP-over-SSL architecture. A client requests the SSL connection from its peer, the SSL server. This request results in a handshake in which the client verifies the identity of the server and in the case when a server requests client's authentication. The two peers also agree on an encryption algorithm and exchange a secret key. Once the connection is established, the client can invoke operations on the server objects in the usual manner. The only difference to the normal IIOP traffic is that the IIOP request and response will be completely encrypted once they reach the socket layer.

Access control requires the identity of the requester and an authorization server, which controls an access control list. X.509 certificates provide the identity of a requester. Alternatively, the identity of a user can be established by a pair of name and password, a cookie or a simi-

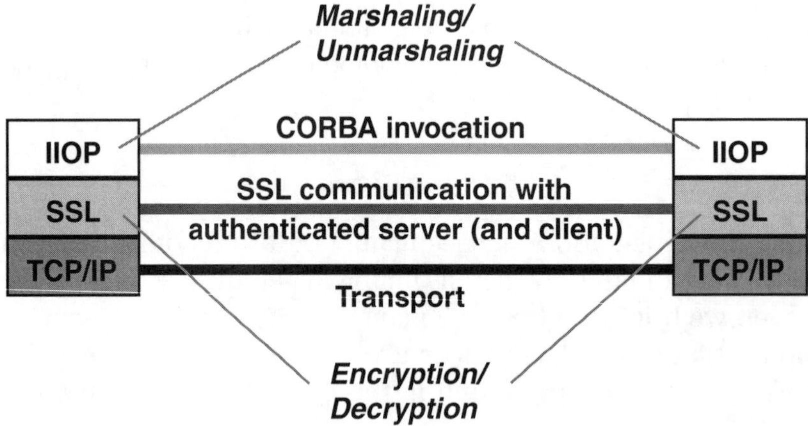


**Figure 4.4** IIOP over SSL.

lar mechanism. When using IIOP-over-SSL with client certificates, the ORB automatically transmits the identity of the client. The invoked object can access the requester's certificate via an SSL current object.

When using other means for determining the identity of the client, the identity can be attached in form of a byte stream to an invocation as part of the corresponding IIOP message. The IIOP specification defines the concept of a service context, which is an array of pairs of identifiers of type long and a value, which is a byte stream. The API to set and get a service context is product specific. Visibroker's interceptors, for example, provide an easy-to-use API for manipulating service contexts. Service contexts are also used by ORB implementations for the implementation of the security or the transaction service.

The authorization object as shown in Figure 4.5 provides the access control. Typically, such an object is just a wrapper for some backend systems; for example, an LDAP server, a Unix password file, or some security-related tables in a database. Access control can be managed on a per-bind or a per-invocation basis.

To instrument an application, bind calls or invocations should be intercepted for authorization before an implementation object is accessed as shown in Figure 4.5. Visibroker's interceptors can be used for this purpose, and some other ORBs provide similar APIs.

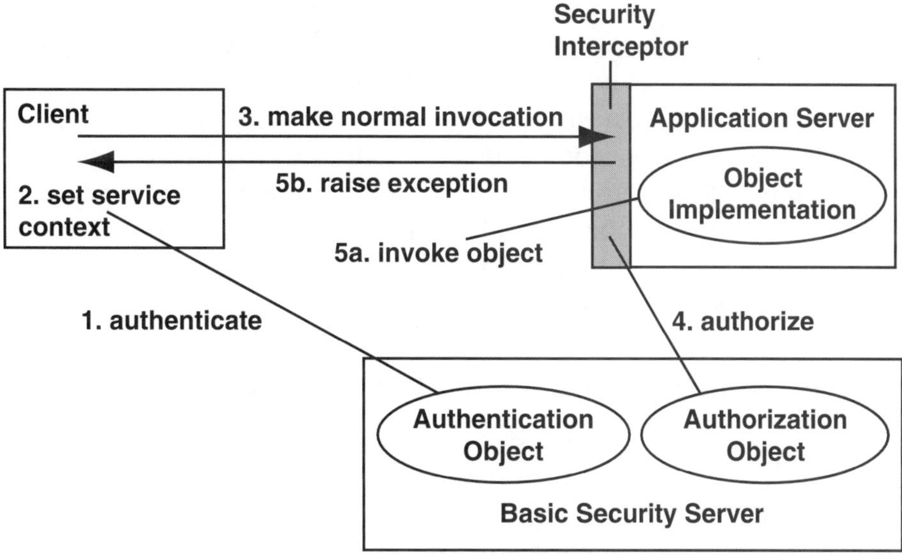


**Figure 4.5** Authentication and access control.

## Management

There are many aspects to the management of a distributed application. Generally distributed application management can be described as *monitoring* of all components of a distributed application and *controlling*; that is, reacting to the events produced by the monitors according to certain rules.

Network management addresses the management of the communication infrastructure, which is comprised of machines, network cards, routers, and so forth. Traditional network management tools are based on SNMP, the Simple Network Management Protocol. As a side note, many of today's network management tools are built with CORBA.

While network management is an important aspect of distributed application management, it is only one of many. Distributed application management also involves higher-level entities such as databases, mainframe applications, application components, and so forth. All these aspects are addressed in conjunction with enterprise-level management tools. Today there are probably only two tools that qualify for this category: Tivoli's TME and Computer Associate's Unicenter.

These enterprise management tools bring a new quality to the operation of a corporation's IT system as they provide an application-centric view on the system through a single management console. Instead of showing the status of various network or application components in isolation, they show if an application or business system is available or not. The necessary abstractions are achieved by defining relationships, in particular hierarchies, and rules between the various entities.

Figure 4.6 illustrates the architecture of an enterprise-level distributed application management tool. Typically such tools can be configured to monitor and control various application components; for example, a mainframe application or a database server. Enterprise management must also manage the network, directly or indirectly, by interfacing to a third-party network management tool.

### *Enterprise Management Tools and CORBA Systems*

CORBA introduces a number of characteristics that have an impact on management; for example, the concepts of Object, Object Adapter and Server, the notion of threads and connections, or the definition of specific services such as Naming, Trading, and Transaction. Enterprise management tools cannot (yet) be expected to understand all of these

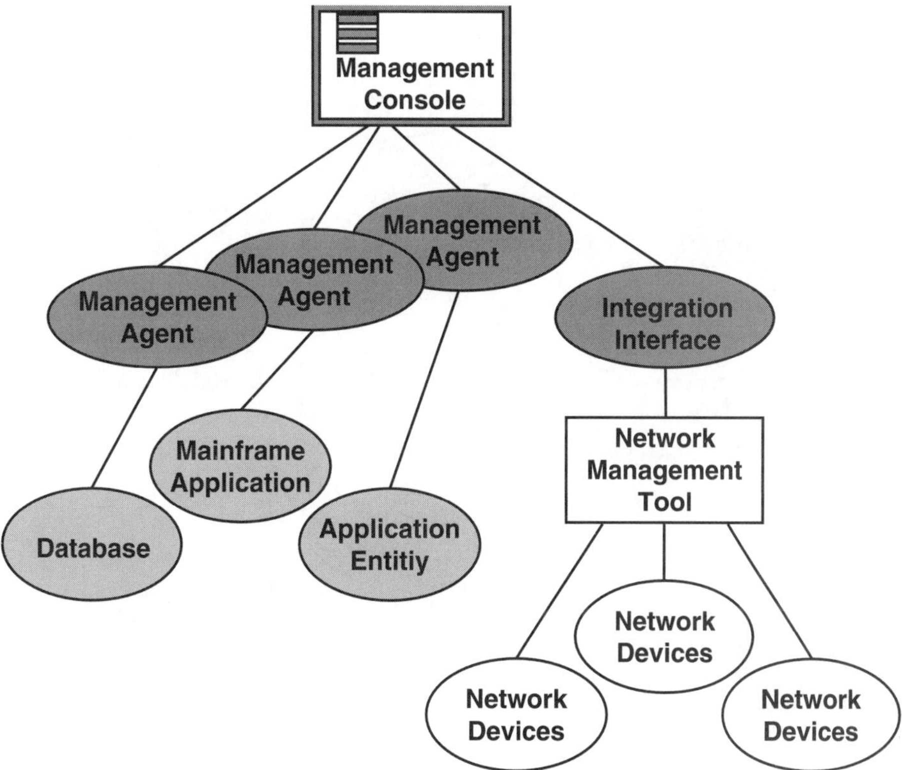


**Figure 4.6** Architecture of enterprise management tools.

CORBA concepts. Furthermore, CORBA applications do not exist in isolation. Typically, they involve a number of the following entities: mainframe applications, databases, web servers, and of course, the network infrastructure.

To address these issues, CORBA management becomes another subcomponent in the enterprise management tool as shown in Figure 4.7. Now a CORBA application can be managed through the same console as other systems of the company. This integration is made possible through management APIs, which are published by the enterprise management tool vendors. Tivoli, for example, has defined the Application Management Specification (AMS).

As application servers are getting more and more in the spotlight of enterprise computing, an application installed in an application server can be considered as a self-contained unit. For example, Inprise's application server comes with an integrated version of Inprise's distributed application management tool AppCenter.

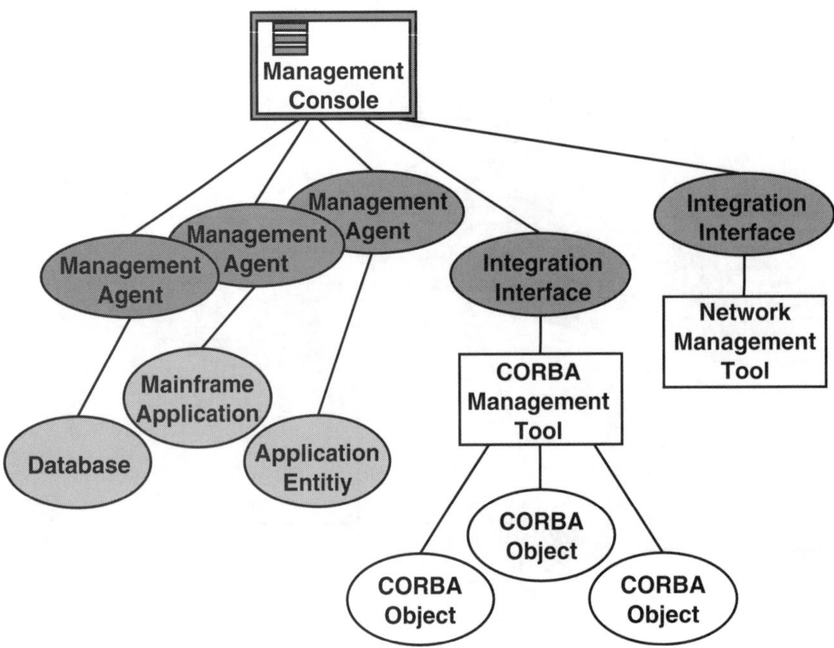


**Figure 4.7** Enterprise management tool and CORBA management.

As installing an enterprise management infrastructure is a nontrivial investment, many companies decide to use application-centric management solutions. Here, application servers with integrated management capabilities are quite useful.

## *Specific Aspects of Managing CORBA Applications*

We have defined distributed application management as monitoring and controlling the components, which form the application. These activities are driven by various requirements, including

**Bootstrapping and shutdown.** Automatically starting various components of an application on certain machines, with certain parameters, in a specified order and shutting down an application or some parts of it in a graceful manner.

**Load balancing.** Starting and maintaining an application with a configuration that provides sufficient resources for the current load. The management may include starting additional instances or changing configuration of an existing application.

**Fault tolerance.** Monitoring an application for failures and reacting accordingly; for example, by redirecting invocations or starting new instances of failed components.

**Security.** Monitoring invocations to detect intruders.

**Debugging.** Monitoring exceptions and failures for software improvements.

**Capacity planning.** Collecting long-term, statistical performance data for prediction of trends and future system load.

So far OMG has not yet produced any substantial specifications for the management of CORBA applications. Existing specifications are mainly concerned with the interoperability of today's management protocols. Hence, the management of CORBA applications is left to the vendors. In the absence of standards, they provide management tools in a proprietary way. An example for the latter is Inprise's AppCenter that manages CORBA applications. Although the tool is not limited to managing Visibroker implemented applications it works best for them as it ties in with Visibroker features such as the OSAgent, Object Activation Demon, the Location Service, and so forth. AppCenter can also be integrated into enterprise management tools and in SNMP-based tools.

### *Management Interface for Graceful Shutdown*

Throughout our sample application we want to address some management aspects, specifically load balancing, fault tolerance, and graceful shutdown. For the latter we're using a couple of interfaces introduced in *Java Programming with CORBA**.

We specify an interface called Maintained to be implemented by all objects you need to gracefully shut down. These are typically factories and manager objects; for example, session managers. Additionally there is an interface Maintainer that is implemented by a tool which you or a system operator would use to control the shutdown. Figure 4.8 illustrates the interfaces and their interactions.

As shown in the following IDL, the interface Maintained has an operation prepareShutdown() which is called by the Maintainer object in the maintenance tool. It provides the IOR of its implementation of the interface Maintainer as an argument. Once the prepareShutdown() method

* *Java Programming with CORBA*, 2nd edition, by Andreas Vogel and Keith Duddy. New York: John Wiley and Sons, 1998.

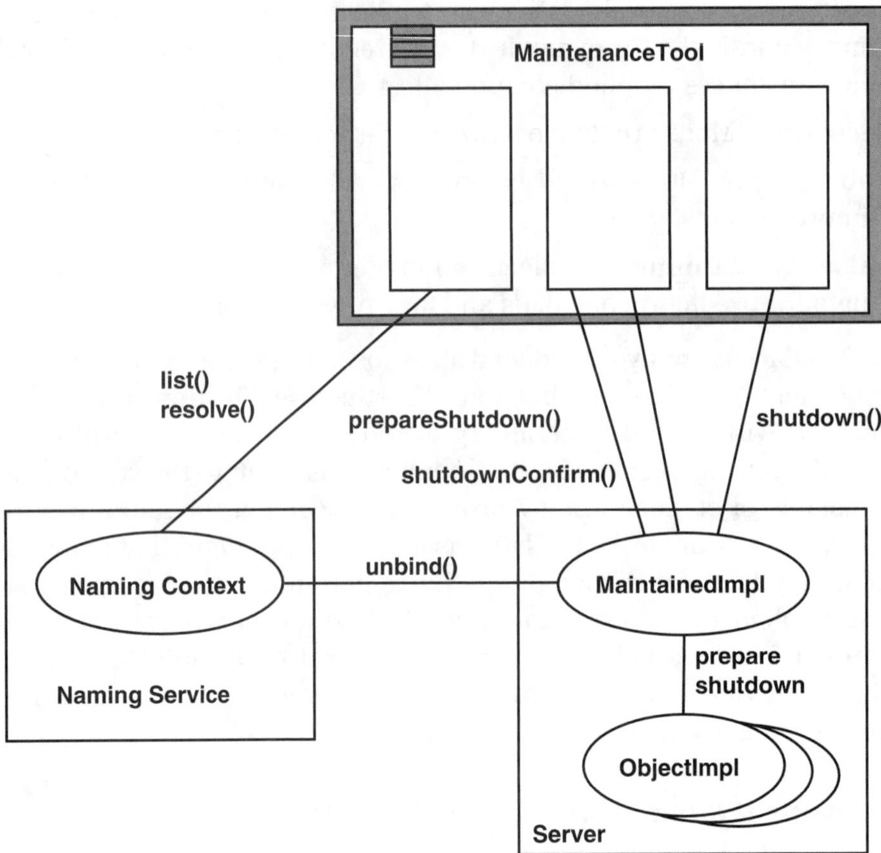


**Figure 4.8** Managing graceful shutdown.

has been called, the receiving object prepares its graceful shutdown, which typically includes the following:

- The object makes itself invisible; for example, it deregisters itself from the naming service, trader, or a proprietary directory service. Now potential clients can't find the object anymore. Additionally, an object can set a shutdown-in-progress flag and raise a CORBA system exception when an invocation is made. That signals the client to look for a replica of the object.
- The object recursively shuts down the objects it controls in a graceful manner. The meaning of "graceful" here is a bit vague since it depends very much on the application. If, for example, the initial object is a session manager, it makes all the session objects grace-

fully shut down. This could mean that a session continues to be active until its client terminates the session or the session times out. All the objects controlled by the Maintained object should be deactivated. This means that the Maintained object and the objects themselves call disconnect() on the ORB or the appropriate operation on the object adapter.

```
module com {
...
module chapter13 {
module maintenance {
   interface Maintainer;
   interface Maintained;
   interface Maintained {
     oneway void prepareShutdown( in Maintainer maintenanceTool );
     oneway void shutdown()
   };
   interface Maintainer {
     oneway void shutdownConfirmation( in Maintained confirmingObject );
   };
};};};};};};
```

Once the Maintained object has prepared the shutdown it notifies the Maintainer object with a call to its shutdownConformation() operation. Once the maintainer has received the callback it can shut down the server that hosts the maintained object by calling shutdown() on the Maintained interface.

## Interface Specification

In this section we specify the IDL data types and interfaces for our flight-booking system. Each of the components follows a particular design pattern, which we explain in the context of the component.

### *Imports*

We import two IDL files into the IDL file for our flight-booking system. The first file, `CosTransactions.idl`, contains data types and interfaces as defined by OTS, which is explained in Chapter 3, "Understanding the CORBA Object Transaction Service." The second file, `maintenance.idl`, contains the maintenance interfaces we introduced earlier.

```
#include "CosTransactions.idl"
#include "maintenance.idl"
```

### Modules

We acknowledge the usefulness of the Java naming conventions for packages and apply the same principle to IDL and CORBA/Java implementations.

One approach to apply the naming convention would be through nested IDL modules; for example,

```
module com {
 module company {
  module division {
    module project {
};};};};
```

This approach works fine for all Java implementations of the interfaces. However, CORBA caters to a wider spectrum of programming languages that may have limited scoping capabilities. Although C++ has a namescope construct, it's not yet widely implemented; therefore, nested IDL modules are often mapped to nested C++ classes, which makes the use of the preceding approach very awkward.

An alternative approach is to remove the outer modules from the IDL definition and apply the packages as an extra parameter to the IDL compilation process. For example, the preceding IDL shrinks to

```
module project {
};
```

We can compile the IDL file with a flag `-package com.company.division` (flags are ORB dependent, see the manual of your ORB for the syntactical details). In both cases, the Java interfaces and classes are generated in a Java package, `com.company.division.project`.

Our application defines a single module called flightBooking. Some interfaces are implemented in Java, others in C++.

```
module flightBooking {
  ...
}
```

### Data Type Definitions

The module flightBooking contains all data types and interfaces of the application. We have four basic structs to describe dates, persons, user profiles, and flights. Note that a flight is only defining a direct connection. We also refer to a single flight as a *leg*. A leg record combines a single flight with a person. For this example, we keep the profile rather simple, but the comments show how it could be extended for a full-blown application.

```
struct SimpleDate {
   long day;
   long month;
   long year;
   long hour;
   long minute;
};

struct Person {
   string title;
   string firstName;
   string middleInitial;
   string lastName;
};

struct Profile {

   Person customer;
   // credit card
   // airline, food, seating preferences
   // frequent flyer numbers
   // etc
};

struct Flight {
   string id;
   string flightNumber;
   string departingAirport;
   string arrivingAirport;
   SimpleDate departureDate;
   SimpleDate arrivalDate;
   string aircraft;
   float price;
};

struct LegRecord {
   Flight leg;
   Person passenger;
};
```

In the following we define flavors of structs for data associated with bookings. The struct BookingRequest contains all the data associated with a booking request. The struct TaBookingRecord is used for the communication between the travel agent and its data access object as shown. Finally, the struct BookingRecord completely describes the data associated with a booking, including a reference to booking object.

```
struct BookingRequest {
  string label;
  ComposedFlight aComposedFlight;
  Person passenger;
  float confirmedPrice;
};

struct TaBookingRecord {
  string label;
  string id;
  string userId;
  IdSeq airlineIds;
  float confirmedPrice;
};

struct BookingRecord {
  string label;
  string id;
  string userId;
  ComposedFlight aComposedFlight;
  Person passenger;
  float confirmedPrice;
  Booking bookingObj;
};

typedef sequence< BookingRecord > BookingRecordSeq;
typedef sequence< TaBookingRecord > TaBookingRecordSeq;
typedef sequence <string> IdSeq;
typedef sequence <Flight> ComposedFlight;
typedef sequence <ComposedFlight> FlightList;
```

We also define sequences of the various bookings. We define a type IdSeq as a sequence of strings, and a composed flight, ComposedFlight, which is defined as a sequence of flights. For example, a flight from San Francisco to Sao Paulo via Los Angeles is a sequence with two flights. The sequence FlightList is used to describe a number of flight alternatives.

We also define a number of exceptions, which are raised by various operations defined in the following sections.

```
exception NotAvailable{ string reason; };
exception NonExistent{ string reason; };
exception InvalidQuery { string reason; };
exception Internal { string description; };
exception NotAuthorized {};
```

```
exception ShutDownInProgress {};
exception NotAuthenticated{};
```

## *Travel Agent*

The travel agent is designed using the session or factory pattern.

### Session Pattern

The session pattern provides a particular object instance, a session object, for each client that uses this service. The server has one initial object, a factory. The factory creates a session object on demand of the clients. The client uses the session object for further processing with the server side. Figure 4.9 illustrates the creation and use of session objects.

The factory typically has one or more operations to create objects. Often these operations are called "create...". The session objects created have a transient object reference and are not registered with a naming, trading, or directory service as they are usually only used by the client that requested their creation.

The factory or session pattern is the ancestor of the EJB stateful session bean.

**Synchronization** Since there is only one client per session object there is no conflict when clients currently access the session object. The

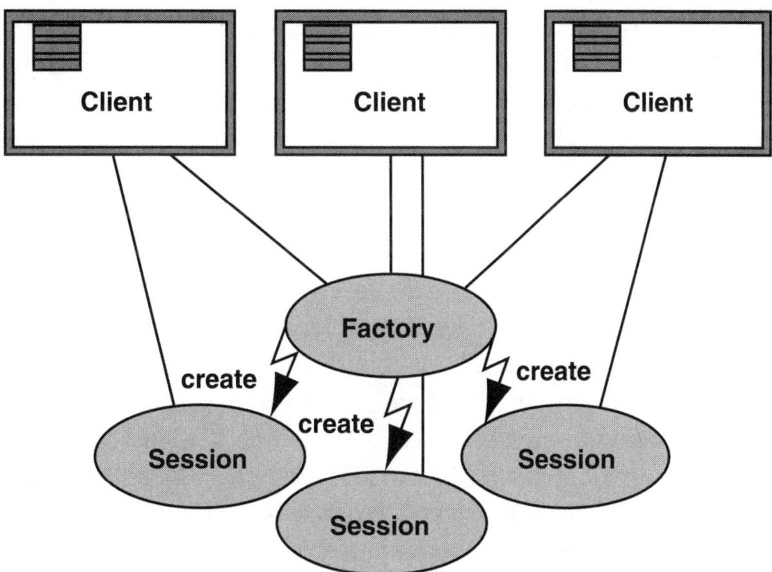


**Figure 4.9** Session pattern.

factory itself follows the stateless server model, which is explained later in the chapter. The factory's create operations must be synchronized if they share state variables.

**Garbage Collection** An ORB cannot and does not provide distributed garbage collection. It is the application's responsibility to manage the life cycle of the objects in the various components of a distributed application. The created session objects should have a *destroy* operation. Using the session pattern, the client controls the life cycle of the session objects. Once a client is finished with a session object it should call the destroy operation on the object.

You have to declare this destroy operation in the IDL interface of the object. You can declare your own destroy operation or the object can inherit the CORBA LifeCycleObject interface and implement its remove() operation.

```
exception NotRemovable { string reason; };
interface LifeCycleObject {
  ...
  void remove()raises( NotRemovable);
  ...
};
```

Note that the Life Cycle Service is a set of IDL interfaces intended as a design pattern you have to implement rather than as an off-the-shelf service such as the Naming or Event Services.

There are two more mechanisms that can be used to remove a session object. They can be used alternatively or in addition to the client explicitly calling the remove operation on the object. In either case, the factory acts as a manager, which controls the complete life cycle of the session objects it creates.

The manager can be triggered in two ways to call remove on an object. Most ORBs provide APIs, which allows monitoring the network connections. An example of such an API is Visibroker's interceptor. They can trigger an event when the server loses a connection due to a disappearing client or a network failure. This event can be propagated to the manager, which destroys the affected server objects. This approach has, however, a number of shortcomings. For example, objects would be removed even during a temporary network failure after which a client may immediately reconnect. The approach doesn't work when the client is not directly connected to a server; for example, an IIOP gateway such as Visibroker's Gatekeeper may be part of the end-to-end connection.

The other way to trigger the manager to destroy an object is based on a time-out mechanism. Each session object gets a certain lifetime when it is created. Once the lifetime has expired, the manager destroys the object. The lifetime can be absolute or relative to the last invocation of the object. This mechanism can be easily implemented by a thread, which is notified by the factory when the session object is created. When using a relative lifetime, the thread must be notified every time the object is invoked. Again, Visibroker's interceptors or similar APIs can be used. The thread periodically checks the elapsed time and once it passes the specified lifetime it will notify the manager to destroy the object. This approach has two advantages in addition to those of other garbage collection mechanisms. It aids resource management in the server, cleaning up objects created for clients that have been inactive for a while. Also, it can assist in implementing security policies that require the time-out of a user session; for example, online banking sessions typically time-out after 15 or 20 minutes.

**Load Balancing** A session object is a transient object, which means it is bound to the server that is hosting it. Once a client has a session object it is bound to this particular process or JVM. Load balancing can be achieved by clients binding to one of many factories that can be distributed across many processes and machines. Additionally, the session object can use load-balancing mechanisms when accessing resources such as databases or mainframe-based applications.

Replicating session objects for load-balancing reasons, usually makes little sense. However, long-lived session objects could be deactivated and reactivated on a different machine. The deactivation must persist the session object's state and the reactivation recreates the object with the original state.

### Interface Specification

The design of the travel agent component in our application follows the session pattern. The component is comprised of two interfaces: the travel agent interface, which is a factory, and the session interface, which provides the functionality to a client.

**Factory** The interface TravelAgent is a factory. It defines one create operation. Instead of naming the operation createSession() or something similar, we called it login() since it creates a session object and provides additional security-related semantics. If the request client is not authorized to create a session object, the exception NotAuthorized is raised. The TravelAgent interface also inherits from the interface Maintained, which we introduced earlier.

```
interface TravelAgent :
  ::com::wiley::compbooks::vogel::chapter13::maintenance::Maintained {

  Session login( in string userId, in string password )
    raises ( NotAuthorized );
};
```

**Session** The session interface inherits from two interfaces, BaseQuery and TransactionalObject. The interface BaseQuery provides query operations to learn about available flights. The session provides the same interface to clients. The interface TransactionalObject enables session objects to participate in OTS-controlled transactions.

```
interface Session:
  BaseQuery,  ::CosTransactions::TransactionalObject {

  Booking createBooking( in BookingRecord aBooking )
    raises ( NotAvailable );

  Booking findBooking( in string bookingId )
    raises ( NotAvailable );

  BookingRecordSeq findAllBookingRecords();

  void remove();
};
```

The session interface defines four operations: three application-specific ones, which are all concerned with creating and finding booking objects, and one remove operation for garbage collection as discussed earlier.

The session interface acts like a manager for booking objects. The operation createBooking() creates a new Booking object. The corresponding interface is defined later in the chapter. The operation accepts a BookingRecord as an in parameter, which contains all information about the flight that a customer wants to book. The session interface also provides the findBooking() operation, which allows a client to obtain an object reference to an existing booking based on a booking identifier. Then there is another find operation, findBooking(), which returns all bookings associated with the person that is associated with the session object. A variant of a find-all operation could additionally return an iterator as described in Chapter 13 of *Java Programming with CORBA*. This is recommended if you expect a large number of booking records to be returned.

## *Flight Query*

The flight query interface follows the stateless server model. In its implementation, we use a database-connection-pooling pattern to optimize data access.

### Stateless Server Pattern

A stateless server provides some functionality or access to data. A client must always provide the complete input data to obtain a result. The server does not keep any information about the client. Figure 4.10 illustrates the interactions with a stateless server.

Typically, a stateless server is a multithreaded program. Exceptions are only made when the server is wrapping a legacy application, which is not thread-safe. Usually, all incoming requests will be associated with a thread, which executes the request. Industrial-strength ORB implementations provide multithreading of concurrent requests. The most effective way to use threads is using a thread-per-request policy and thread pools. That means, at start up, the object adapter creates a thread pool with a certain number of threads. Whenever an invocation occurs a thread is taken from the pool. Once the invocation is processed and the response is sent, the thread is released to the pool.

**Synchronization** Since all clients access the same object instance via different threads, you must take care of the synchronization of concurrent invocations. Avoid state variables wherever possible. If you need them, synchronize the access to them. This can be done with the Java *synchronize* construct. When using other programming languages you have to implement your own locks or use a mutex provided by a third-party library.

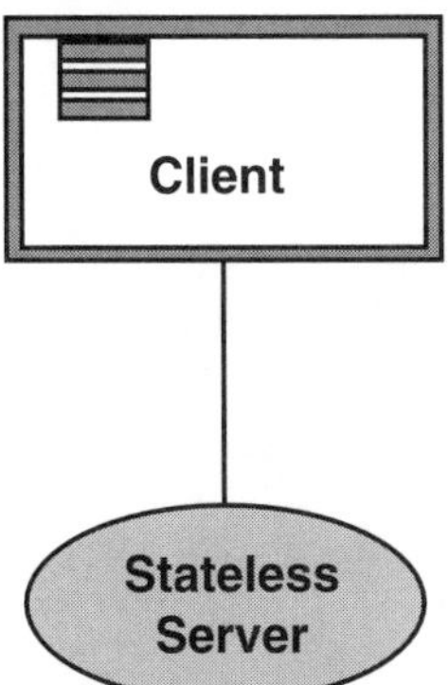


**Figure 4.10** Stateless server pattern.

**Garbage Collection** Since there is only one object, which provides the service, there is no garbage collection issue.

**Load Balancing** The stateless server object does not keep any state; hence, a client can invoke different instances of the same object, in particular the least-loaded one. This decision can be made at bind time or at invocation time. Note that there is a trade-off between always getting the least-loaded instance and the effort it takes to find them and to potentially establish a new connection. Usually, for large numbers of clients and similar loads per client, it is sufficient to statistically distribute the load between different instances. Round-robin or random algorithms can be used to achieve such a distribution. The CORBA Object Trading Service, proprietary services such as Visibroker's OSAgent, or your own implementation of a load-balancing directory service can be used to balance the load. The Trading Service provides a "random" policy, the OSAgent uses a round-robin algorithm for bind calls.

### Database Connection Pooling

Often a stateless server is a CORBA frontend to a database. The access to a database is constrained through the number of connections the

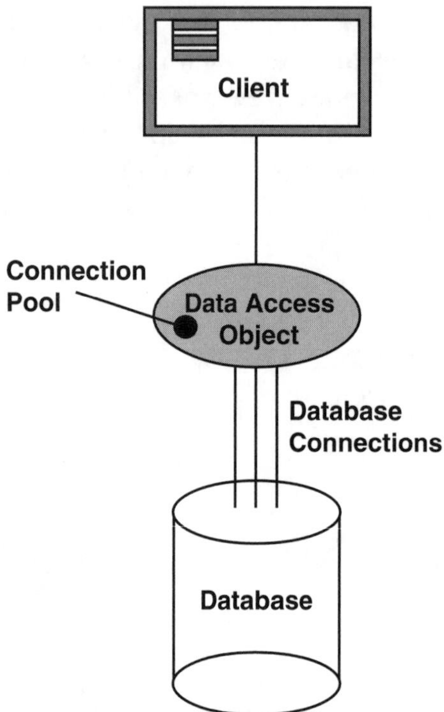


**Figure 4.11** Database connection pooling.

database provides. This is not so much a technical issue but a licensing one. There is also a certain overhead involved with the creation and the closing of a database connection.

When the data access object is started it opens a number of connections to the database and creates a connection pool, which manages the connections. Every time an invocation needs to access the database, it obtains a connection from the pool. Once it is finished it returns the connection to the pool. If all connections are in use, a requester waits—it will be notified by the pool when connections become available. An implementation of a database connection pool is illustrated in Figure 4.11 and explained in the section, "Design and Implementation," later in the chapter. The JDBC 2 specification defines connection pooling; hence, the application programmer is freed from this task.

### Interface Specification

We define two interfaces, BaseQuery and Query. The interface BaseQuery contains the query operation queryAvailableFlights() which searches for (composed) flights around a certain departure time.

```
interface BaseQuery {

  FlightList queryAvailableFlights(
   in string from,
   in string to,
   in SimpleDate departureDate )
  raises( InvalidQuery, Internal, ShutDownInProgress );
 };
```

The operation raises a number of exceptions that have the following semantics:

- InvalidQuery. Invalid query; for example, a nonexistent airport name or an invalid date.
- Internal. An internal problem occurred that cannot be handled by the invoked object; for example, the database is down.
- ShutDownInProgress. The invoked object is shutting down and therefore is not accepting new invocations. The invoking program should obtain an IOR of a replica of the object.

```
interface Query :
  BaseQuery,
  ::com::wiley::compbooks::vogel::chapter13::maintenance::Maintained {
```

```
    Flight getFlight(
      in string flightNumber,
      in SimpleDate departureDate )
    raises( NotAvailable, Internal, ShutDownInProgress );
};
```

The interface Query combines the interface BaseQuery and the interface Maintained. This separation is done due to the fact that the interface Session also inherits the query functionality, but a session object is not a managed object. The session factory provides the management interface.

Additionally, the extended interface adds an additional operation getFlight(), which returns a struct Flight determined by the flight number and the departure date.

## *Bookings*

Bookings follows the persistent object pattern.

### Persistent Object Pattern

A persistent object is an object that represents some data in a database and provides behavior associated with this data as shown in Figure 4.12. Essentially, the lifetime of such objects is determined by the lifetime of the corresponding entry in the database. There are, however, different mechanisms of referencing the object.

**Primary key.** The ultimate handle to the data associated with a persistent object. An instance of the object can be created at any time from a primary key.

**IOR.** There are transient and persistent object references.

**Transient IOR.** References a particular instance of the object. Once the instance goes away due to the deactivation by the server or due to the termination of the server, the object reference becomes invalid.

**Persistent IOR.** References a particular instance of the object. It also contains additional data, usually the primary key, which allows the ORB to create a new instance of the object if necessary. CORBA describes this process as *object activation*. The POA specification defines operations for activating and deactivating objects.

There are two handles to a persistent object: its primary key, or a persistent object reference. Eventually, both represent some data stored in the database. The object reference provides a handle on the object abstraction layer; however, its representation, a stringified IOR, is rather

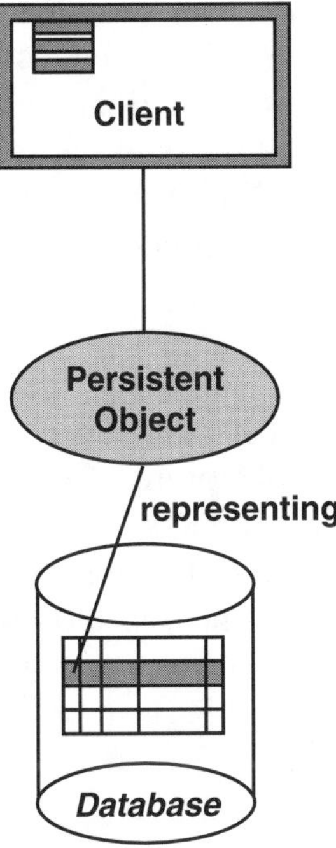


**Figure 4.12** Persistent object pattern.

awkward and should be avoided for human interaction. A primary key could be created in a more compact manner; for example, as a relatively short string as known from confirmation numbers of today's reservation systems. If the handle does not need to be exposed to a human, then an IOR is more suitable.

**Synchronization** Persistent objects can be shared objects. When clients concurrently access a persistent object to modify it, the object must serialize the invocations that modify its data. Alternatively, the implementation can provide a more fine-grained synchronization and locking mechanisms.

**Garbage Collection** The lifetime of a persistent object concurs with and is determined by the lifetime of the corresponding entry in the database. There is however, the lifetime of an instance of the object. This is managed either by the application code or by the ORB. *Deactivating* an instance means to garbage collect the object. *Reactivating* means to create a new instance of it. The mechanisms used in the application code or mechanisms provided by the older ORB versions may vary. The POA provides a corresponding API.

**Load Balancing** There can be multiple servers hosting persistent objects that are associated with a database. Incoming client requests must be balanced between the different servers. This can be done by a CORBA Object Trading Service or similar means as discussed earlier. Usually a single instance of a persistent object is sufficient. However, one could easily have multiple instances of a persistent object, as the database would take care of the data integrity.

#### Interface Specification

The interface Booking is a persistent object. It encapsulates the data associated with a single booking from the travel agent's point of view. The session object is the creator and finder of booking objects.

The interface Booking exposes a unique booking identifier that is a primary key in the travel agent's database. There are also set and get methods to access and manipulate the data associated with a booking.

```
interface Booking :
   ::CosTransactions::TransactionalObject {

   readonly attribute string BookingId;

   BookingRecord getBookingData();
   void setBookingData( in BookingRecord aBookingRecord );
 };
```

### *Airlines*

We specify two interfaces for the airlines, the interface Airline and the interface AirlineWithResource. They both provide the same functionality except the latter is a Resource object since it inherits from the interface CosTransactions::Resource. We need this differentiation as we provide two implementations. The C++ implementation uses Oracle as a resource via an XA interface. In this case we don't need to expose the resource interface since Inprise has an implementation of the Resource object. The Java implementation has a faked resource similar to what we demonstrated in Chapter 1, "Quick Start to EJB, JTS, and OTS."

Both interfaces are examples of a stateless server. They provide operations to book and cancel a leg. The book operation takes LegRecord as an argument and stores it in the database. The lookup and the cancel operation use the booking id to locate a booking record and return or delete it, respectively.

```
interface Airline :
  ::com::wiley::compbooks::vogel::chapter13::maintenance::Maintained,
  ::CosTransactions::TransactionalObject {

  string bookLeg( in LegRecord leg )
    raises ( NotAvailable );

  void cancel( in string id )
    raises ( NonExistent );

};

interface AirlineWithResource :
  Airline,
  ::CosTransactions::Resource {
};
```

Additionally, we have the interface AirlineQuery, which is a lookup operation for leg records.

```
interface AirlineQuery :
  ::com::wiley::compbooks::vogel::chapter13::maintenance::Maintained {

  LegRecord lookUpById( in string id )
    raises ( Internal, NonExistent );
};
```

Logically, the operation belongs to Airline interface. We made the separation since we implemented the transactional operations in C++ and the lookup operation in Java. If you want to make a different implementation choice you can easily combine the interface via inheritance.

### Directory

Finally we have a simple directory interface that we use to manage the users of the system. For this example we restrict the functionality to authentication of users and to obtaining user profiles. Both operations are invoked when a user logs in and requests a session object.

```
interface Directory {

    void authenticate(
      in string userId,
      in string passWord )
      raises( NotAuthenticated );

    Profile getProfile( in string userId )
      raises( NotAvailable );
};
```

Other architectural choices include the use of an IDL wrapper for an LDAP/X.500 or some other existing directory mechanisms. It is beyond the scope of this example to provide a sophisticated access control and better user profiling mechanism.

## Design and Implementation

In this section we explain the interfaces specified in the previous sections. We show Java and C++ implementations. Wherever possible we have chosen Java; however, there are no XA implementations in Java available at the time of writing. The reason is that the JDBC 2.0 specification that employs XA interface for providing distributed transactions was not yet finalized at the time of writing. Hence, we have chosen a twofold approach. We provide a Java implementation with a fake resource. This means that we implement the operations needed for OTS' two-phase commit. We only provide an illustrative implementation. Additionally, we show a C++ implementation, which is using Oracle's XA API.

Figure 4.13 summarizes all the interfaces and implementations. We only show interfaces that correspond to an implementation. Interfaces that are inherited and implemented by the class for the derived interface are omitted from the illustration. An example of such an interface is BaseQuery. Java implementation classes are shown in white, C++ classes in gray. We have structured this section as follows:

- Implementation of the flight query object—in Java Flight query object implementation
  - Database connection pool implementation
  - Flight query server implementation
- Implementation of airline objects
  - Fake Java airline object implementation
  - C++/Oracle airline object implementation
  - Java airline query object implementation
- Implementation of travel agent objects
  - C++/Oracle travel agent data access object implementation
  - Java booking object implementation
  - Java session object implementation
  - Java travel agent query implementation

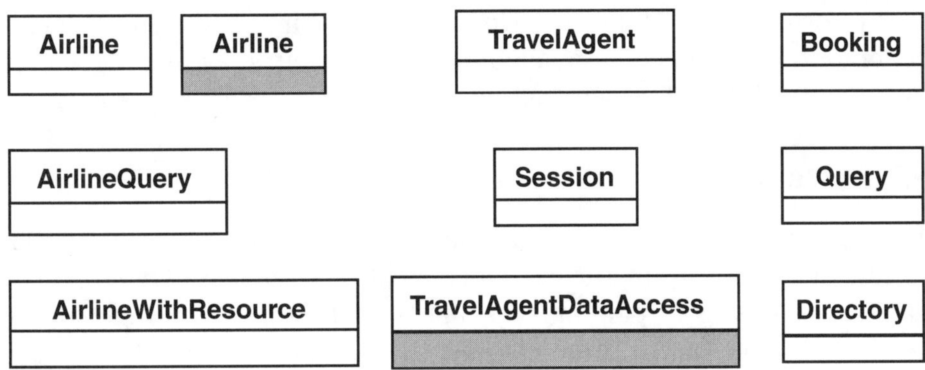


**Figure 4.13** Design of the implementation.

- Java travel agent object implementation
- Java travel agent server implementation

- Directory implementation in Java
- Client implementation in Java

The POA is defined and mapped to Java and C++; however, ORB implementations, which provide the Java and C++ mapping, the POA and OTS were not available at the time of writing. We have used the Inprise Application Server (Visibroker for Java and C++ and Inprise ITS) for the implementation of this example. We have used standard compliant features wherever possible and we point out where we use proprietary ones. We have used the Visibroker's BOA. Throughout the implementation classes you find three BOA specific calls:

- `BOAInit()` on the ORB to obtain a BOA pseudo object
- `obj_is_ready()` on the BOA to register an object with the object adapter
- `impl_is_ready()` on the BOA to keep the server up and running

The corresponding methods in the POA context are

- `resolve_initial_references( "Root_POA")` on the ORB to obtain the root POA pseudo object
- `activate_object()` on the POA to register an object with the object adapter
- `run()` on the ORB to keep the server up and running

The corresponding lines of code can be easily updated once the next-generation ORBs become available. ORB vendors may also decide to maintain BOA APIs for backward compatibility.

## Flight Query

The flight query object is not a transactional object. It is part of the application and illustrates the design patterns of the stateless server and the database connection pooling. The implementation of the flight query component consists of three classes: the implementation class of the IDL interface FlightQuery; the class that manages the database connection pool; and a server class, which is hosting instances of the first two.

### *Implementation of the IDL interface FlightQuery*

The class is part of the package `vogel.transaction.chapter6.flightBookingImpl`, which contains all of the server-side implementation classes for this example. We import Java packages for SQL/JDBC and vectors, the CORBA package, and two packages from the book *Java Programming with CORBA**. These packages handle CORBA naming and some aspects of the management of CORBA objects. We also import the package, which contains the interfaces and classes, generated from our interface specification by the IDL compiler.

```
package vogel.transaction.chapter6.flightBookingImpl;
import java.sql.*;import java.util.*;
import org.omg.CORBA.*;
import com.wiley.compbooks.vogel.chapter8.naming.*;
import com.wiley.compbooks.vogel.chapter13.maintenance.*;
import vogel.transaction.chapter6.flightBooking.*;
```

We declare a public class `QueryImpl` that extends the base class `_QueryImplBase`, which is generated by the IDL compiler. We define a number of private variables in the class. The class `ConnectionPool` is explained later, the class `EasyNaming` is taken from *Java Programming with CORBA*. It provides an easy API to the naming service.

```
public class QueryImpl extends _QueryImplBase {  private ConnectionPool
connectionPool = null;
  private EasyNaming easyNaming;
  private String context;
  private String name;
  private String URL;
```

* *Java Programming with CORBA*, 2nd edition, by Andreas Vogel and Keith Duddy. New York: John Wiley and Sons, 1998.

```
private String userId;
private String password;
private ORB orb;
private int departureTimeInterval;
private int changeTimeInterval;
```

In the constructor, we initialize the private variables of the class with values, which get passed as arguments to the constructor. We explicitly call the constructor of the superclass that makes the object references of instances of this class persistent. In the case of Visibroker, the instance is registered with the OSAgent. We also create a connection pool. We chose 2 for the number of connections and pass the values of the database URL, the username, and the password. Typically, one would choose a larger number of connections. We have chosen two for testing the pool. We also declare two variables for search policies, which are explained later.

```
public QueryImpl( ORB orb, EasyNaming easyNaming,String context,
  String name, String URL, String userId, String password ) {

    super( name );

    this.orb = orb;
    this.easyNaming = easyNaming;
    this.context = context;
    this.name = name;
    this.URL = URL;
    this.userId = userId;
    this.password = password;

    connectionPool = new ConnectionPool( 2, URL, userId, password );
    connectionPool.start();

    departureTimeInterval = 2; // hours
    changeTimeInterval = 60; // minutes
}
```

In the IDL interface we defined two operations, getFlight() and queryAvailableFlights(). The first operation lets a client find out about a connection between two airports. We have implemented the method with the following hard-coded search policies.

- A flight does not exceed three legs.
- The actual departure date is plus/minus two hours of the desired time.
- The connection time is less than one hour.

We create three different select statements, for one-leg, two-leg, and three-leg flights. The query for a two-leg flight qualifies the following criterion: *Is there a flight F1 from A to X and a flight F2 from X to B, where the departure time of flight F1 is within two hours of our desired departure time, and the departure time of F2 is not later than one hour after arrival time of Flight F1?* The full string constructor for this case is shown next. The other two cases are following the same pattern.

```
public Flight[][] queryAvailableFlights(
    String from,
    String to,
    SimpleDate departureDate )
    throws InvalidQuery, Internal, NotAvailable, ShutDownInProgress {

    int i, j;
    String[] selectStatement = new String[3];
    ResultSet[] resultSets = new ResultSet[3];
    Statement[] statement = new Statement[3];
    Flight[][] flights = null;
    Vector flightVector = new Vector();
    Connection c;

    // create the three select statements

    selectStatement[0] = new String(
      "select * from flight_type ft, flight_instance fi where ..." +

    selectStatement[1] = new String(
      "select * from flight_type ft1, flight_instance fi1," +
      " flight_type ft2, flight_instance fi2 where " +
      " ft1.from_airport = '" + from + "' and " +
      " ft2.to_airport = '" + to + "' and " +
      " ft1.to_airport = ft2.from_airport and " +
      " ft1.flight_number = fi1.flight_number and " +
      " ft2.flight_number = fi2.flight_number and " +
      " fi1.departure_date = to_date('" +
      departureDate.month + "-" + departureDate.day + "-" +
      departureDate.year + "', 'MM-DD-YY') and" +
      " ft1.departure_hour - " + departureTimeInterval +
      " < " + departureDate.hour + " and" +
      " ft1.departure_hour + " + departureTimeInterval +
      " > " + departureDate.hour + " and" +
      " (ft2.departure_hour * 60 + ft2.departure_minute) -" +
      " (ft1.arrival_hour * 60 + ft1.arrival_minute) > " +
      changeTimeInterval );

    selectStatement[2] = new String(
      "select * from flight_type ft1, flight_instance fi1," +
      " flight_type ft2, flight_instance fi2," +
      " flight_type ft3, flight_instance fi3 where ..." +
```

Now we get a connection from the connection pool. In case there are any connections left in the pool, the operation blocks until a connection is returned from another thread. Once we have the connection, we create three JDBC statements and execute them.

```
try {
  // get connection from pool
  c = connectionPool.getConnection();

  // create statements and execute queries
  for( i = 0; i < 3; i++ ) {
    try {
      statement[i] = c.createStatement();
      resultSets[i] = statement[i].executeQuery(selectStatement[i]);
    }
    catch( Exception ex ) {
      System.out.println( ex );
      System.out.println( "no connection with " + i + " stops" );
      throw new Internal();
    }
}
```

Then we process the result sets that are returned from the execution of the statements. For each of the result sets, we iterate through the rows and populate flight objects by extracting the appropriate elements from the row. In some cases, the type conversion is straightforward (integers and strings). In the case of dates, we first populate a temporary variable of type `Timestamp` (defined in the `java.sql` package) and then we populate the appropriate fields into our IDL-defined `SimpleDate` objects. We collect the flight objects, we create from the result sets in a vector called `FlightVector`.

```
// process result sets - collect flights in a vector
Timestamp timestamp;

for( i = 0; i < 3; i++ ) {
  if( resultSets[i] == null ) {
    System.out.println("no connection with " + i + " legs");
  }
  else {
  while( resultSets[i].next() ) {
      Flight[] flight = new Flight[i+1];
      for( j = 0; j < i+1; j++ ) {
        flight[j] =  new Flight();

        flight[j].flightNumber = resultSets[i].getString(11*j+1);
        flight[j].departingAirport =
          resultSets[i].getString(11*j+2);
```

```
                    flight[j].arrivingAirport =
                      resultSets[i].getString(11*j+3);
                    timestamp = resultSets[i].getTimestamp(11*j+9);
                    flight[j].departureDate = new SimpleDate(
                      timestamp.getDate(),
                      timestamp.getMonth() + 1,
                      timestamp.getYear(),
                      resultSets[i].getInt( 11*j+4 ),
                      resultSets[i].getInt( 11*j+5 ) );
                    timestamp = resultSets[i].getTimestamp(11*j+10);
                    flight[j].arrivalDate = new SimpleDate(
                      timestamp.getDate(),
                      timestamp.getMonth() + 1,
                      timestamp.getYear(),
                      resultSets[i].getInt( 11*j+6 ),
                      resultSets[i].getInt( 11*j+7 ) );
                    flight[j].aircraft = resultSets[i].getString( 11*j+11 );
                  }
                  flightVector.addElement( flight );
                }
              }
            }
```

Now we close all of our statement handles. We also convert the vector, which contains our flight objects, into an array. The array conforms to the Java mapping of the IDL sequence, which we specified as the return type of the operation queryAvailableFlights().

```
            // close statements
            for( i = 0; i < 3; i++ ) {
              try {
                statement[i].close();
              }
              catch( Exception ex ) {
                System.out.println( ex );
              }
            }

            //copy vector into array
            if( flightVector.size() == 0 ) {
                flights = new Flight[0][];
            }

            flights = new Flight[flightVector.size()][];
            flightVector.copyInto( flights );
          }
          catch( Exception e) {
            System.out.println("database access error: " + e );
            throw new Internal();
          }
```

Finally, we return the connection to the pool. We also check if there are any flights in the array we want to return. If not, we raise the exception `NotAvailable`. Otherwise, we return the array `flights`.

```
        connectionPool.releaseConnection( c );

        // if there are no matching flights throw an exception
        if( flights.length == 0 ) {
          throw new NotAvailable("No flights match this query");
        }
        // otherwise return flights
        return flights;
    }
```

The other operation of the interface is implemented by the method `getFlight()`. The approach is the same as described earlier. We construct a string, which holds our SQL query, get a connection from the connection pool, execute the query, and process the result set. Finally, we return the connection to the pool and return the flight data, which belongs to the requested flight number and departure date.

```
public Flight getFlight( String flightNumber, SimpleDate departureDate )
    throws Internal, NotAvailable, ShutDownInProgress {

    int i, j;
    String selectStatement;
    ResultSet resultSet;
    Statement statement;
    Flight flight = null;
    Connection c = null;

    selectStatement = "select * from FLIGHT_TYPE ft,
      FLIGHT_INSTANCE fi   where " +
      "ft.flight_number = '" + flightNumber +"' and " +
      "fi.flight_number = '" + flightNumber +"'";

    try {
      // get connection from pool
      c = connectionPool.getConnection();

      statement = c.createStatement();
      resultSet = statement.executeQuery(selectStatement);
    }
    catch( Exception ex ) {
      connectionPool.releaseConnection( c );
      throw new Internal();
    }

    // process result sets
```

```
    Timestamp timestamp;
    if( resultSet == null ) {
      connectionPool.releaseConnection( c );
      throw new NotAvailable();
    }
    try {

      resultSet.next();

      // extract data from result set and create flight objects
      flight =  new Flight();
      flight.id = "";
      flight.flightNumber = resultSet.getString(1);
      flight.departingAirport = resultSet.getString(2);
      flight.arrivingAirport = resultSet.getString(3);
      timestamp = resultSet.getTimestamp(9);
      flight.departureDate = new SimpleDate(
        timestamp.getDate(),
        timestamp.getMonth() + 1,
        timestamp.getYear(),
        resultSet.getInt( 4 ),
        resultSet.getInt( 5 ) );
      timestamp = resultSet.getTimestamp(10);
      flight.arrivalDate = new SimpleDate(
        timestamp.getDate(),
        timestamp.getMonth() + 1,
          timestamp.getYear(),
        resultSet.getInt( 6 ),
        resultSet.getInt( 7 ) );
      flight.aircraft = resultSet.getString( 11 );
    }
    catch( Exception e ) {
      connectionPool.releaseConnection( c );
      throw new NotAvailable();
    }
    connectionPool.releaseConnection( c );
    return flight;
  }
```

We must also implement the operations we have defined in the IDL interface Maintained. This interface provides a pair of operations, which allow the graceful, two-phase shutdown of CORBA objects.

The method `prepareShutdown()` unbinds this instance from the naming service using the method `unbind_from_string()` of the Easy-Naming class. We also notify the connection pool, so that it can shut down the connection to the database in a graceful manner. Once this all done we call back the maintainer object reporting that we are ready to shut down.

```
  public void prepareShutdown( Maintainer maintainer ) {
    // unbind from the naming service
```

```
        try {
          easyNaming.unbind_from_string( context + name );
        }
        catch ( Exception ex ) {
          System.err.println( ex );
        }

        connectionPool.prepareShutdown();

        // confirm shutdown
        maintainer.shutdownConfirmation( this );

        return;
      }
```

In the `shutdown()` method, we call the shutdown operation on the ORB. When using the BOA, this method invocation makes `impl_is_ready()` return, which usually terminates the server process.

```
    public void shutdown() {
        orb.shutdown();
        return;  }
    }
```

### *Implementation of the Connection Pool*

The connection pool manages the connection to a database. At creation time, the constructor obtains a number of connections to the database and puts them in a pool. Whenever an object needs to access the database, a connection is taken from the pool and given to the object. Once the object is finished with its database access it returns the connection to the pool.

There are two advantages, which are achieved by database connection pooling.

- An application can get optimal use out of a limited number of database connections. This is important as database vendors usually charge by the number of concurrently available connections.
- The time required to open and close database connections creates a substantial performance overhead, which is avoided by connection pooling.

There is, however, one issue with connection pooling: security. Once the connection pool is created it logs into the database under a single user. All connections in the pool and consequently all application clients have the privileges/limitation of this user. Typically this is not a problem as applications have a need for a higher-level access control anyway. Also, clients cannot directly query the database with arbitrary SQL statements. The middle layer prevents this.

Our class ConnectionPool extends the Java class Thread. This is necessary to make the event notification work, which is used to notify threads waiting for a connection. The pool itself is a private variable of type Stack (as defined in the package java.util). There is also a flag, which indicates if the connection pool is shutting down. The variable poolSize depicts how many connections the pool contains.

```
package vogel.transaction.chapter6.flightBookingImpl;
import java.sql.*;import java.util.*;import
vogel.transaction.chapter6.flightBooking.ShutDownInProgress;

public class ConnectionPool extends Thread {

  private Stack pool;
  private boolean shutdown;
  private int poolSize;
```

In the constructor, we initialize our variables and get the connection. We have to load a JDBC driver. The JDK only provides the JDBC interfaces. The implementations are provided by various vendors. In this example, we load the Oracle JDBC driver. Then we initiate the connections and put them in the connection pool.

```
  public ConnectionPool(
    int poolSize, String URL, String name, String password  ) {

    shutdown = false;
    this.poolSize = poolSize;
    pool = new Stack();

    try {

      // load the Oracle JDBC driver
      DriverManager.registerDriver(
        new oracle.jdbc.driver.OracleDriver() );

      for( int i = 0; i < poolSize; i++ ) {
        // get new connection to the database
        Connection c = DriverManager.getConnection(
          URL,name,password);
        // put new connection in the pool
        pool.push( c );
      }
```

```
    }
    catch( Exception e ) {
      System.err.println( "Database access error: " + e);
    }
  }
```

The method `getConnection()` returns a connection from the pool. It is essential that the method is declared `synchronized` to make the event notification work.

First we check if the shutdown flag is set. If so, we throw the exception `ShutDownInProgress`. The idea of our implementation of a graceful shutdown is that during the shutdown process no new requests for connections are accepted. However, connections, which are already given out, continue to operate (for a limited time).

To obtain a connection to be returned we check if the pool is empty. If so, we wait. The `wait()` call is interrupted when another method in the same object sends an event. Once we receive the event, that is, we return from `wait()`, we check again if the pool is empty.

If there is a connection available in the pool, we pop a connection from the pool (stack) and return it.

```
  public synchronized Connection getConnection()
    throws ShutDownInProgress {

    if( shutdown ) {
      throw new ShutDownInProgress();
    }
    while( pool.empty() ) {
      System.out.println("pool is empty: wait");
      try {
        wait();
      }
      catch( java.lang.InterruptedException ie ) {
        System.out.println( ie );
      }
      System.out.println("received event");
    }
    System.out.println("pop connection");
    Connection connection = (Connection) pool.pop();

    return connection;
  }
```

The method `releaseConnection()` must also be declared as `synchronized`. We return (push) the released connection to the pool and send out an event by calling `notifyAll()`.

```
public synchronized void releaseConnection( Connection c ) {
  pool.push( c );
  notifyAll();
}
```

In the method `prepareShutdown()` we first set the shutdown flag. Then we wait for outstanding connections to be returned. To avoid deadlocks we use a time-out of five seconds on the waits. Once we have reclaimed/timed out all connections we close the connections and return.

```
public synchronized void prepareShutdown() {

  // set shutdown flag
  shutdown = true;
  while( pool.size() < poolSize ) {
    try {
      wait( 5000 );
    }
    catch( InterruptedException ie ) {
      System.out.println("interupt exception");
    }
  }

  //close all database connections
  Connection c;
  for( int i = 0; i < poolSize; i++ ) {
    c = (Connection) pool.elementAt( i );
    try {
      c.close();
    }
    catch( SQLException se ) {
      System.out.println("problem when closing connections: " + se );
    }
  }
}
```

### *Implementation of Server*

We want to run the `FlightQuery` object as a standalone object; hence, we need a server class, which hosts it. We call this class `QueryServer`. As usually in such CORBA server classes we only implement the `main()` method. First, we check for the right number of arguments (zero in this case).

```
package vogel.transaction.chapter6.flightBookingImpl;

import java.util.*;import org.omg.CORBA.*;
import org.omg.CosNaming.NamingContextPackage.*;
import com.wiley.compbooks.vogel.chapter8.naming.*;
import vogel.transaction.chapter6.flightBooking.*;

public class QueryServer {

  public static void main(String[] args) {

    if( args.length != 0 ) {
      System.out.println(
        "Usage: vbj" +
        "vogel.transaction.chapter6.flightBookingImpl.QueryServer");
      System.exit( 1 );
    }
```

Then we initialize the ORB, the object adapter and the EasyNaming class. We also create an instance of our class `QueryImpl`. We pass references to the ORB, the `EasyNaming` instance, the naming context name, the object name, the URL for the database instance, a database username and password into the constructor of the class. The pair "scott"/"tiger" is the default user in Oracle databases.

```
    String context = new String("/schedules/");
    String name = new String("Central Flight Schedule");

    try {
      // init ORB, OA and EasyNaming
      Properties orbProps = new Properties();
      orbProps.put("ORBservices", "CosNaming");
      ORB orb = ORB.init( args, orbProps );
      BOA boa = orb.BOA_init();
      EasyNaming easyNaming = new EasyNaming( orb );

      // create the query object
      Query query = (Query) new QueryImpl(
        orb, easyNaming, context, name,
        "jdbc:oracle:oci7:@", "scott", "tiger" );
```

We then notify the object adapter of the existence of our instance, register the object (that is, its IOR), with the naming service. Note that the rebind method overrides existing entries of the same name. Then we print out a notification and wait for incoming requests.

```
      // export the object reference
      boa.obj_is_ready(query);
```

```
        // register with the naming service
        easyNaming.rebind_from_string( context + name, query );

        // wait for requests
        System.out.println(
          "Query Server <schedules/Central Flight Query> is ready");

        boa.impl_is_ready();
      }    catch(Exception e) {
        System.err.println(e);
      }
    }
  }
```

## Airline

We explain an illustrative Java implementation of the airline object and full C++ implementation, which is based on the Oracle XA integration into the OTS; we use (Visibroker ITS). We also explain the Java implementation of the Airline Query object.

### *Fake Java Implementation*

The implementation involves two classes, the Airline implementation class and the server class, which is hosting the object.

#### Implementation of the Interface AirlineWithResource

The class `AirlineImpl` implements the IDL interface AirlineWithResource, which inherits the IDL interfaces Airline, CosTransactions::Resource and com::wiley::compbooks::vogel::chapter13::maintenance::Maintained. The implementation class inherits the implementation base class `_AirlineWithResourceImplBase`.

We include the usual set of packages. The new package we import here is `org.omg.CosTransactions.*`. The implementation class extends the implementation base class generated by the IDL compiler. In the constructor we copy arguments into local variables of the object.

```
package vogel.transaction.chapter6.flightBookingImpl;

import java.util.*;

import org.omg.CORBA.*;
import org.omg.CosTransactions.*;
import org.omg.CosNaming.NamingContextPackage.*;
```

```
import com.wiley.compbooks.vogel.chapter8.naming.*;
import com.wiley.compbooks.vogel.chapter13.maintenance.*;

import vogel.transaction.chapter6.flightBooking.*;

public class AirlineImpl extends _AirlineWithResourceImplBase {

  private ORB orb;
  private EasyNaming easyNaming;
  private String context;
  private String name;

  public AirlineImpl(
    ORB orb, EasyNaming easyNaming, String context, String name ) {

    super( name );
    this.orb = orb;
    this.easyNaming = easyNaming;
    this.context = context;
    this.name = name;
  }
```

The implementation of the operations follows the same pattern, which we explain using the `boolkLeg()` method. These methods are performed within a distributed transaction. We use the current interface to employ indirect context management. We obtain the current interface by invoking the method `resolve_initial_references()` on the ORB providing the string "TransactionCurrent" as an argument. As usual, we narrow the IOR obtained and check for a null reference. You have to obtain the current object within the scope of the method, as it is different for each invocation. Each invocation belongs to a different transaction, which is described by the current object.

```
public String bookLeg( LegRecord legRecord )
    throws NotAvailable {

    try {
      // obtain current object
      System.err.println("resolve transaction current");
      org.omg.CORBA.Object obj =
        orb.resolve_initial_references("TransactionCurrent");
      org.omg.CosTransactions.Current current =
        org.omg.CosTransactions.CurrentHelper.narrow( obj );
      if( current == null ) {
        System.err.println("current is not of expected type");
        System.exit( 1 );
      }
```

From the current object we get the control object, and from control we get the coordinator. We register the resource that is the object itself with the coordinator. Note that this class implements the IDL interface AirlineWithResource, which inherits from the OTS Resource interface. Finally, we return a made-up booking number. We also catch possible exceptions and throw our IDL-defined exception `NotAvailable`.

```
Control control = current.get_control();
      Coordinator coordinator = control.get_coordinator();

      // register resource
      RecoveryCoordinator recCoordinator =
        coordinator.register_resource( this );

      System.out.println("Airline: booking made");
      // return booking number
      String bookingId = new String( name + "00000815" );
      return bookingId;
    }
    catch( Exception ex ) {
    System.err.println("Airline.book: " + ex );
      throw new NotAvailable();
    }
  }

  public void cancel( String id ) throws NonExistent {
    // ...

  }
```

The implementation of the `cancel()` is the same with respect to the transaction management. Since we have not stored the booking information, there isn't anything to cancel in this implementation.

Now we implement the Resource interface by illustrating the call flow. When running this implementation it demonstrates the two-phase commit protocol as implemented by OTS. For each of the operations that can take part in the protocol we simply print out a statement saying which method has been invoked. The `prepare()` method returns VoteCommit status to indicate that we have arbitrarily chosen to commit the transaction.

```
// implement methods of the Resource interface

  public Vote prepare() {
    System.out.println("Resource: prepare(): VoteCommit");
    return Vote.VoteCommit;
  }

  public void rollback() {
    System.out.println("Resource: rollback()");
```

```
}

public void commit() {
  System.out.println("Resource: commit()");
}

public void commit_one_phase() {
  System.out.println("Resource: commit_one_phase()");
}

public void forget() {
  System.out.println("Resource: forget()");
}
```

If you wish to fully implement the `resource` interface, you will have to program the following main tasks:

- `prepare()`. Store the state changes caused by the method invocation temporarily but persistent. If successful, return `VoteCommit`; otherwise, `VoteRollback`.
- `commit()`. Move the temporarily stored state changes to the corresponding entry in your persistent storage.
- `rollback()`. Roll back the memory state and remove the temporary stored state changes.
- Constructor. In case your resource object crashed during a transaction, you must synchronize the state of a restarted object from the temporary storage and persistent storage and the OTS.

Finally, we implement the interface Maintained. The method `prepareShutdown()` unbinds from the naming service and notifies the `maintainer`. The `shutdown()` method calls the shutdown method on the ORB.

```
public void prepareShutdown( Maintainer maintainer ) {

    // unbind from the naming service
    try {
      easyNaming.unbind_from_string( context + name );
    }
    catch ( Exception ex ) {
      System.err.println( ex );
    }

    // confirm shutdown
    maintainer.shutdownConfirmation( this );

    return;
  }
```

```
    public void shutdown() {
      orb.shutdown();
    }
  }
```

### Implementation of the Airline Server

The implementation of the server class follows the usual pattern: initializing the ORB and the object adapter, creating an instance of the object, registering it with the object adapter, and waiting for invocation. The only difference in this server is that we initialize the ORB with different properties. We have here two ORB services, the CORBA Naming Service as well as the Object Transaction Service. The properties are ORB specific.

```
package vogel.transaction.chapter6.flightBookingImpl;

  ...
public class AirlineServer {

  public static void main(String[] args) {

    ...
    try {
      Properties orbProps = new Properties();
      orbProps.put(
        "ORBservices",
        "CosNaming,com.visigenic.services.CosTransactions");
      ORB orb = ORB.init( args, orbProps );
    ...
}
```

## C++ Implementation Using Oracle XA

The implementation of the C++/Oracle airline object has three pieces: the header, the airline object implementation, and the server implementation.

### Implementation of the Interface Airline

The implementation of the airline interface consists of a header file `AirlineImpl.h` and a corresponding implementation file `Airline-Impl.cpp`. The header file defines the C++ signature of the class, which implements the IDL interface.

**Header** We include the header file for the ITS session manager, the header file generated for the IDL file which contains the interface for this application, and the interface for the graceful shutdown. We also include C header files for the Oracle Call Interface (OCI).

```
#define _INC_FSTREAM
#include <VISSessionManager_c.hh>
#include "Chapter6_s.hh"
#include "maintenance_s.hh"

extern "C"
{
#include <ociapr.h>
#include <ocidem.h>
}
```

Then we declare the implementation class `AirlineImpl`, which inherits from the IDL-generated skeleton. We publicly declare the constructor and the methods, which correspond to the operations we defined in the IDL interface. The parameters and return types are according to the IDL/C++ mapping.

```
class AirlineImpl : public _sk_flightBooking::_sk_Airline {

public:

  //constructor

  AirlineImpl(const char *name, const CORBA::ORB_var& orb);


  // implement Airline interface

  virtual char* bookLeg( const flightBooking::LegRecord& leg );

  virtual void cancel( const char* _id );

  virtual void shutdown();

  virtual void prepareShutdown(
    com::wiley::compbooks::vogel::chapter13::maintenance::Maintainer *
    maintainer );

};
```

**Implementation** AirlineImpl.cpp contains the code for the implementation of the `AirlineImpl` class. AirlineImpl.h contains the class definition and timeb.h to use the time-related utilities. We define some Oracle-related constants that are required for the OCI calls. The `report_error()` function handles all the runtime errors. We also declare some variables on the class level. Since those variables can be accessed concurrently by different threads we must protect them. We do these with a mutex, and choose the one provided by the Visibroker for C++ distribution for illustrative purposes.

```
#include "AirlineImpl.h"
#include "sys/timeb.h"

#define DEFER_PARSE      1
#define NO_DATA_FOUND    1403
#define VERSION_7        2

static void report_error( Lda_Def *lda, Cda_Def *cda );

const char* _name;
long _counter;
com::wiley::compbooks::vogel::chapter13::maintenance::Maintainer *
_maintainer;
CORBA::ORB_var _orb;
VISMutex _mutex;
```

In the constructor we just copy the values we receive and initialize the counter for unique (within this airline) booking identifiers. We increase the counter after every booking made.

```
AirlineImpl::AirlineImpl(const char *name, const CORBA::ORB_var& orb ) :
    _sk_flightBooking::_sk_Airline( name ) {

    _name = name;
    _orb = orb;

    counter = init_counter();
}
```

Airline interface provides two methods for booking and cancellation of a leg. Both operations must be executed in the context of a distributed transaction since a flight has usually more than one leg and the creation/cancellation of booking spans over all of the legs.

```
// implement Airline interface

char* AirlineImpl::bookLeg( const flightBooking::LegRecord& leg ) {

  try
  {
    CORBA::Object_var obj =
      _orb->resolve_initial_references("TransactionCurrent");
    CosTransactions::Current_var _current =
      CosTransactions::Current::_narrow( obj );
  }
  catch(const CORBA::Exception& ex)
  {
    cerr << "Can't get Current: " << ex << endl;
    throw;
  }
```

Now we declare some OCI-related variables, a string for a SQL insert statement and a string for the confirmation number of the booking we want to create. Since the confirmation number is a variable shared between different threads we protect it with a mutex. In the critical section we increment the booking id counter by 1. Then we create the string for the SQL insert statement.

```
Lda_Def* lda;
  Cda_Def cda_var;
  Cda_Def* cda = &cda_var;

  char sql_insert[256];
  char confirmationNumber[10];

  _mutex.lock();
    sprintf( confirmationNumber, "%s%8.8u", _name, _counter++ );
  _mutex.unlock();
  cout << "##" << confirmationNumber << "##" << endl;

  sprintf( sql_insert,
    "INSERT INTO FLIGHT_BOOKING VALUES( '%s', '%s', '%s', '%s', '%s',
TO_DATE('%02u-%02u-%02u', 'MM-DD-YY'), %8.2f, '%s' )",
    leg.passenger.title,
    leg.passenger.firstName,
    leg.passenger.middleInitial,
    leg.passenger.lastName,
    leg.leg.flightNumber,
    leg.leg.departureDate.month,
    leg.leg.departureDate.day,
    leg.leg.departureDate.year,
    leg.leg.price,
    confirmationNumber );
  cout << sql_insert << endl;
```

Now declare and initialize the Visibroker session manager and its connection pool. Then we get a connection from the connection pool. The session manager supports different profiles, which determine the kind of connection. For this example it contains a flag that we want to use the Oracle XA interface. For details we refer to the Inprise ITS user and programming manuals, as it is a vendor-specific offering and outside the scope of this book.

Eventually we get a connection handle and deal with the various exceptions that can occur.

```
VISSessionManager::Connection_var smconn = NULL;
  try
  {
```

```
    // obtain a reference to the Session Manager connection pool
    CORBA::Object_var initRef =
      _orb->resolve_initial_references(
      "VISSessionManager::ConnectionPool");

    // narrow this reference to the correct type
    VISSessionManager::ConnectionPool_var pool =
      VISSessionManager::ConnectionPool::_narrow(initRef);

    // now, get a connection using the connection profile "booking"
    smconn = pool->getConnection("booking");

    //  get a connection handle to use for native OCI calls
    lda = (Lda_Def*) smconn->getNativeConnectionHandle();
  }
  catch(const VISSessionManager::ConnectionPool::ProfileError& ex)
  {
    // we received an error with this profile.
    cerr << "Profile error:\n"
         << "  " << ex.code
         << ": " << ex.reason
         << endl;
        throw CORBA::PERSIST_STORE();
  }
  catch(const VISSessionManager::Error& ex)
  {
    cerr << "Session Manager error:\n";
    // print out all the error messages
    for(CORBA::ULong i = 0; i < ex.info.length(); i++)
    {
      cerr << "  " << ex.info[i].subsystem
           << "-"  << ex.info[i].code
           << ": " << ex.info[i].reason
           << endl;
    }
        throw CORBA::PERSIST_STORE();
  }
  catch(CORBA::PERSIST_STORE)
  {
    cerr << "resolve_initial_references on the Session "
         << "Manager Connection Pool failed" << endl;
    throw;
  }
```

Now that we have the connection handle, we obtain a cursor from it and start processing out a SQL insert statement. First we parse the statement, then we execute it, and since we don't expect any results, we close the cursor right afterward.

```
  // open the cursor
  cout << "open the cursor" << endl;
  if(oopen(cda, lda, 0, -1, -1, 0, -1))
  {
    report_error(lda, cda);
    throw CORBA::PERSIST_STORE();
  }

  // parse the SQL statement
  cout << "parse the SQL statement" << endl;
  if(oparse(cda, (text*) sql_insert, -1, 0, VERSION_7))
  // if(oparse(cda, (text*) sql_insert, -1, DEFER_PARSE, VERSION_7))
  {
    report_error(lda, cda);
    throw CORBA::PERSIST_STORE();
  }

  if(oexec(cda))
  {
    report_error(lda, cda);
  }

  oclose(cda);
```

Finally, we release the connection and return the confirmation number.

```
smconn->release(VISSessionManager::Connection::MarkSuccess);

  return strdup( confirmationNumber );
}
```

The implementation of the cancel method is pretty much the same, the only difference is in the SQL statement shown in the following code.

```
void AirlineImpl::cancel( const char* confirmationNumber ) {

  ...
  char sql_delete[256];

  sprintf( sql_delete,
    "DELETE FROM FLIGHT_BOOKING WHERE CONFIRMATIONNUMBER = '%s'",
    confirmationNumber );
  ...
}
```

The implementation of the Maintenance interface is simple. In the shutdown preparation we immediately send acknowledgment to the maintainer, and in the shutdown we call shutdown on the ORB.

```
void AirlineImpl::prepareShutdown(
  com::wiley::compbooks::vogel::chapter13::maintenance::Maintainer *
    maintainer ) {

  cout << "Prepare shutdown on Airline " << _name << " called" << endl;
  maintainer->shutdownConfirmation( this );
  cout << "Airline " << _name << ": shutdown confirmed" << endl;
};

void AirlineImpl::shutdown() {

  cout << "Shutdown on Airline " << _name << " called" << endl;
  _orb->shutdown();
};
```

### Implementation of the Airline Server

The implementation of the airline server follows the standard server pattern. In the main routine, we initialize the ORB and the object adapter. We also initialize the C++ version of the `EasyNaming` class, taken from the book *C++ Programming with CORBA**. We also check for the correct number of arguments.

```
#include "AirlineImpl.h"
#include "EasyNaming.h"

int main(int argc, char* const* argv) {

  try {

    // Initialize the ORB.
    CORBA::ORB_var orb = CORBA::ORB_init(argc, argv);

    // Check the command line arguments
    CORBA::BOA_var boa = orb->BOA_init(argc, argv);

    // Initialize EasyNaming
    EasyNaming *easy_naming = new EasyNaming( orb );

    // Check the arguments.
    if(argc < 2) {
      cerr << "Usage: " << argv[0] << " <airline>" << endl;
      return 1;
    }
```

We create an instance of the airline implementation object and register it with the object adapter and the naming service. Then we print its

* *C++ Programming with CORBA*, Andreas Vogel, et al. New York: John Wiley and Sons, 1999.

name and stringified IOR, and wait for incoming events. Finally, we catch and handle possible exceptions.

```
      const char* airline_name = argv[1];

      // Create the airline object
      flightBooking::Airline_var airline =
        new AirlineImpl(airline_name, orb);

      // Export the object reference.
      boa->obj_is_ready( airline );

      // register object with Naming Service
      easy_naming->rebind_from_string(
          strcat("/airlines/", airline_name ),
          airline );
      cout << "bound to " << strcat("/airlines/", airline_name ) << endl;

      // Wait for incoming requests
      boa->impl_is_ready();
    }
    catch(const CORBA::Exception& e) {
      cerr << "Exception: " << e << endl;
      return 1;
    }
    catch(...) {
      cerr << "Uncaught Exception" << endl;
      return 1;
    }
    return 0;
  }
```

### Airline Query Implementation

The implementation of the airline query interface is quite similar to the flight query interface. We use the same structure, including the connection pool object. We only show the essential parts of the implementation.

```
public class AirlineQueryImpl extends _AirlineQueryImplBase {
  ...
  public AirlineQueryImpl( ORB orb, EasyNaming easyNaming,
    String context, String name,
    String URL, String userId, String password ) {
    ...
  }

  public LegRecord lookUpById( String id )
    throws Internal, NonExistent {
```

```
LegRecord legRecord;
// ...

// create the sql query
selectStatement = new String(
  "select * from FLIGHT_BOOKING where CONFIRMATIONNUMBER = '"
  + id + "'" );

// get connection from pool
// ...
// create statements and execute queries
// ...

// process result sets
// collect flights in a vector
Timestamp timestamp;
if( resultSet == null ) {
  System.out.println("no entry");
  throw new NonExistent();
}
```

Since we are expecting a single record back, we only query the result set once. We then create a new `LegRecord` instance and initialize with all the data available from the query. For the data, which is not available, we fill in dummy values.

```
// we only process the first entry
resultSet.next();

legRecord = new LegRecord();
legRecord.passenger = new Person();
legRecord.leg = new Flight();

// extract data from result set and create leg record
// passenger data
legRecord.passenger.title = resultSet.getString(1);
legRecord.passenger.firstName = resultSet.getString(2);
legRecord.passenger.middleInitial = resultSet.getString(3);
if( legRecord.passenger.middleInitial == null )
  legRecord.passenger.middleInitial = new String("");
legRecord.passenger.lastName = resultSet.getString(4);

// leg data
legRecord.leg.flightNumber = resultSet.getString(5);
timestamp = resultSet.getTimestamp(6);
legRecord.leg.departureDate = new SimpleDate(
  timestamp.getDate(),
  timestamp.getMonth() + 1,
  timestamp.getYear(),
```

```
        -1, // undefined
        -1  // undefined
      );
      legRecord.leg.price = resultSet.getInt(7);
      legRecord.leg.id = resultSet.getString(8);

      // complete the legRecord with dummy data
      // this date is known from the flight query entry
      // for this particular flight
      legRecord.leg.aircraft = new String("");
      legRecord.leg.arrivalDate = new SimpleDate(
        -1, -1, -1, -1, -1 );
      legRecord.leg.arrivingAirport = new String("");
      legRecord.leg.departingAirport = new String("");

      // close statements
      // ...
    return legRecord;

}
```

The implementation of the server class follows the usual pattern and the explanation is omitted.

## Travel Agent

The travel agent is the centerpiece of the application. It is the single point of access for the client and has references to various backend systems and subcomponents. The backend systems are the various airline objects and the central flight query as shown earlier. The subcomponents are

**Travel agent data access.** Stores bookings in local database.

**Session objects.** The travel agent is a session factory.

**Booking objects.** The session objects act as a booking factory.

**Directory.** Provides user and profile management.

In the remainder of this section we look at the implementations of the various objects and finally the implementation of the travel agent server.

### *Travel Agent Data Access*

The travel agent data access objects provide transactional access to the database, which is private to the travel agent. We have chosen to implement this object in C++ as it allows us to embed access to an Oracle database within a distributed transaction through its XA interface. The implementation of the interface TravelAgentDataAccess is similar to the Airline interface.

### Header

The following code shows the declaration of the implementation class.

```
#include <VISSessionManager_c.hh>
#include "Chapter6_s.hh"
#include "maintenance_s.hh"

extern "C"
{
#include <ociapr.h>
#include <ocidem.h>
}

class TravelAgentDataAccessImpl :
  public _sk_flightBooking::_sk_TravelAgentDataAccess {

public:

  //constructor

  TravelAgentDataAccessImpl(
    const char *name, const CORBA::ORB_var& orb);


  // implement TravelAgentDataAccess interface

  virtual void createBooking(
    const flightBooking::BookingRecord& aBooking );

  virtual void cancelBooking( const char* bookingId );

  virtual void shutdown();

  virtual void prepareShutdown(
    com::wiley::compbooks::vogel::chapter13::maintenance::Maintainer *
    maintainer );

};
```

### Implementation

In the implementation of the class, we follow the same idea as shown in the airline implementation class. This includes the initialization and the management of the unique identifiers. Now we use them for complete booking from a travel agent's point of view rather than only for a single leg in the airline case.

When we create a booking, we construct a special field, which is the concatenation of all of the leg identifiers. Since the data in our example has fixed length, it will be easy to pull the record apart, when retrieving it from the database.

```
#include "TravelAgentDataAccessImpl.h"

...

void TravelAgentDataAccessImpl::createBooking(
    const flightBooking::BookingRecord& aBooking ) {

char sql_insert[256];
  char legIds[50];

  strcpy( legIds, "");
  for( int n = 0; n < (int) aBooking.aComposedFlight.length(); n++ ) {
    strcat( legIds, aBooking.aComposedFlight[n].id );
  }

  sprintf( sql_insert,
    "INSERT INTO TA_BOOKING VALUES('%s', '%s', '%s', '%s', %8.2f)",
    aBooking.id,
    aBooking.label,
    aBooking.userId,
    legIds,
    aBooking.confirmedPrice );
  ...
}

void TravelAgentDataAccessImpl::cancelBooking( const char*
confirmationNumber ) {
  ...
char sql_delete[256];

  sprintf( sql_delete,
    "DELETE FROM TA_BOOKING WHERE ID = '%s'", confirmationNumber );
  ...
}
```

Since the Travel Agent Data Access object is implemented in C++, it cannot run in the same process as the travel agent. The implementation must be packaged as a C++ server. We have omitted the explanation of it here since it contains the same code as the airline server shown earlier.

## Booking Object

The Booking object is the middle-tier representation of a database entry, which describes a flight booking from the perspective of the travel agent. It defines the relationship of a customer with the bookings of multiple legs with potentially various airlines.

### Implementing a Persistent Object

A persistent object can simply represent an entry in a database table, or be the runtime representation of an object stored in an object-oriented database. A persistent object can also be a sophisticated business object, which represents data stored in various tables or even in different databases as in our example.

In any case, whenever the state of a persistent object changes it must persistify these changes in the data store(s). The locking of data or the notification of state changes to clients is not part of the pattern and must be added as needed.

### Booking Object Implementation

The booking object is implemented in Java. The implementation class has the usual package declaration and imports. The implementation class extends the implementation base class. We declare a number of private variables. The variable `bookingRecord` contains the state of the objects. We also keep a hashtable with the airline objects and a reference to the travel agent's data access objects.

```
package vogel.transaction.chapter6.flightBookingImpl;

import java.util.*;

import org.omg.CORBA.*;
import org.omg.CosTransactions.*;

import vogel.transaction.chapter6.flightBooking.*;

class BookingImpl extends _BookingImplBase {

    private ORB orb;
    private BookingRecord bookingRecord;
    private TaBookingRecord taBookingRecord;
    private Hashtable airlines;
    private TravelAgentDataAccess taDataAccess;
    private Query query;
```

We have defined a couple of constructors. The first one creates an uninitialized booking object. We just provide the booking object with the necessary object references. The booking record is set later. The second constructor sets the booking record and creates a fully initialized object.

```
public BookingImpl( ORB orb, Hashtable airlines,
      TravelAgentDataAccess taDataAccess ) {

      this.orb = orb;
      this.airlines = airlines;
      this.taDataAccess = taDataAccess;
    }
```

We also store all the arguments in local variables in the second constructor. The main task is that we get a travel agent booking record. This record describes a flight booking completely, by pointing into the databases of the airlines that are involved with the particular booking.

```
    public BookingImpl( ORB orb,
      Hashtable airlines, Hashtable airlineQueries,
      TravelAgentDataAccess taDataAccess,
      TaBookingRecord taBookingRecord,
      Query query ) {

      Vector flightVector = new Vector();
      this.orb = orb;
      this.airlines = airlines;
      this.taDataAccess = taDataAccess;
      this.taBookingRecord = taBookingRecord;
      this.query = query;
```

The state of a booking object is described in a booking record. We create a new one and initialize it with the data directly available from the travel agent booking record.

```
      bookingRecord = new BookingRecord();
      // get data from ta record
      bookingRecord.confirmedPrice = taBookingRecord.confirmedPrice;
      bookingRecord.id = taBookingRecord.id;
      bookingRecord.label = taBookingRecord.label;
      bookingRecord.userId = taBookingRecord.userId;
```

To complete the booking record, we get the remaining data from the airlines via their Airline Query interface. The travel agent booking record has a field that contains the airline booking id for the legs of the composed flight. In the context of this sample application, we have defined the following format for the airline booking ids: <two-character airline id><eight-character number>, for example “UA12345678” is a United Airlines booking id.

We loop through the list of airline booking ids. First we extract the leading two characters, which specify the airline identifier. We use the airline identifier to obtain the object reference for the airline's query interface. The hashtable `airlineQueries` is keyed by airline identifiers.

```
try {
  // get booking data from airlines and query
  for( int i = 0; i < taBookingRecord.airlineIds.length; i++ ) {
    String airline = taBookingRecord.airlineIds[i].substring(0,2);
    AirlineQuery airlineQuery =
      (AirlineQuery) airlineQueries.get(airline);
```

From the airline query interface we get a `LegRecord` for the particular leg by calling `lookUpById()`. In the first iteration we also copy the passenger information into the booking record.

```
    if( airlineQuery != null ) {
      Flight f = new Flight();
      LegRecord legRecord =
        airlineQuery.lookUpById( taBookingRecord.airlineIds[i] );
      if( i == 0 ) {
        // set passenger
        bookingRecord.passenger = legRecord.passenger;
      }
      f = legRecord.leg;
```

We obtain the remaining information about the flight from flight query object. Once we have completed the flight we put it in a vector.

```
      Flight f1 = query.getFlight(
        legRecord.leg.flightNumber, legRecord.leg.departureDate );
      f.aircraft = f1.aircraft;
      f.arrivalDate = f1.arrivalDate;
      f.arrivingAirport = f1.arrivingAirport;
      f.departingAirport = f1.departingAirport;
      f.departureDate = f1.departureDate;

      flightVector.addElement( f );
    }
  }
  bookingRecord.aComposedFlight = new Flight[flightVector.size() ];
  flightVector.copyInto( bookingRecord.aComposedFlight );
}
catch( Exception e ) {
  System.err.println( e );
}
}
```

Once we have finished looping through the legs we assign the contents of the vector to the booking record's compose flight field. Now we have a fully initialized instance of a booking object.

The method `bookingId()` implements the read-only attribute of the IDL interface by returning the value of a booking record field. The method `getBookingData()` returns the complete booking record.

```
public String bookingId() {

      return bookingRecord.id;
    }

    public BookingRecord getBookingData()
      throws Internal {

      return bookingRecord;
    }
```

The method `setBookingData()` sets the booking record of the booking object and stores the data in the database via the travel agent data access object. This method is always executed in the context of a transaction where the session object, which invokes this operation, is the transaction originator.

```
public void setBookingData( BookingRecord bookingRecord )
      throws Internal {

      try {
        // update local database
        this.bookingRecord = bookingRecord;
        taDataAccess.createBooking( bookingRecord );
      }
      catch( Exception ex ) {
        System.err.println( "Booking: " +  ex );
        throw new Internal();
      }
      return;
    }
```

The `cancel()` method cancels a booking. This involves the cancellation of the different legs with the different airlines and the removal of the entry from the travel agent's database. The cancellation of a booking is a distributed transaction, which is controlled by the booking object. The booking object acts as the transaction originator. It obtains a transaction current and starts the transaction.

```
public void cancel()
      throws Internal {

      try {
        // get current
        org.omg.CosTransactions.Current current = getCurrent();

        System.err.println("start transaction");
        // start transaction
        current.begin();

        // print transaction status (should be "active")
        System.err.println(
          "transaction status: " + current.get_status() );
```

First we cancel all the legs. We obtain the names of the airlines from the booking record and the matching airline IORs from the hashtable `airlines`. We call `cancel()` on the airline object of each of the legs providing the airline identifier. We have this identifier stored as part of the flight structure.

```
try {

  for( int i = 0;
    i < bookingRecord.aComposedFlight.length; i++ ) {

        // get airline
        String airlineId =
          bookingRecord.aComposedFlight[i].flightNumber
            .substring(0, 2);
        Airline airline = (Airline) airlines.get( airlineId );

        // cancel leg
        airline.cancel( bookingRecord.aComposedFlight[i].id );
      }
```

Then, still in the same transaction, we update the booking entry in the travel agents database via the travel agent data access object. Once all of the updates have been successful we commit the transaction. If an error occurred, we rollback the complete transaction and throw an exception.

```
        // update travel agent's database
        taDataAccess.cancelBooking( bookingRecord.id );

        // commit transaction
        current.commit( true );
      }
      catch( Exception ex ) {
        System.err.println( "Cancel failed, roll back: " +  ex );
```

```
            current.rollback();
            throw new Internal();
          }
        }
        catch( Exception ex ) {
          System.err.println( "Booking: " +  ex );
          throw new Internal();
        }
        return;
      }
```

We check for general exceptions. If one exists, we propagate it as an exception of type `Internal`. If everything went fine we just return.

```
  private org.omg.CosTransactions.Current getCurrent() {

      System.err.println("Session: resolve transaction current");
      try {
        org.omg.CORBA.Object obj =
          orb.resolve_initial_references("TransactionCurrent");
        org.omg.CosTransactions.Current current =
          org.omg.CosTransactions.CurrentHelper.narrow( obj );
        if( current == null ) {
          System.err.println("current is not of expected type");
        }
        return current;
      }
      catch( org.omg.CORBA.ORBPackage.InvalidName in ) {
        System.err.println( in );
        return null;
      }
    }
  }
```

Finally, the helper method `getCurrent()` obtains a transactional current from the ORB and narrows it to the expected type.

### Other Aspects of Persistent Objects

There are two other aspects that are typically associated with the life cycle of a persistent object: activation and deactivation. Typically, a persistent object is deactivated for memory management reasons. The deactivation means to release the memory associated with the object by keeping the state in the database and the handles of the object valid. There are two types of handles:

- IORs, which can be persistent in conjunction with activators
- Primary keys, such as booking identifiers in our example

There are pros and cons for both types of handles. IORs seem to be more suitable for programs to keep, where humans may prefer a compact unique identifier: a 6- to 10-character reservation code is easier to handle than a stringified IOR, which is a few hundred characters long.

Persistent objects often have explicit activate and deactivate methods. The POA specification provides operations for the activation/deactivation of objects. Typically the deactivation is triggered by some kind of manager object; for example, the factory object, according to a time-out policy. The activation is triggered by a client, which tries to access the object.

In our example, the lifetime of a booking object is coupled to the lifetime of a session. That means when the session is created, all the booking objects that are associated with the user are created and activated. Once the user terminates the session, all the booking objects are deactivated. In this example, we use the identifier as the handle to the booking objects, and the find operations activate the objects.

### Session Objects

Our implementation of the session object has a one-to-one relationship with a user. Furthermore, our session object keeps state. This state is also known as *conversational* state.

```
package vogel.transaction.chapter6.flightBookingImpl;

import java.util.*;

import org.omg.CORBA.*;
import org.omg.CosTransactions.*;

import vogel.transaction.chapter6.flightBooking.*;

public class SessionImpl extends _SessionImplBase {

  private Hashtable airlines;
  private org.omg.CORBA.ORB orb;
  private org.omg.CORBA.BOA boa;
  private org.omg.CORBA.Object obj;
  private Query query;
  private Directory directory;
  private Hashtable bookings;
  private BookingIdDispenser bookingIdDispenser;
  private String userId;
  private TravelAgentDataAccess taDataAccess;
  private Profile profile;
```

In the constructor of the session object we initialize all the private variables with the arguments passed from the server.

```
public SessionImpl(
    ORB orb, BOA boa, String userId,
    BookingIdDispenser bookingIdDispenser,
    Hashtable airlines, Query query, TravelAgentDataAccess taDataAccess,
    Directory directory ) {

    this.orb = orb;
    this.boa = boa;
    this.userId = userId;
    this.airlines = airlines;
    this.query = query;
    this.directory = directory;
    this.taDataAccess = taDataAccess;
    this.bookingIdDispenser = bookingIdDispenser;

    bookings = new Hashtable();
```

We obtain the user's profile from the directory and all the booking records associated with the user who is requesting the session. We create booking objects for each of the bookings. Booking object constructor fully initializes the booking objects. To obtain a full booking record we must first obtain the data from the travel agent's database, and then auxiliary data from the airlines. We store all the existing booking objects in a hashtable.

```
try {

      // get user profile from directory
      profile = directory.getProfile( userId );

      // get existing booking records
      // from travel agent data access object
      BookingRecord[] bookingRecords =
        taDataAccess.getBookingsForPerson( userId );

      // go to the airlines and fully initialize the booking record
      ...

      // create booking objects from the records
      for( int i = 0; i < bookingRecords.length; i++ ) {
        Booking booking  = (Booking) new BookingImpl(
          orb, airlines, taDataAccess, bookingRecords[i] );
        boa.obj_is_ready( booking );
        bookings.put(  booking.bookingId(), booking );
      }
```

```
    }
    catch( Exception ex ) {
      System.err.println( "Booking constructor: " + ex );
    }
  }
```

The method `queryAvailableFlights()` is just a proxy for the query object. We invoke the same method on the query object and return the results. The motivation for not exposing the query object to the client is to provide the travel agent a single point of access.

```
  public Flight[][] queryAvailableFlights(
    String from,
    String to,
    SimpleDate departureDate )
  throws InvalidQuery, Internal, NotAvailable, ShutDownInProgress {

    return query.queryAvailableFlights( from, to, departureDate );
  }
```

The method `createBooking()` creates a booking object from a booking request. This method starts a new distributed transaction, which coordinates the updates in the airlines' databases and the updates in the travel agent's database.

```
public Booking createBooking( BookingRequest bookingRequest ) {

    Booking booking = null;
    String[] legIds = new String[ bookingRequest.aComposedFlight.length
];
    bookingRequest.passenger = profile.customer;
    Flight[] composedFlight = bookingRequest.aComposedFlight;
```

After collecting all the available data in the right form, we get the transaction current object from the ORB and start a new transaction. For the illustrative and debug purposes we obtain and print the transaction status, which should be "active."

```
    try {
          org.omg.CosTransactions.Current current = getCurrent();


      current.begin();

          System.err.println("transaction status: " +
            current.get_status() );
```

In the context of the transaction, we loop through the legs of the booking request's composed flight. We first get the IOR of the airline object involved in the flight we want to book. We extract the two leading characters of the flight number (for example, "UA4321"), which determines the airline. UA stands for United Airlines in our example. These strings are the key for the airline hashtable. Then we create a fully initialized `LegRecord` and book the leg.

```
try {

  for( int i = 0; i < composedFlight.length; i++ ) {
    // get airline
    String airlineId =
      composedFlight[i].flightNumber.substring(0,2);
    Airline airline = (Airline) airlines.get( airlineId );

    // book leg at airline
    LegRecord legRecord = new LegRecord(
      composedFlight[i],
      bookingRequest.passenger,
      bookingRequest.confirmedPrice );
    composedFlight[i].id = airline.bookLeg( legRecord );
  }
```

Once we have made all the individual bookings we create a booking record and initialize it. Then we create a noninitialized booking record and set the booking record on the booking object, which stores the booking data in the travel agent's database.

```
  System.err.println("create booking record");
  BookingRecord bookingRecord = new BookingRecord();
  bookingRecord.aComposedFlight = bookingRequest.aComposedFlight;
  bookingRecord.confirmedPrice = bookingRequest.confirmedPrice;
  bookingRecord.label = bookingRequest.label ;
  bookingRecord.passenger = bookingRequest.passenger ;
  bookingRecord.id = bookingIdDispenser.newId();
  bookingRecord.userId = userId;

  // create a booking object
  booking = (Booking) new BookingImpl(orb, airlines, taDataAccess );
  boa.obj_is_ready( booking );
  bookingRecord.bookingObj = booking;

  booking.setBookingData( bookingRecord );
}
```

If something fails in the transaction, an exception is thrown. The exception is caught in the catch clause. An exception causes the rollback of the transaction and we complete the method invocation by raising the exception NotAvailable. Otherwise, we commit the transaction, store the booking object in the bookings hashtable, and return the booking object to the client.

```
        catch( Exception e ) {
          // something failed
          // rollback the transaction and throw an exception
          current.rollback();
          throw new NotAvailable();
        }
        // commit transaction
        System.err.println("commit booking");
        current.commit( true );
        bookings.put( booking.bookingId(), booking );
      }
      catch( Exception e ) {
        System.err.println( e );
      }
      return booking;
    }
```

The method findBooking() returns a booking object determined by its identifier. We just look it up in the cache, the bookings hashtable. If it is not there, we raise the exception NotAvailable.

```
  public Booking findBooking( String bookingId )
      throws NotAvailable {

      Booking b;
      if( (b = (Booking) bookings.get( bookingId )) != null ) {
        return b;
      }
      else {
        throw new NotAvailable();
      }
    }
```

The method findAllBookingRecords() goes through all the booking objects in the hashtable, retrieves their booking records, puts them in an array, and finally returns the array to the caller.

```
  public BookingRecord[] findAllBookingRecords()
      throws NotAvailable {

      // return all booking (for a particular user) from cache
      try {
        BookingRecord[] bookingRecords =
          new BookingRecord[ bookings.size() ];
```

```
        Enumeration e = bookings.elements();
        for( int i = 0; e.hasMoreElements(); i++ ) {
          bookingRecords[i] =
            ((Booking) e.nextElement()).getBookingData();
        }
        return bookingRecords;
      }
      catch( Exception e ) {
        System.out.println( e );
        throw new NotAvailable();
      }
    }
```

The `remove()` operation is a life cycle operation. The object adapter is the only place where a reference is held to the session object. Once we call `deactivate_obj()`, the object is ready for garbage collection. We also have to deactivate all the CORBA objects we have created during the session, like the booking objects.

```
  public void remove() {

      // deactivate all booking objects
      Enumeration e = bookings.elements();
      for( int i = 0; e.hasMoreElements(); i++ ) {
        boa.deactivate_obj( (Booking) e.nextElement() );
      }

      // deactivate the session object so that it can be garbage collected
      boa.deactivate_obj( this );
    }
```

Note that in other implementations the factory may act as a manager by keeping references to the created objects. In this case, the manager must release the object reference to the session object.

```
  private org.omg.CosTransactions.Current getCurrent() {
      // as above
    }
```

### *Travel Agent Query Object*

The travel agent booking object is a data access object, which allows the travel agent to obtain data from its own database. It uses JDBC and the connection pool object, which we introduced earlier in the context of the flight query object. Its structure is the same as the query object.

```
package vogel.transaction.chapter6.flightBookingImpl;

import java.sql.*;
import java.util.*;

import org.omg.CORBA.*;

import com.wiley.compbooks.vogel.chapter8.naming.*;
import com.wiley.compbooks.vogel.chapter13.maintenance.*;

import vogel.transaction.chapter6.flightBooking.*;

public class TravelAgentQuery {

  private ConnectionPool connectionPool = null;
  private String URL;
  private String userId;
  private String password;

  public TravelAgentQuery (
    String URL, String userId, String password ) {

    this.URL = URL;
    this.userId = userId;
    this.password = password;

    connectionPool = new ConnectionPool( 2, URL, userId, password );
    connectionPool.start();
  }
```

The method `getBookings()` returns a sequence of TA booking records. These records contain all the information, which is stored in the travel agent's database, about a particular booking. Note that this information is complete, but relative through keys into the airline's databases.

```
public TaBookingRecord[] getBookings( String id )
    throws Internal, NonExistent {

    int i, j;
    String selectStatement;
    ResultSet resultSet;
    Statement statement;
    TaBookingRecord[] taBookingRecords;
    Vector taVector = new Vector();
    Connection c;
```

First we create the simple select statement for querying the database. Then we get a database connection from the pool and execute the query. In case of an exception, we propagate the `Internal`.

```
selectStatement = new String(
      "select * from TA_BOOKING where USERID = '" + id + "'" );

    try {
      // get connection from pool
      c = connectionPool.getConnection();

      // create statements and execute queries
      try {
        statement = c.createStatement();
        resultSet = statement.executeQuery(selectStatement);
      }
      catch( Exception ex ) {
        System.out.println( ex );
        throw new Internal();
      }
```

If the result set is empty, `NonExistent` exception is raised. Otherwise, we loop through the entries in the result set. For each entry, we create a new `TaBookingRecord` object and populate its various fields.

```
      Timestamp timestamp;
      if( resultSet == null ) {
        System.out.println("no entry");
        throw new NonExistent()
      }
      while( resultSet.next() ) {

        // extract data from result set and create leg record
        TaBookingRecord taBookingRecord = new TaBookingRecord();
        taBookingRecord.id = resultSet.getString(1);
        taBookingRecord.label = resultSet.getString(2);
        taBookingRecord.userId = resultSet.getString(3);
        taBookingRecord.confirmedPrice = resultSet.getInt(5);
```

Special care is needed for the airline identifiers. These identifiers are the primary keys for the tables in the databases of the various airlines. We have simplified things here, assuming that each of the identifiers has exactly 10 characters. The travel agent database holds all the identifiers as a concatenated string. We now unparse the string, extract the individual identifiers, and assign them to the airline identifier array.

```
        String airlineIds = resultSet.getString(4);
        airlineIds.trim();
        int length = airlineIds.length() / 10;
        System.out.println("length: " + airlineIds.length() +
          ":"+ length );
        taBookingRecord.airlineIds = new String[ length ];
        for( i = 0; i < length; i++ ) {
```

```
          taBookingRecord.airlineIds[i] =
            airlineIds.substring( i*10, (i+1)*10 ); ;
          System.out.println( taBookingRecord.airlineIds[i] );
        }
        taVector.addElement( taBookingRecord );
      }
```

We collect all the TA booking records in a vector, `taVector`. Once we are finished looping through the result set, we close the statement and release the connection back to the pool. Finally, we assign the contents of the vector to an array of TA booking records, which we return as the result of the method.

```
      try {
        System.out.println("close statement" );
        statement.close();
      }
      catch( Exception ex ) {
        System.out.println( ex );
      }
      System.out.println("return the connection to the pool" );
      connectionPool.releaseConnection( c );
    }
    catch( Exception e) {
      System.out.println("database access error: " + e );
      throw new Internal();
    }
    taBookingRecords = new TaBookingRecord[ taVector.size() ];
    taVector.copyInto( taBookingRecords );
    return taBookingRecords;
  }
}
```

### *Travel Agent Object*

The travel agent object is the primary object of the travel agent server. It has three major tasks:

- Initializing the travel agent by obtaining references to all related objects such as airlines
- Creating a travel agent data access object
- Implementing the session factory functionality in the `login()` method

First we have the usual package, import, and class declarations. Within the class we define a number of private variables.

```
package vogel.transaction.chapter6.flightBookingImpl;

import java.util.*;

import org.omg.CORBA.*;
import org.omg.CosTransactions.*;
import org.omg.CosNaming.*;

import com.wiley.compbooks.vogel.chapter8.naming.*;
import com.wiley.compbooks.vogel.chapter13.maintenance.*;

import vogel.transaction.chapter6.flightBooking.*;

class TravelAgentImpl extends _TravelAgentImplBase {

  private Hashtable airlines;
  private Hashtable airlineQueries;
  private org.omg.CORBA.ORB orb;
  private org.omg.CORBA.BOA boa;
  private org.omg.CORBA.Object obj;
  private org.omg.CosTransactions.Current current;

  private EasyNaming easyNaming;

  private Query query;
  private String context;
  private String contextName;
  private String scheduleContextName;
  private String airlineContextName;
  private String airlineQueryContextName;
  private String securityName;
  private String daName;
  private String queryName;
  private String name;
  private NamingContext airlineContext;
  private NamingContext airlineQueryContext;
  private BookingIdDispenser bookingIdDispenser;
  private TravelAgentDataAccess taDataAccess;
  private Directory directory;
  private TravelAgentQuery travelAgentQuery;
```

The constructor receives references to the ORB, the object adapter, the EasyNaming object, a context and an absolute name for the registration with the naming service as arguments. We call the superclass' constructor with the name as arguments. This gives the object a persistent object reference when using Visibroker 3.x. Then we assign the arguments to local variables we declared earlier. We also create an instance of the `BookingIdDispenser` class and the Travel Agent Query. We pass the URL to Travel Agent Query for the database/JDBC driver and a user id and password for the database. We have chosen the default user "scott" for logging in to the Oracle database.

```
public TravelAgentImpl(
  ORB orb, BOA boa,
  EasyNaming easyNaming,
  String context, String name ) {

  super( name );

  this.orb = orb;
  this.boa = boa;
  this.easyNaming = easyNaming;
  this.name = name;
  this.context = context;
  airlines = new Hashtable();
  airlineQueries = new Hashtable();
  bookingIdDispenser = new BookingIdDispenser();
  travelAgentQuery = new TravelAgentQuery(
    "jdbc:oracle:oci7:@", "scott", "tiger" );
```

Now we start retrieving object references from the naming service. The objects we need at the travel agent are

- The flight query object
- The travel agent data access object
- The directory object
- All airline objects that are registered with the naming service

In the first three cases, we have only one instance each with a distinct name. To get these objects we make a single lookup using the full string name and the EasyNaming class. Note that you must narrow all object references received from the naming service and must test for null object references.

```
try {

    // get query object from naming service
    scheduleContextName = new String("/schedules/");
    queryName = new String("Central Flight Schedule");
    query = QueryHelper.narrow( easyNaming.resolve_from_string(
      scheduleContextName + queryName ) );
    if( query == null ) {
```

```
      System.err.println("no query object");
      System.err.println("exiting ...");
      System.exit( 1 );
    }

    // get TravelAgentDataAccess object from naming service
    contextName = new String("/data access/");
    taDataAccess = TravelAgentDataAccessHelper.narrow(
      easyNaming.resolve_from_string( contextName + name ) );
    if( taDataAccess == null ) {
      System.err.println("no data access object");
      System.err.println("exiting ...");
      System.exit( 1 );
    }

    // get directory object from naming service
    contextName = new String("/directories/");
    directory = DirectoryHelper.narrow(
      easyNaming.resolve_from_string( contextName + name ) );
    if( directory == null ) {
      System.err.println("no directory object");
      System.err.println("exiting ...");
      System.exit( 1 );
    }
```

There is the agreement that all airline objects are registered in the same context named "airlines" and that this context only contains airline objects. To obtain all the airline objects, first we have to obtain the IOR to the airline context object.

```
    // get airline context
    airlineContextName = new String("/airlines");
    airlineContext = NamingContextHelper.narrow(
      easyNaming.resolve_from_string( airlineContextName ) );
    if( airlineContext == null ) {
      System.err.println("airlineContext is not valid");
      System.err.println("exiting ...");
      System.exit( 1 );
    }
```

Then we can list the names of all objects registered with the airline context. The naming service's list operation uses the iterator pattern. That means that we ask for a specific number of names returned immediately. The remaining names can be retrieved from the iterator object. We receive its IOR as an out parameter of the list method.

We create a binding list holder object and a binding iterator holder object according to the IDL/Java mapping conventions for out parameters. Then we invoke the list operation on the airline context. First we process the names we have obtained in the binding list. We loop through the list and resolve each name the IOR is associated with. We narrow the generic (of type CORBA::Object) IOR to an airline IOR. If we succeed we store it in the airlines hashtable.

```
BindingListHolder blHolder = new BindingListHolder();
BindingIteratorHolder biHolder = new BindingIteratorHolder();

airlineContext.list( 2, blHolder, biHolder );

for( int i = 0; i < blHolder.value.length; i++ ) {
  obj = airlineContext.resolve( blHolder.value[i].binding_name );
  Airline airline = AirlineHelper.narrow( obj );
  if( airline != null ) {
    airlines.put( airline._object_name(), airline );
    System.err.println(airline._object_name() );
  }
  else {
    System.err.println("airline: narrow failed");
  }
}
```

The iterator `biHolder.value`, is used to obtain remaining names, by calling the method `next_one()` on it. This method returns a TRUE indicating that there are more entries. The operation also has an out parameter, of type `BindingHolder`. For each of the binding we get the name and then resolve it to the airline context, narrow it to an airline, and put it in the hashtable as described previously.

```
BindingHolder bHolder = new BindingHolder();

if( biHolder.value != null ) {
while( biHolder.value.next_one( bHolder ) ) {
    if( bHolder.value != null ) {
      obj = airlineContext.resolve( bHolder.value.binding_name );
      Airline airline = AirlineHelper.narrow( obj );
      if( airline != null ) {
        airlines.put( airline._object_name(), airline );
      }
      else {
        System.err.println("airline: narrow failed");
      }
    }
    else {
      System.err.println("airline: no element in binding
        iterator");
    }
  }
}
```

The same steps are repeated for airline query objects. We have omitted the explanation for this part of the implementation. The final catch clause completes the constructor.

```
        // get airline query context
        // ...
      }
      catch( Exception ex ) {
        System.err.println( ex );
        System.err.println("exiting ...");
        System.exit( 1 );
      }
    }
```

The `login()` method provides the factory functionality. The travel agent application is based on a user id/password security mechanism. We avoid elaborate explanation of the security issues since it is out of the scope of this book.

The user id and password are passed as arguments to the directory's `login()` operations (as explained earlier). If an exception is raised by the directory, we throw the exception `NotAuthorized`, which means that the identified client is not known by the directory and hence not authorized to log in as the travel agent.

```
    public Session login( String userId, String password )
      throws NotAuthorized {

      try {
        directory.authenticate( userId, password );
      }
      catch( Exception e ) {
        throw new NotAuthorized();
      }
```

Now that we passed the authorization, we act as a factory and create a new `Session` object, register it with the object adapter, and return it to the client.

```
      SessionImpl session = new SessionImpl( orb, boa, userId,
        bookingIdDispenser,
        airlines, airlineQueries, query, taDataAccess, directory,
        travelAgentQuery );
      boa.obj_is_ready( session );
      return session;
    }
```

Finally, we have method implementations for the `Maintained` interface. Again we have kept the implementation rather simple, as the focus of this example implementation is not on management issues. A fully featured application would propagate the prepare-shutdown event to all session objects created as well as to other objects it controls.

```
public void prepareShutdown( Maintainer m ) {

    // could tell sessions to shutdown

    m.shutdownConfirmation( this );
    return;
  }

  public void shutdown() {
    orb.shutdown();
  }
}
```

### *Travel Agent Server*

The travel agent server determines a particular configuration of objects running in the same JVM. We have chosen a configuration in which the server hosts the directory object and the travel agent object.

```
package vogel.transaction.chapter6.flightBookingImpl;

import java.util.*;
import org.omg.CORBA.*;
import org.omg.CosNaming.NamingContextPackage.*;
import com.wiley.compbooks.vogel.chapter8.naming.*;
import vogel.transaction.chapter6.flightBooking.*;

public class TravelAgentServer {

  public static void main(String[] args) {

    String taContextName, dirContextName, strName;
    TravelAgent travelAgentImpl;
    Directory directoryImpl;
    EasyNaming easyNaming;
    Properties orbProps;
    ORB orb;
    BOA boa;

    if( args.length != 2 ) {
      System.out.println(
```

```
        "Usage: vbj " +
        "vogel.transaction.chapter6.flightBookingImpl.TravelAgentServer"
        + " <travel agent>, <directory file>");
      System.exit( 1 );
    }

    taContextName = new String("/travel agents/");
    dirContextName = new String("/directories/");
```

We initialize with the properties for the CORBA Naming and the CORBA Object Transaction Service. We create an instance of the Easy-Naming object and get an object adapter.

```
    try {
      //init orb and oa
      orbProps = new Properties();
      orbProps.put("ORBservices",
         "CosNaming,com.visigenic.services.CosTransactions");
      orb = ORB.init( args, orbProps );

      easyNaming = new EasyNaming( orb );
      boa = orb.BOA_init();
```

An instance of the directory object is created and registered with the object adapter. We also register the object with the naming service under the name "/directories/<args0>". Then we do the same for the travel agent object. We register it in the context called "/travel agents".

```
      directoryImpl = (Directory) new DirectoryImpl( args[0], args[1] );
      boa.obj_is_ready(directoryImpl);
      strName = dirContextName + args[0];
      easyNaming.rebind_from_string( strName, directoryImpl );

      travelAgentImpl = (TravelAgent)
          new TravelAgentImpl(orb, boa, easyNaming, taContextName,
            args[0]);
      boa.obj_is_ready(travelAgentImpl);
      strName = taContextName + args[0];
      easyNaming.rebind_from_string( strName, travelAgentImpl );

      // waiting for requests
      System.out.println("travel agent is ready");
      boa.impl_is_ready();
    }
    catch(Exception e) {
      System.err.println(e);
    }
  }
}
```

## Directory Object

The directory object manages users of the travel agent system. Specifically, it handles the authentication of users and the user profiles.

The implementation follows the usual pattern. We have a Java implementation class `DirectoryImpl` for the IDL interface. We use the inheritance approach and extend the implementation base class `_DirectoryImplBase`. We don't have a server class. The directory object is instantiated by the travel agent server as shown previously.

```
package vogel.transaction.chapter6.flightBookingImpl;

import java.util.*;
import java.io.*;
import org.omg.CORBA.*;
import vogel.transaction.chapter6.flightBooking.*;

public class DirectoryImpl extends _DirectoryImplBase {

  private Hashtable userTable;
  private Hashtable profileTable;
```

We keep the user data in two hashtables, one for the security data, the other for the user profiles. Both tables are initialized with the data from a file. In this example we use the following syntax to represent the data in the file:<userId>:<password>:<title>:<firstName>:<middleInitial>: <lastName>:. In the constructor, we open the named file, parse its contents, and initialize the hashtables. We have omitted the parsing, as it is not relevant to main topics of the book.

```
  public DirectoryImpl( String name, String fileName ) {

    super( name );

    userTable = new Hashtable();
    profileTable = new Hashtable();

    // initialize the hashtables from file
  }
```

The IDL interface Directory specified two operations, which we implement here in the Java class. The method `authenticate()` takes a pair of user id and password as input. If the pair is found in the user table, the method returns silently; otherwise, it raises the `NotAuthenticated` exception.

```
public void authenticate( String userId, String passwd )
    throws NotAuthenticated {

    // login is valid if the user id exists and the password matches
    if( userTable.containsKey( userId ) &&
      ((String)userTable.get( userId )).equals( passwd ) )
      return;
    else
      throw new NotAuthenticated();
  }
```

The other operation deals with the user profile. For simplicity and clarity of the example, we have restricted the user profile to a person record. A full-scale application would use a more sophisticated data type. The method `getProfile()` takes a user id as input. The method returns the profile from the profile hashtable, if there is an entry for the user. Otherwise, it raises the `NotAvailable` exception.

```
  public Profile getProfile( String userId )
    throws NotAvailable {

    if( profileTable.containsKey( userId ) )
      return (Profile) profileTable.get( userId );
    else
      throw new NotAvailable();
  }
}
```

## Client

The client is a Java GUI application that provides the basic functionality of the application. We omit most of the GUI code and concentrate on the CORBA- and transaction-related parts. The client consists of the following classes:

**TravelAgentClient.java.** This is the main class that declares and creates the frame.

**TravelAgentFrame.java.** This is the class that holds the application together. It initializes the CORBA-related variables and the GUI elements, such as buttons and panels. The class also handles the major events and has methods corresponding for each of the events. The menubar has two dropdown menus, File and Help, with the items ..., Query, Quit, and About.

**BookingPanel.java.** This is the main panel of the client. On the left-hand side it shows the booking of a customer, and on the other side the details of a selected booking. There are three more buttons at the bottom of the panel that allow you to create new bookings, modify existing bookings, and delete bookings.

**TravelAgentFrame_AboutBox.java.** The about box displays information about the application.

**TravelAgentFrame_LoginBox.java.** The login box lets you log in to the system. It prompts you for a user id and a password and presents a choice of travel agents registered with the Naming Service.

**TravelAgentFrame_QueryBox.java.** The query box is a popup window, which allows you to get information about flights according to your requirements. It also allows you to select a flight and make a booking.

### *Initialization*

In the class `TravelAgentFrame` we declare and initialize the relevant CORBA variables, the ORB, and the `easyNaming` object in the method `corbaInit()`.

```
// CORBA related initialization

  private void corbaInit() throws Exception {

    try {
      Properties orbProps = new Properties();
      orbProps.put("ORBservices", "CosNaming");
      orbProps.put("DSVCnameroot", "WileyRoot");
      orb = ORB.init( (String[]) null, orbProps );
      easyNaming = new EasyNaming( orb );
    }
    catch( Exception ex ) {
      System.err.println( ex );
    }
  }
```

As you can see, we do not initialize the client's ORB with the transaction service. As explained earlier, there are two ways for building transactional systems. Our client does not initiate the distributed transactions; instead, it makes “normal” CORBA calls to the travel agent. The travel agent initiates the distributed transactions, which run under OTS control.

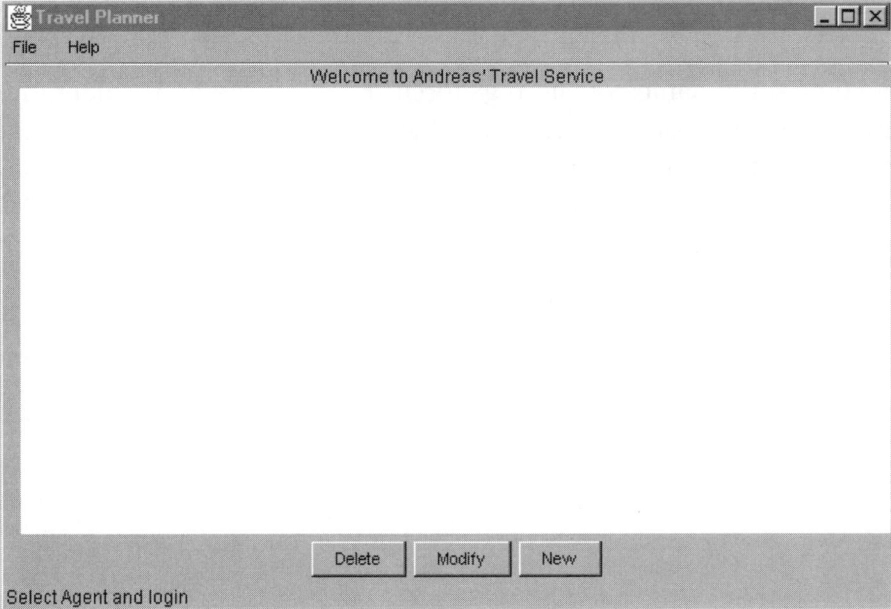


**Figure 4.14** Client GUI in its initial state.

### *Login*

The next step is that a customer logs in to the system. Once the login menu is selected we pop up the login box. `corbaInit()` is done from the constructor.

The first thing we have to do is to get the names of all the travel agents available so that we can populate the login window as shown in Figure 4.14. A travel agent is considered available when it is registered with the naming services in the context "/travel agents". We obtain the context object through Easy Naming's `resolve_from_string()` method.

```
void corbaInit() {

    org.omg.CORBA.Object obj;

    try {
      // get travel agent context
      String contextName = new String("/travel agents");
      System.err.println("context: " + contextName );
      NamingContext context = NamingContextHelper.narrow(
        easyNaming.resolve_from_string( contextName ) );
      if( context == null ) {
        System.err.println("context " + context + " is not valid");
        System.err.println("exiting ...");
```

```
        System.exit( 1 );
      }
```

We obtain the names of the registered travel agents by invoking the `list()` operation on the `context` object. We copy the elements from the name sequence into a vector `agents` and add the ones we get from the iterator. We use the vector `agents` to initialize the swing list `agentList`, which is used to display the agents in the window.

```
      // get all travel agents from naming service
      BindingListHolder blHolder = new BindingListHolder();
      BindingIteratorHolder biHolder = new BindingIteratorHolder();

      context.list( 2, blHolder, biHolder );
      for( int i = 0; i < blHolder.value.length; i++ ) {
        agents.addElement( blHolder.value[i].binding_name[0].id );
      }

      // get remaining travel agents from the iterator
      BindingHolder bHolder = new BindingHolder();
      if( biHolder.value != null ) {
        while( biHolder.value.next_one( bHolder ) ) {
          if( bHolder.value != null ) {
            agents.addElement( bHolder.value.binding_name[0].id );
          }
          else {
            System.err.println(
              "travel agents: no element in binding iterator");
          }
        }
      }
    }
    catch( Exception ex ) {
      System.err.println( ex );
      System.err.println("exiting ...");
      System.exit( 1 );
    }
    agentList.setListData( agents );
  }
```

The completed box window is shown in Figure 4.15.

The method `setAgent()` is invoked when a customer tries to log in. First we obtain the name of the travel agent selected from the list.

```
  void setAgent() {

    // picked the name of the agent
    int index = agentList.getSelectedIndex();
```

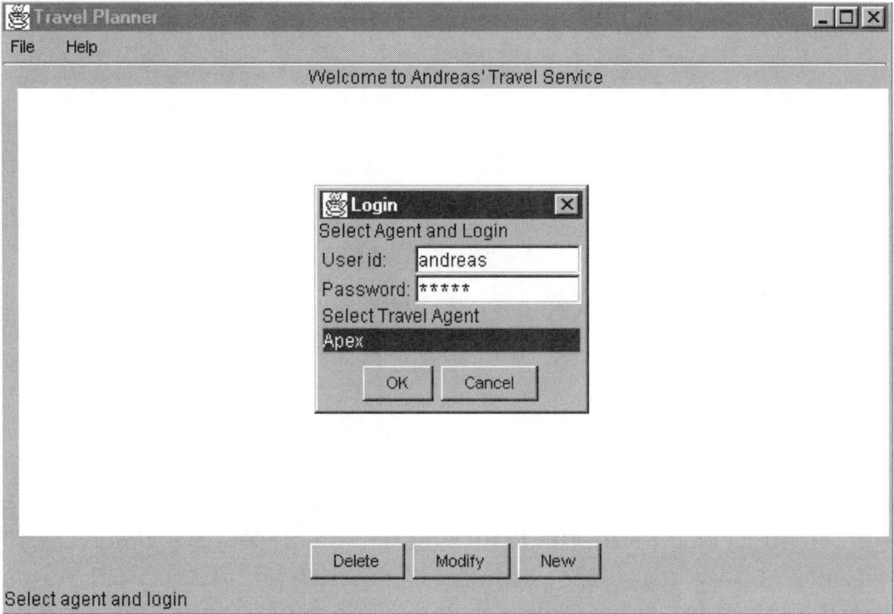


**Figure 4.15** Completed login box.

```
String travelAgentName = (String) agents.elementAt( index );
String travelAgentContext = new String("/travel agents/");
```

Once we get the name, we obtain the object reference of the agent from naming service. After the IOR is successfully narrowed, we invoke the `login()` operation on it. We obtain the values of the user id and password text fields which we pass as arguments to the `login()` operation. A successful login returns an IOR to a session object; otherwise, an exception is raised. The outcome of the `login()` operation is shown in the status line, or in the exception case, in the header label of the login box.

```
try {
 // now get the IOR of the agent from the naming service
 taf.travelAgent = TravelAgentHelper.narrow(
  taf.easyNaming.resolve_from_string(
  travelAgentContext + travelAgentName ) );
 if( taf.travelAgent != null ) {
   // try to log in at the selected travel agent
   taf.session = taf.travelAgent.login(
     idTextField.getText(), passwordField.getText() );
   taf.statusBar.setText("logged in travel agent " +
     travelAgentName );
   taf.showBookingList();
   dispose();
```

```
        }
        else {
          headerLabel.setText("travel agent " +
          travelAgentName + " is unavailable");
        }
      }
      catch( NotAuthorized na ) {
        headerLabel.setText("not authorized");
      }
      catch( Exception e ) {
        headerLabel.setText("travel agent " +
        travelAgentName + " is unavailable");
      }
      headerLabel.repaint();
      this.validate();
      this.repaint();
    }
```

If the login is successful, the login box will be closed. We also want to obtain all the bookings the customer already has and display them in a list on the left side of the booking panel. The functionality is encapsulated in the method `showBookingList()` of the class `TravelAgentFrame`. The method is called from the login window as shown previously. The implementation of the method is shown in the next code listing.

We call the operation `findAllBookingRecords()` on the session object. There is no need for a parameter, as the (server-side) session object has the user id from the login operation. The operation returns a sequence of booking records, which we put into a vector. Then we display the labels of the bookings in a swing list on the left side of the booking panel.

```
public void showBookingList() {

  try {
    bookingRecordSeq = session.findAllBookingRecords();
    bookingRecordVector = new Vector();
    bookingLabelVector = new DefaultListModel();
    for( int i = 0; i < bookingRecordSeq.length; i++ ) {
      bookingRecordVector.addElement( bookingRecordSeq[i] );
      bookingLabelVector.addElement( bookingRecordSeq[i].label );
    }
    bookingList = new JList( bookingLabelVector );
    mouseListener = new MouseAdapter() {
      public void mouseClicked( MouseEvent e ) {
        if( e.getClickCount() == 2 ) {
          int index = bookingList.locationToIndex( e.getPoint() );
          showBooking( (BookingRecord)
```

```
            bookingRecordVector.elementAt( index ) );
          }
        }
      }
      bookingList.addMouseListener( mouseListener );
      leftPanel.add( bookingList, null );
      this.validate();
      this.repaint();
    }
    catch( Exception e ) {
      statusBar.setText( e.toString() );
    }
  }
```

Figure 4.16 shows the GUI client after a successful login with a previous booking displayed on the left side of the booking panel.

### Making Queries

The next step in a typical usage of the client is to make queries for possible connections. Therefore, we pop up a new window, an instance of the class `TravelAgentFrame_QueryBox`. This window, as illustrated in Figure 4.17, allows you to enter your travel request, which includes

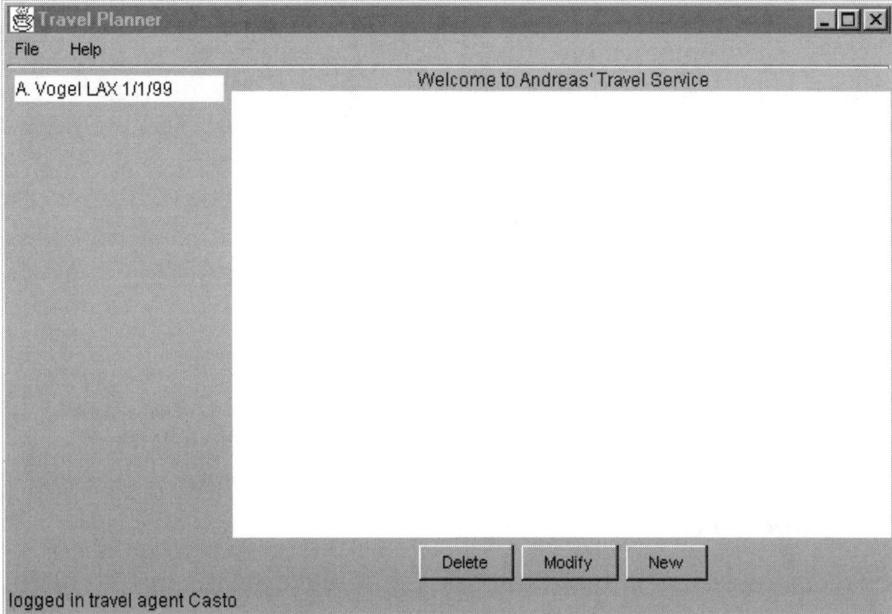


**Figure 4.16** GUI with booking history.

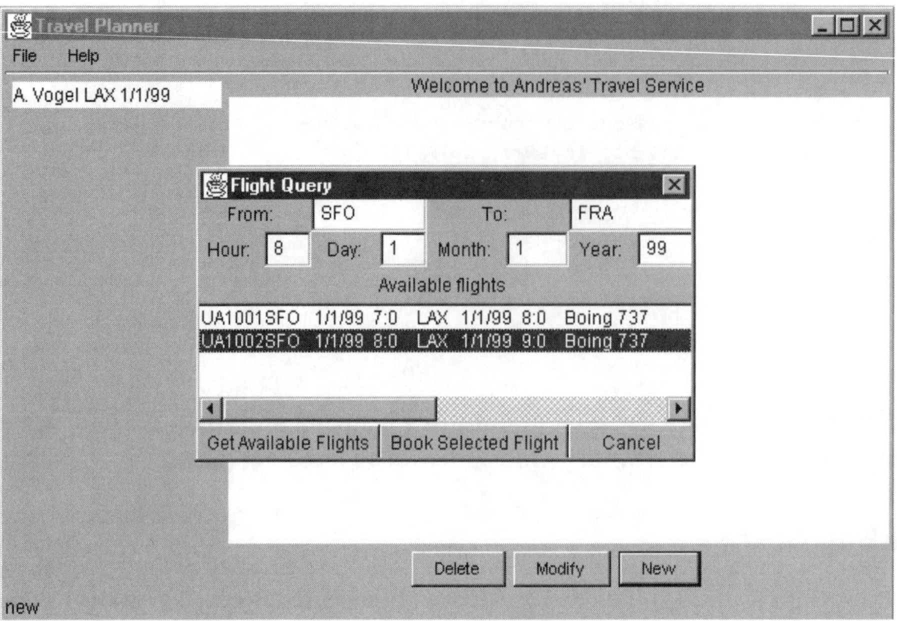


**Figure 4.17** Query window.

travel information like departure and arrival airport and the preferred date and time for the trip.

Once we have obtained the input data for the text fields, we invoke the `queryAvailableFlights()` operation on the session object. The arguments are the departure airport, the arrival airport, and the departure date (of IDL-defined type `SimpleDate`).

```
// make the query on the session object
flights = taf.session.queryAvailableFlights(
  fromTextField.getText(),
  toTextField.getText(),
  d );
```

The session object only acts as a proxy for the Query object as explained earlier.

### *Making Bookings*

Once a customer has found a suitable flight, the booking can be made. From the information we obtained through the query, we create and initialize a `BookingRequest` object (IDL struct). It is passed as an argument to the `createBooking()` operation on the session object. The operation returns the IOR to a booking object, which has been created by the session object upon our request.

```
Booking booking = taf.session.createBooking( bookingRequest );
```

### Cancel a Booking

To cancel a booking we invoke the `cancel()` operation on the selected booking object.

```
( (BookingRecord) bookingRecordVector.elementAt(
        bookingList.getSelectedIndex())).bookingObj.cancel();
```

From the JList `BookingRecordList`, we get the index of the selected booking. Using this index, we selected `BookingRecord` from the Vector `BookingRecordVector`, as shown in Figure 4.18. The selected `BookingRecord` lets us get the IOR to the associated booking object on which we eventually invoke the `cancel()` operation.

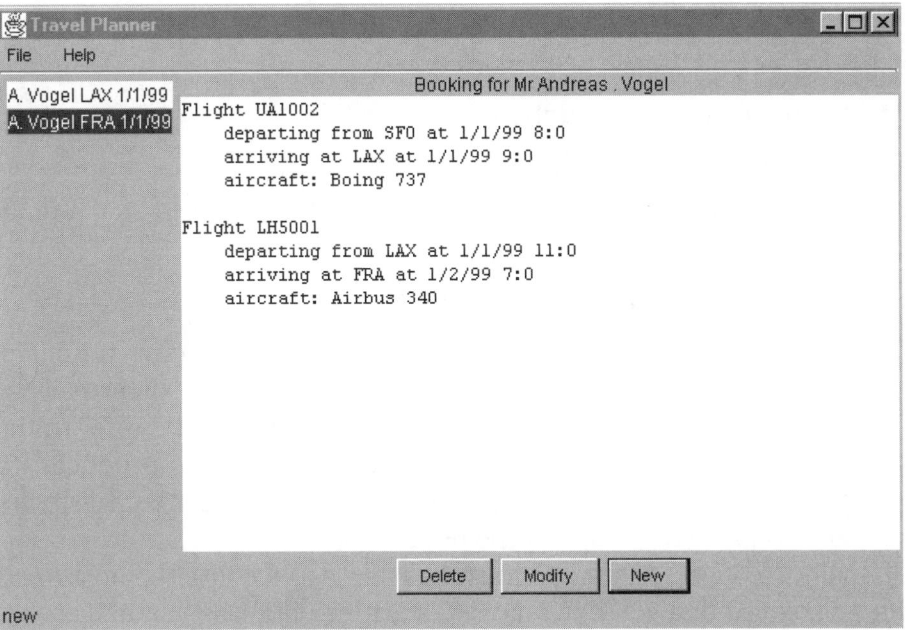


**Figure 4.18** Displaying booking details.

### Life Cycle

Once a customer is finished and leaves the client GUI, we must clean up on the server side. This means that we have to destroy the session object, which exists for this client in the middle tier. We can do this via the `remove()` operation, which we have defined and implemented on the session interface.

```
public void fileExit_actionPerformed(ActionEvent e) {
    try {
      session.remove();
    }
    catch( SystemException se ) {
      ;
    }
    System.exit(0);
  }
```

We already discussed that the server cannot rely on the discipline of the client implementation and user behavior to invoke the `remove()` operation, and it must take precautions to avoid stale objects.

## Running the Application

To run the application follow these steps:

1. Configure and start databases.
2. Configure and start OTS/ORB system.
3. Start additional services such as naming and directory and administration tools.
4. Start application servers and clients.

Note that the configuration details are given for specific products: Oracle database, Visibroker ITS, Visibroker for Java, and Visibroker for C++. For details on the configuration of other products we refer to the appropriate product documentation. Even for the chosen products we do not provide all the details, as product configurations are proprietary and hence outside the scope of the book.

Usually, a database service is installed as a service into the host operating system so that you don't have to start the database manually.

## Configuring and Starting Databases

In our application we have three entities that need databases. These are the fight query server, the airlines, and the travel agent. In a real-world scenario, no assumptions can be made about the type of the database, the database product, and the way information is stored in the database.

The sample configuration for the application is simple. We use the same tables for the same type of services. We used NT 4.0 as our host operating system, which was run on a laptop. We used a single Oracle database for testing the application. Even though the application is simple, it illustrates most of the features offered by an OTS product like Inprise ITS.

### *Flight Query Database*

We use two tables for flight queries, as shown in Tables 4.1 and 4.2.

### *Airline Database*

The airlines need to store information about all the legs that they serve. We have defined the table FLIGHT_BOOKING to store this information, as shown in Table 4.3.

### *Travel Agent Database*

The travel agent stores information about complete bookings; in other words, composed flights that can have legs served by different airlines.

**Table 4.1** FLIGHT_TYPE for Storing All the Flight Information Associated with a Flight Number

| NAME | DATA TYPE | LENGTH |
|---|---|---|
| Flight_Number | char | 6 |
| From_Airport | char | 3 |
| To_Airport | char | 3 |
| Departure_Hour | number | 2 |
| Departure_Minute | number | 2 |
| Arrival_Hour | number | 2 |
| Arrival_Minute | number | 2 |

**Table 4.2** FLIGHT_INSTANCE for Storing All the Flight Instances (the Association of a Flight Date with a Departure Date and Aircraft Type)

| NAME | DATA TYPE | LENGTH |
|---|---|---|
| Flight_Number | char | 6 |
| Departure_Date | Date | |
| Arrival_Date | Date | |
| Aircraft | char | 20 |

We use the table TA_BOOKING, as shown in Table 4.4. Note that we store dependencies to data stored in the airlines database. A real implementation would probably replicate the data for caching data, to gain independence of other servers and for auditing purposes.

## Configuring and Starting OTS/ORB System

Visibroker relies for bootstrapping and other features on its OSAgent. It can be registered as an NT service or started from the command line.

Windows platforms:

```
> osagent -C
```

Unix platforms:

```
> osagent &
```

Visibroker ITS requires to start an ITS instance; here we use a standalone ITS server rather than an in-process configuration and an XA resource director.

**Table 4.3** Flight Booking

| NAME | DATA TYPE | LENGTH |
|---|---|---|
| Title | char | 2 |
| FirstName | char | 25 |
| MiddleInitial | char | 1 |
| LastName | char | 25 |
| FlightNumber | char | 6 |
| DepartureDate | Date | |
| Price | Number | |
| ConfirmationNumber | char | 10 |

**Table 4.4** TA Booking

| NAME | DATA TYPE | LENGTH |
|---|---|---|
| Id | char | 30 |
| Label | char | 30 |
| UserId | char | 25 |
| LegIds | char | 50 |
| Price | number | |

```
> its &
> xa_resdir -SMprofile_name booking &
```

Note that you have to create and register a profile, as for example the profile `booking` that we use. We refer to Visibroker ITS manual for details on profiles, as this is a product-specific detail outside the scope of OTS.

## Starting Services and Tools

Our application relies on the CORBA Naming Service to locate objects. We use a maintenance tool for the graceful shutdown of our objects.

### *Naming Service*

The Visibroker implementation of the CORBA Naming Service is started as shown here:

```
> vbj -DORBservices=CosNaming
com.visigenic.vbroker.services.CosNaming.ExtFactory
WileyRoot ns.log
```

The first parameter is the name of the root context, the second one is the name of a file for persistently storing the naming information.

### *Maintenance Tool*

The maintenance tool is started like any other Visibroker for Java application, using the two flags for the use of the Naming Service and the full class name.

```
> vbj -DORBservices=CosNaming -DSVCnameroot=WileyRoot
com.wiley.compbooks.vogel.chapter13.maintenanceImpl.MaintenanceTool
```

The maintenance tool brings up a console as shown in Figure 4.19. It lets you find objects, which implement the Maintained interface and are registered in a certain namespace. Figure 4.19 shows maintained airline objects in the context "/airlines". The left panel lets you select an object for sending a prepare-shutdown message. Once the object is prepared and has made a callback to the tool, its name will appear in the right panel. Now you can send the final shutdown message.

The maintenance tool deals only with one aspect of distributed object management. For production systems, fully featured tools such as Inprise's AppCenter should be used, which deals with a wide range of management tasks.

## Start Application Servers and Clients

The application has four major component types: the flight query server, the airlines, the travel agents, and the clients.

### *Starting Flight Query Server*

The flight query service is a Java implementation. We just pass the name of the root context so that the server can be bootstrapped in the right naming domain. In our configuration, we start only one flight query server.

```
> vbj -DSVCnameroot=WileyRoot
vogel.transaction.chapter6.flightBookingImpl.QueryServer
```

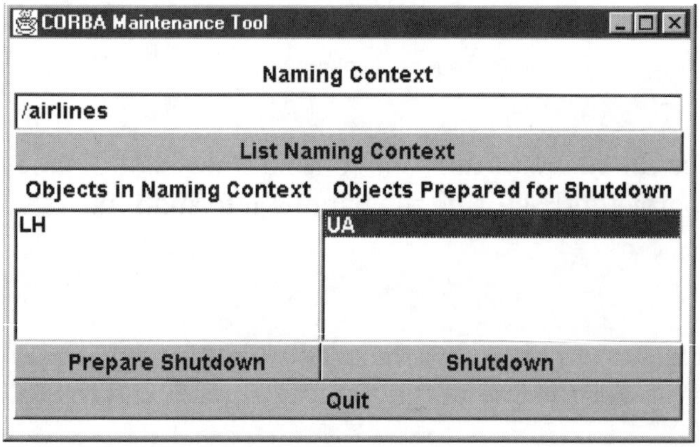

**Figure 4.19** Maintenance tool console.

### Starting Airline Servers

An airline is represented by two servers, the airline server and the airline query server for implementation reasons we explained earlier. The airline server is a C++ server, we start and pass the configuration parameters for the naming and the transaction service as command-line options. We also provide the name of the airline as an argument. The airline query service is implemented as a Java server and is started with the arguments the name of the root context and the name of the airline. For our sample configuration we have a pair of servers, United Airlines UA and Lufthansa LH.

```
> ../../cpp/AirlineServer -SVCnameroot WileyRoot -ORBservices
CosNaming,com.visigenic.services.CosTransactions UA

> ../../cpp/AirlineServer -SVCnameroot WileyRoot -ORBservices
CosNaming,com.visigenic.services.CosTransactions LH

> vbj -DSVCnameroot=WileyRoot
vogel.transaction.chapter6.flightBookingImpl.AirlineQueryServer UA

> vbj -DSVCnameroot=WileyRoot
vogel.transaction.chapter6.flightBookingImpl.AirlineQueryServer LH
```

### Starting Travel Agents

A travel agent is again represented by two servers: a C++ server for the transactional data access, and a Java server for the main functionality. Command-line options are the same as explained previously. The travel agent data access server just has the name argument. The travel agent server has the travel agent name and filename for the directory as arguments since the travel agent server is configured to host the directory object, too.

```
> ../../cpp/TravelAgentDataAccessServer -SVCnameroot WileyRoot -
ORBservices CosNaming,com.visigenic.services.CosTransactions Casto

> vbj -DSVCnameroot=WileyRoot
vogel.transaction.chapter6.flightBookingImpl.TravelAgentServer Casto
dir.data
```

The file dir.data contains authentication information and user profiles. The file format is the following:

*<user id>":"<password>":"<title>":"<first name>":"<middle initial>":"<last name>":"* and the our sample file's content is

```
andreas:vogel:Mr:Andreas::Vogel:
meta:meta:Ms:Meta:J:Hillmann:
```

### *Starting Clients*

The client is a Java application. We start the clients in the same naming domain as the servers by giving it the same root context name.

```
> vbj -DSVCnameroot=WileyRoot
vogel.transaction.chapter6.travelAgentClient.TravelAgentClient
```

The snapshots of the client can be seen in Figures 4.14 through 4.18.

# Configuration Alternatives

The application can be configured in different ways to suit different purposes. An interface is the atomic unit for configuration. We have a look at different configuration options for our flight-booking application in this section.

The configuration of an application has two different aspects: the kind of clients, which access the server-side objects, and the grouping of the server-side objects.

## Different Types of Clients

In the implementation section earlier in the chapter we outlined the implementation of a Java application that provides a simple GUI interface to our application. Here we explain different options for clients. The server-side of the application is independent of the type of the client.

In either case, the CORBA part of the client is fairly simple and always the same. The client must resolve an initial reference to the Naming Service and get an IOR to a travel agent from it. The client gets its session objects and does its business.

Figure 4.20 illustrates the different types of clients.

**GUI Client.** A GUI client is an application implemented in Java, C++, or any other language for which an IDL mapping exists. Such clients would be typically used when the application is deployed in an intranet.

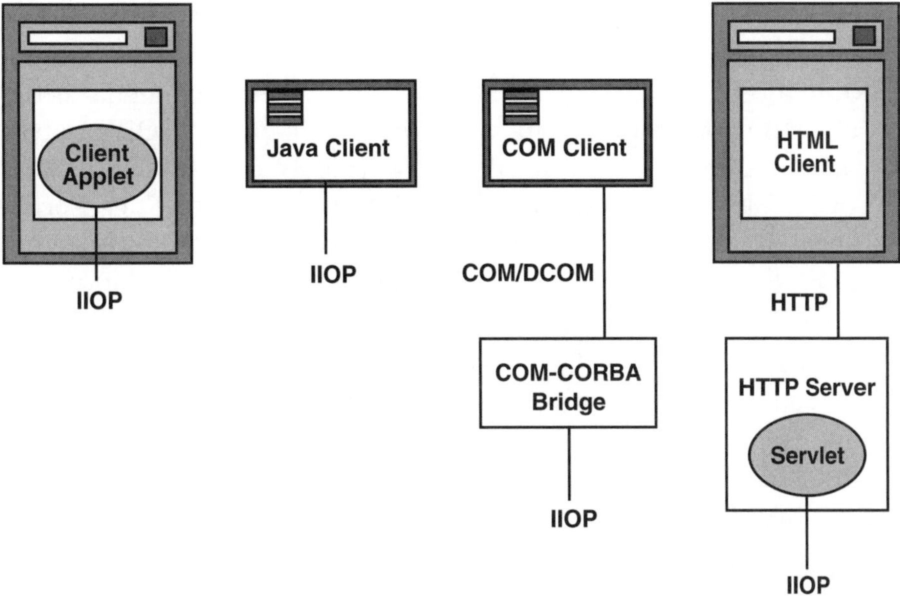


**Figure 4.20** Various client configurations.

**Applet.** Creates two new requirements that must be addressed by specific configuration choices:

**Applet Sandboxing.** Prevents an (unsigned) applet from opening network connections to hosts that are different from the one the applet has been downloaded from. This problem can be overcome with an IIOP gateway such as Visibroker's Gatekeeper. The IIOP gateway must be placed on the machine where the applet has be loaded from. It receives all requests from the applet and forwards them to the target object.

**Firewalls.** There are client-side and server-side firewalls. Client-side firewalls can be overcome by tunneling IIOP traffic through HTTP—the IIOP gateway also acts as a specialized Web server. Server-side firewalls can be configured to enable traffic to the IIOP gateway and to the CORBA servers on predefined ports and IP addresses.

Applet clients can be used in Internet, extranet, and intranet applications.

**Servlet.** Servlets are the best way to provide HTML clients. The client becomes a servlet, which acts as a non-GUI CORBA client. It adds an HTML form parser and an HTML generator to the CORBA part of the client.

**COM Object.** COM objects are an important class of clients as they allow the integration of functionality provided by a CORBA object into an ActiveX document. The most typical example is to include a COM object, which accesses a CORBA object, into an Excel spreadsheet. CORBA has defined a COM-CORBA interworking specification, which is implemented by multiple vendors. Furthermore, there are products that bridge between Java and COM.

**Test Client.** Test clients are command-line driven clients that implement one or multiple use cases of the application. Such clients are used to test functional completeness, performance, and scalability of the server-side components.

There are a number of client configurations from which to choose and most applications implement more than one. Almost always there is a need for a test client. If the application is targeted for browser users, it makes sense to provide both: an HTML/servlet client for the occasional users (to avoid long downloads), and an applet client (which can be cached for superior functionality and performance).

Applet and Java application clients can be derived from the code base. The main applet class has to provide both a `main()` and an `init()` method. COM clients are used as an addition or alternative to applet or application clients as they nicely fit in the world for spreadsheets.

Furthermore, there's the issue of where to initiate a distributed, OTS-controlled transaction, which we discussed earlier in this chapter.

## Configuration of Server-Side Objects

An instance of a class, which implements an IDL interface, is the smallest unit of configuration. A configuration is an operating system process, which is equal to JVM for Java applications. This process is also known as *CORBA server* or just as *server*. However, not all objects can be hosted by an individual server. This applies specifically to the objects following the session pattern.

### *Objects per Server*

The initial configuration of a server is defined in the main routine of the server program. There you define which initial CORBA objects are created. Typically, object instances are created and registered with the object adapter. This is usually done for factories and stateless server objects. Session objects are created by the factory and hence hosted by the same server. The factory controls the life cycle of objects: creation, destruction, deactivation, and reactivation.

The object adapter, in particular, the POA, allows for different mechanisms. For example, it can fabricate an IOR for an object without creating a instance of the object. Once a client tries to invoke an operation on the IOR, the POA will create an instance on the fly, using servant activators for example. This technique is particularly useful for persistent objects. Activating the object means to read the object's state from the database and represent it as a memory object.

### *Replicated Objects*

Replicating objects over multiple processes and machines is a technique used to achieve fault tolerance and scalability. Replicating stateless objects and factories is a straightforward thing to do as the different instances are in no runtime relationship. Persistent objects can also be easily replicated as long as their state management is completely left to the database.

The replication of stateful objects is more complex as the state changes need to be synchronized. However, usually there seems to be little need for replicating these objects for scalability reasons as they are only used by an individual client.

### *Servers per Machine*

A server represents an operating system process. If you want to use a single server or multiple servers depends mainly on the quality of the operating system; specifically, the way it handles lightweight threads. For example, if you use a JVM with green threads you may want to use multiple instances; in case of a JVM with native threads, one instance may be sufficient.

# PART Three

# EJB

CHAPTER

5

# Understanding Enterprise JavaBeans

In this chapter we present Sun's Enterprise JavaBeans (EJB) specification. The specification is primarily focused on developers of EJB containers and servers, which form the infrastructure in which an enterprise bean is deployed. We present the EJB specification from a programmer's or, in EJB terms, an enterprise bean provider's and application assembler's point of view.

First we investigate what Enterprise JavaBeans are and what their purpose is, and in the second section, we explain the EJB infrastructure. The main focus of the chapter is on APIs used by an enterprise bean provider and assembler. In the section "EJB Development," we explain those interfaces and classes defined by the EJB specification and illustrate their use.

The APIs defined for the deployer are under change as we write. While the EJB specification 1.0 uses serialized Java objects to capture deployment information, the subsequent release defines XML as the language for deployment information. However, we do not expect the deployer to be directly confronted with any of these formats when using an EJB product. Commercially relevant EJB servers must provide tool support in the form of wizards or similar tools to handle deployment information. Hence we concentrate in the section "EJB Deployment" on the explanation of the deployment properties and policies.

The EJB specification does not provide much detail about the enterprise bean assembly. In the section "Application Assembling," we explain how an application assembler uses the EJB APIs and the Java Naming and Directory Interface (JNDI) to build distributed enterprise applications.

Finally, we present how EJB and CORBA can be integrated. The EJB specification 1.0 defines how CORBA clients, implemented in any of the programming languages that CORBA defines a mapping from IDL to, can interact with enterprise beans. However, that is another area of the specification under revision and thus we concentrate on the general aspects such as protocol interoperability, transaction coordination, and security.

We return to Enterprise JavaBeans development in Chapter 6, "Programming with EJB," where we implement a comprehensive example.

## Why Enterprise JavaBeans?

Distributed systems are complex. Building distributed applications, particularly when dealing with distributed transactions, is difficult and requires highly specialized and experienced people with skills in different areas.

Enterprise JavaBeans is an approach to overcome this problem. The idea is to apply the divide-and-conquer approach to distributed systems. In this context, it means to divide the building of a distributed application into different tasks. These tasks can then be executed by different people with different levels and different areas of expertise. The main benefit for an application developer is that certain tasks are taken over by vendors. EJB containers provide a number of features that in the past had to be addressed by the application programmer.

The Enterprise JavaBeans specification identifies the following roles that are associated with a specific task in the development of distributed application.

**Enterprise Bean Provider** is typically an expert in the application domain; for example, in the financial or telecommunications industry. The bean provider implements the business task without being concerned about the distribution, transaction, security, and other nonbusiness-specific aspects of the application.

**Application Assembler** is also a domain expert. The application assembler composes an application from various prefabricated building blocks (that is, enterprise beans) and adds other components such as GUI clients, applets, and servlets to complete the application. While composing an application, an assembler is only concerned with the interfaces to enterprise beans, but not with their implementation.

**Deployer** is specialized in the installation of applications. The deployer adapts an application, composed of a number of enterprise beans, to a target operation environment by modifying the properties of the enterprise beans. The deployer's tasks include, for example, the setting of transaction and security policies and JNDI names by setting the appropriate properties in the deployment descriptor, and the integration with enterprise management software.

**EJB Server Provider** is typically a vendor with expertise in distributed infrastructures and services. The server provider implements a platform, which facilitates the development of distributed applications and provides a runtime environment for them. There can also be specialized containers that wrap a certain class of legacy applications or systems.

**EJB Container Provider** is an expert in distributed systems, transactions, and security. A container is a runtime system for one or multiple enterprise beans. It provides the glue between enterprise beans and the EJB server. A container can be both, prefabricated code as well as a tool, that generates code specific for a particular enterprise bean. A container also provides tools for the deployment of an enterprise bean and hooks into the application for monitoring and management.

**System Administrator** is concerned with a deployed application. The administrator monitors the running application and takes appropriate actions in the case of abnormal behavior of the application. Typically, an administrator uses enterprise management tools that are connected to the application by the deployer through the hooks provided by the container.

Note that the current version of the EJB specification does not define nor exactly draw the line between the two components. In fact, people often refer to it as a single entity. The current specification also does not define APIs for the management of deployed enterprise beans.

Figure 5.1 illustrates the relationships between the various components that are provided by the people or vendors that fulfill the roles described earlier. A "traditional" application programmer now becomes

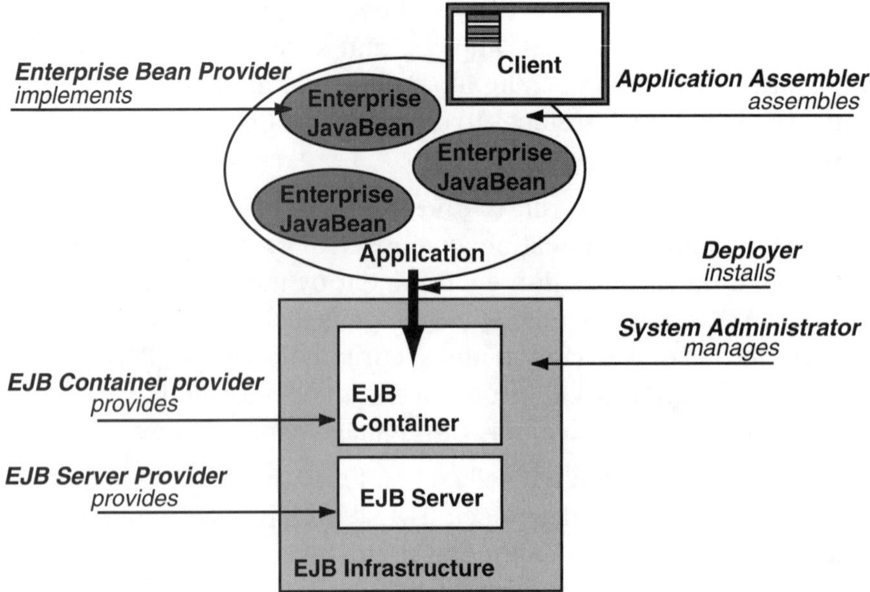


**Figure 5.1** Tasks, roles, and components.

an enterprise bean provider and application assembler, which allows her or him to focus on the business problem. The deployer defines and sets the deployment policies when installing the enterprise bean. The complexity of implementing mechanisms for executing the deployment policies is delegated to specialized vendors. Although the complexity of distributed applications cannot be reduced in total, the application programmer's job becomes easier as much complexity is addressed by EJB server and container providers.

The EJB specification achieves the aforementioned goals by introducing a number of predefined design patterns and naming conventions. This restricts the freedom in the application architecture, but allows the container and service providers to make assumptions about the application design and support them in an efficient manner.

There are three major design patterns for building object-based multitier distributed systems: *stateless server* approach, the *factory/session* model, and the *persistent object* approach. The stateless server is an object that provides certain functionality through its operations without keeping conversational state. That means that clients cannot refer to state information provided in previous operations on the same object.

The session-oriented design creates an object in the middle tier, a session, that is acting as an agent for the client. Typically, the lifetime of a session object is determined by the client and the server program that is hosting it. A client can remove the object once it is finished with it. The server can timeout a session object, and when the server terminates, references to the session object become invalid.

The persistent object design models wraps a certain piece of data (typically stored in a database) and provides operations to manipulate this data. Persistent objects are shared among multiple clients. The lifetime of a persistent object is determined by the lifetime of the data storage, which contains its data.

The EJB specification takes these three design patterns and defines them as *Stateless Session Bean*, *Stateful Session Bean*, and *Entity Bean*. The stateless session bean is modeled after the stateless server approach, the stateful session bean after the session-oriented design approach, and the entity bean after persistent object design. For each design, it defines a number of interfaces and naming conventions, which we explain in detail next.

## EJB Infrastructure

The container and service providers implement the EJB infrastructure. This infrastructure deals with distribution aspects, transaction management, and security aspects of an application. The EJB specification only defines the Java APIs, which determine the various features, and does not prescribe which technology, platforms, protocols, and so forth are used to implement them.

Figure 5.2 illustrates the various requirements for the EJB infrastructure. In fact, we have added a few requirements beyond those from the EJB specification that we see as essential for successful enterprise applications. The EJB infrastructure must provide communication channels to clients and other enterprise beans. Although not required by the EJB specification, communication channels for clients' access beans via the Internet must be secured. The EJB infrastructure must also be able to enforce access control to enterprise beans.

The persistence of the data contained by enterprise beans must be ensured. An EJB infrastructure must provide integration capabilities to existing systems and applications to be useful in an enterprise computing environment. This requirement is stated in the specification, but no APIs are provided. All communication to and from a bean can be part of a distributed transaction that needs to be managed by the EJB infrastructure. For a successful deployment, the EJB infrastructure must provide hooks

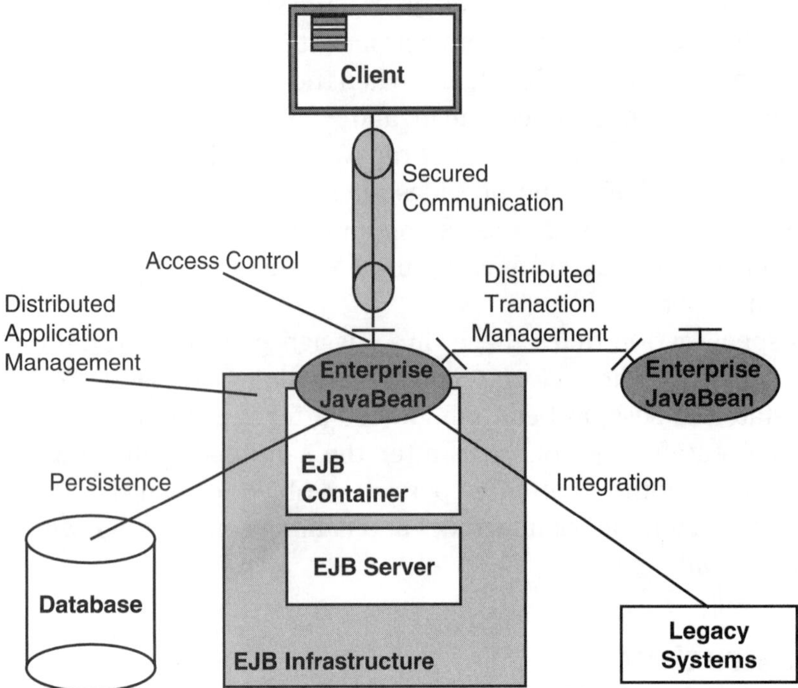


**Figure 5.2** Enterprise beans, containers, and servers.

into a distributed application management tool. Again, the specification does not define any management APIs.

The EJB specification leaves it up to the container and EJB server providers on how to satisfy these requirements. However, it defines a number of interfaces and conventions on the container level, which we present next. Later in the section we review different EJB container and server implementations and investigate how they satisfy the requirements stated earlier.

## Container

The container is probably the single most important concept in the enterprise beans approach as it provides the most benefit to the developer. Object-based middleware platforms like CORBA or RMI free a distributed application developer from the networking aspects of the application by providing mechanisms for object location, data marshaling, and so forth. The concept of a container takes this idea a step further by simplifying other nontrivial aspects of a distributed application such as security, transaction coordination, and data persistence.

Once an enterprise bean is ready for deployment, it is packed in a standard Java archive file, called an *ejb-jar* file. The ejb-jar file can contain one or multiple enterprise beans. For each enterprise bean, it contains its interfaces, classes, and a deployment descriptor. The ejb-jar file also contains a manifest file that identifies the enterprise beans in the file.

The enterprise bean provider has to supply three things to the ejb-jar file:

- The enterprise bean's *remote interface* to the enterprise bean, which specifies the application-specific methods
- Its *home interface*, which helps to create and locate instances of the enterprise bean
- The *implementation* of the application semantics of the enterprise bean

The policies and properties that determine the execution of a particular enterprise bean are provided by the deployer using the deployment descriptor. The EJB1.0 specification defines the deployment descriptor as a serialized instance of the class `javax.ejb.deployment.SessionDescriptor` or `javax.ejb.deployment.EntityDescriptor`. This API has been deprecated in the subsequent version and XML is used instead for defining deployment descriptors. Details on the deployment descriptor are given later in the chapter.

Deploying an enterprise bean means to install the ejb-jar file into a container, as illustrated in Figure 5.3. The installation process deals with the following issues:

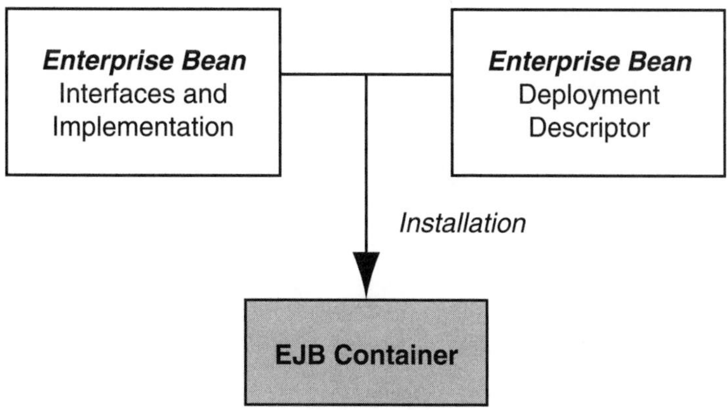


**Figure 5.3** Enterprise beans and containers.

- Gluing the different pieces of the enterprise bean together
- Registration of the enterprise bean with a name service
- Providing access to the enterprise bean through the EJB server's communication system
- Executing the transaction management and security policies

There can be any number of different enterprise beans installed in a container. Besides the installation and execution of an enterprise bean, a container also provides tools for the deployment of an enterprise bean, which are explained in the section, "EJB Deployment," later in the chapter. The interfaces to a container are currently not standardized in the EJB specification.

## Identifying an Enterprise Bean

A client always invokes methods on an enterprise bean's remote interface. This interface is referenced by a *portable remote object reference*. Additionally, an enterprise bean can be referenced by a *handle*, which is a more abstract identifier.

### *Portable Remote Object Reference*

The portable remote object reference identifies remote interfaces and the home interfaces of enterprise beans. It is an opaque data type that contains all the necessary information to enable a client to make invocation on the interfaces. Similar to a CORBA Interoperable Object Reference (IOR), it comprises address information such as IP addresses, port numbers, and information about the type and the instance of the referenced object.

### *Handle*

A handle is a more abstract way of referencing a remote object to an enterprise bean. It is defined by the following interface that must be implemented by all enterprise bean handles.

```
public interface javax.ejb.Handle {
  public abstract EJBObject getEJBObject()
    throws java.rmi.RemoteException;
}
```

It can be used to persistently store a reference to an EJB object by serializing an instance of the class that implements the handle interface, which is similar to a stringified CORBA IOR. Therefore, implementations of the interface must also implement the interface `java.io.Serializeable`. Handle implementations are typically provided by a container.

## Container Implementation

The EJB specification neither defines the interface to a container nor does it prescribe the technologies used to implement a container. In this section we give an example of an EJB container based on CORBA technology and discuss the concept of a specialized container. The main purpose of this is to illustrate how the magic functionality provided by the container can be implemented.

### *CORBA Container Implementation*

A CORBA-based implementation of an EJB container is typically based on the following components (summarized in Table 5.1): CORBA core and IIOP as the communication infrastructure, OTS for the transaction management, a JNDI wrapper of the CORBA Naming Service, and the CORBA Security Service. Figure 5.4 shows how these CORBA components fit into the EJB container picture.

A CORBA-based container implementation is a native Java implementation using OMG's Java-to-IDL mapping. Besides the Java platform features, availability, and portability, CORBA provides one major additional advantage. The interoperability between enterprise beans is guaranteed by OMG's industry standards: IIOP and standardized IDL interfaces for underlying services, specifically OTS.

Furthermore, CORBA has been designed and proven to be a very efficient mechanism for integrating legacy systems into new applications. Object Transaction Service's compliance with the X/A allows for seamlessly accessing heterogeneous resources and integration with legacy systems.

**Table 5.1** EJB Server with CORBA Technology

| ISSUE | CORBA TECHNOLOGY |
|---|---|
| Communication protocol | RMI over IIOP (including OTS transaction id in the service context) |
| JNDI | JNDI over CORBA Naming Service |
| Transactions | CORBA Object Transaction Service |
| EJB activation and deactivation | POA |
| Security | IIOP over SSL |

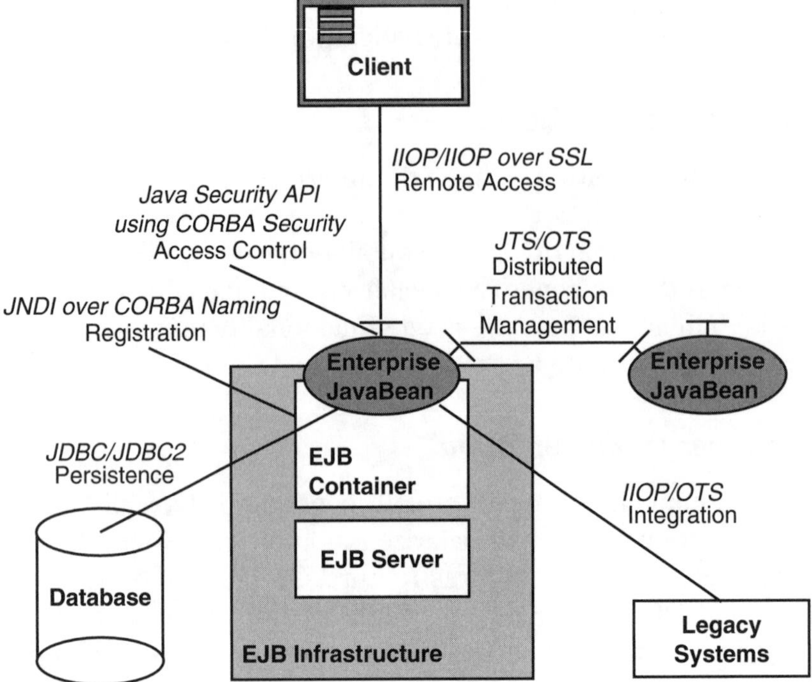


**Figure 5.4** CORBA container.

CORBA implementations have also proven the scalability and robustness expected for enterprise systems. CORBA is deployed today in critical business applications in intranet, extranet, and Internet environments as well as backend systems. These deployments are across all major industry sectors, including finance, telecommunications, and healthcare.

The examples of enterprise beans we present in this book have been deployed in a CORBA-based container, the Inprise EJB Server. This EJB server is based on Visibroker for Java, Visibroker Naming, Visibroker ITS, and Visibroker SSL. JBuilder integrates tool supports for development, deployment, and debugging aspects. Inprise AppCenter provides the management of an EJB application deployed in the Inprise container.

## Specialized Container Implementation

A specialized container is an EJB wrapper around a legacy system—the container and the enterprise beans installed become a single entity. Arbitrary enterprise beans may not necessarily be installable into such a container. The container would, however, expose the functionality of the legacy system through EJB home and remote interfaces.

An enterprise bean is a proxy for the program, which is executed by a legacy system. For example, the only enterprise beans installed in this container can be proxies, which communicate, for example, via CICS to a mainframe program. Instead of having independent enterprise bean providers, the vendor, who provides the container, would also provide tools to automatically generate enterprise beans, which interface with the backend system. Specialized containers require a standard protocol for communication and transaction control. Otherwise the use would be quite limited.

Figure 5.5 shows a possible scenario of a specialized container. It depicts the different components used by a container front-ending CICS. The remote access to the enterprise bean would be via RMI (over IIOP).

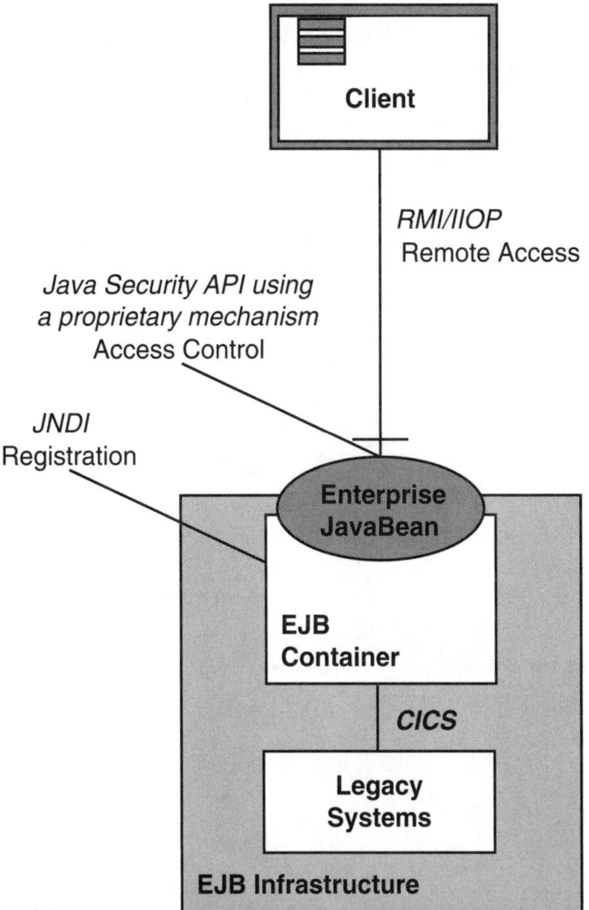


**Figure 5.5** Specialized container implementation.

The bean is registered with JNDI, using any JNDI implementation. The security mechanisms and the transaction management are tightly integrated with the backend systems. Mainframes have sophisticated access control mechanisms, which would be wrapped with Java Security APIs. Transactions could be managed by CICS, or via integration with JTS.

## EJB Development

The enterprise bean provider is concerned with a number of tasks:

- Defining the Remote Interface
- Defining the Home Interface
- Defining the Primary Key class (for entity beans)
- Implementing the enterprise bean; that is, the functionality defined in the remote and home interface

Figure 5.6 illustrates the relationships among the remote interface, the home interface, the implementation of the enterprise bean, and other components supplied by the infrastructure.

The EJB provider defines the remote and the home interface and implements the enterprise bean. Every enterprise bean must have a home interface, which always provides methods to locate or to create instances of the remote interface. The remote interface specifies methods according to the application logic encapsulated by the enterprise bean.

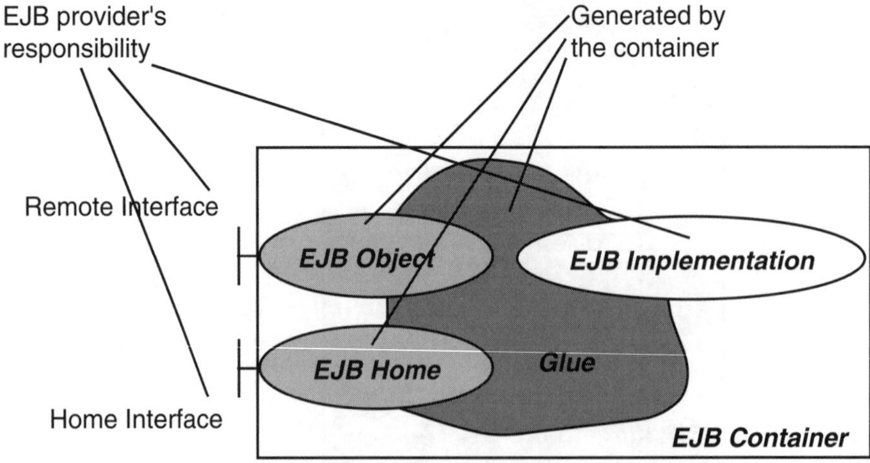


**Figure 5.6** Components of an enterprise bean.

An EJB object is an implementation of functionality declared in the enterprise bean's home and remote interface. The remote and home interface and the bean implementation are in no formal (inheritance or implementation) relationship; however, their methods must match according to a number of rules and naming conventions defined by the EJB spec. Application-specific methods must have the same signatures. The container provides the glue between the home and remote interface and the enterprise bean implementation class where the bean provider defines the semantics of the enterprise bean. The container ensures, at compile time or runtime, that the remote interface and the enterprise bean implementation match.

Figure 5.6 only shows the relationships between interfaces and classes. The glue between the home and remote interface and the enterprise bean implementation is not specified by the EJB specification, and its realization is left to the container provider.

## Remote Interface

An enterprise bean has a remote interface that defines the application-specific operations. Clients to the enterprise bean access it through its remote interface.

An enterprise bean's remote interface is a public Java interface extending the interface `javax.ejb.EJBObject`, which is the base interface of all remote interfaces.

```
package javax.ejb;
public interface EJBObject extends java.rmi.Remote {
  EJBHome getEJBHome() throws java.rmi.RemoteException;
  Object getPrimaryKey() throws java.rmi.RemoteException;
  void remove() throws java.rmi.RemoteException, RemoveException;
  Handle getHandle() throws java.rmi.RemoteException;
  boolean isIdentical (EJBObject p0) throws java.rmi.RemoteException;
}
```

The method `getEJBHome()` allows you to get the associated home interface. For entity beans, you can get the primary key of the entity bean using the method `getPrimaryKey()`. The `remove()` method deletes the enterprise bean; we explain details in the context of the life cycle of the various types of enterprise beans. The method `getHandle` returns the handle, as explained earlier, of the enterprise bean, and the `isIdentical()` allows you to compare enterprise beans.

The remote interface defines public methods, which can be invoked by clients. All methods must throw the exception `java.rmi.RemoteException`.

We already defined a remote interface for the ATM session bean in Chapter 1, "Quick Start to EJB, JTS, and OTS." The parts of the following interface definition that are in bold type are required by the EJB specification.

```
package vogel.transaction.chapter1.ejb;

public interface Atm extends javax.ejb.EJBObject {

  public void transfer(
    String source, String target, float amount )
    throws java.rmi.RemoteException, InsufficientFundsException;
}
```

The definition of the remote interface of session and entity beans follows the same rules.

## Home Interface

An enterprise bean's home interface controls the life cycle of a bean. It provides operations to create, find, and remove an EJB object; that is, an instance of enterprise bean. Session and entity beans have different life cycles due to their respective design patterns. Consequently, the types of their home interfaces must define different methods.

In either case, the home interface defines the interface and the implementation is provided by the container and by the enterprise bean implementation class.

### *Home Base Interface*

Every home interface extends the interface `javax.ejb.EJBHome`. This interface is defined as follows:

```
package javax.ejb;

public interface EJBHome extends java.rmi.Remote {

  void remove(Handle handle)
    throws java.rmi.RemoteException, RemoveException;

  void remove(Object primaryKey)
```

```
    throws java.rmi.RemoteException, RemoveException;

  EJBMetaData getEJBMetaData()
    throws RemoteException;
}
```

There are two `remove()` methods provided to remove EJB object instances. The first `remove()` method removes an instance identified by a handle, the second one by a primary key. A handle is a unique EJB object identifier, which we introduced earlier. A handle has the same lifetime as the EJB object it is referencing. In the case of an entity object, a handle can be valid for multiple instantiations of an EJB object; for example, it is valid even if a server crashed that hosted the EJB object, or when the EJB object moves between different servers and machines. A serialized handle is a concept very similar to a stringified CORBA object reference.

The other `remove()` operation on the `EJBHome` interface uses a primary key to determine the object to be removed. A primary key can be of any Java type extending the Java `Object` class and must implement the Java `Serializable` interface. Primary keys are the main means of identification for entity beans. A primary key is typically a key in a database table which uniquely defines the data, represented by the entity object.

The method `getEJBMetaData()` returns metadata of the EJB object. The metadata type is defined by a Java interface, which provides methods to obtain the `EJBHome` interface, the type (class) of the home and the remote interface, as well as the type of the primary key. It also provides a method to find out if the object hosted by this home interface is a session or entity bean.

```
package javax.ejb;

public interface EJBMetaData {

  EJBHome getEJBHome();

  Class getHomeInterfaceClass();

  Class getRemoteInterfaceClass();

  Class getPrimaryKeyClass();

  boolean isSession();

}
```

### *Session Bean Home*

The session bean pattern mandates that each client has an individual session bean instance. The home interface becomes a session bean factory by defining one or more `create()` methods. The EJB specification defines a naming convention for these `create()` methods:

- Return type is the remote interface type
- Method name is always "create", parameters can vary
- Throws the exception `java.rmi.RemoteException`
- Throws `javax.ejb.CreateException`
- Parameters of the method are used to initialize the new EJB object

The following example shows different create methods at a session home interface. Required parts are shown in bold.

```
package vogel.transaction.chapter1.ejb;

public interface AtmHome extends javax.ejb.EJBHome {

  Atm create()
    throws java.rmi.RemoteException, javax.ejb.CreateException;
  Atm create( Profile preferredProfile )
    throws java.rmi.RemoteException, javax.ejb.CreateException;
}
```

Note that session home interface must not define finder methods to locate objects, as stateful session beans are intended to be used only by their creator.

### *Entity Bean Home*

Similar to the session's home interface, the entity home interface can provide create methods following the same pattern. However, the primary means of locating an entity bean is by using finder operations, since entity beans are long lived and typically already exist and a client just has to find the one it wants to invoke.

An entity home interface has to provide the default finder method, which returns an object of the bean's remote interface type and takes primary key as an argument. The type of the primary key can be of any Java type, which extends the Java Object class. As part of the deployment description, you tell the container the type of the primary key.

```
<entity bean's remote interface> findByPrimaryKey(
  <primary key type> key )
  throws java.rmi.RemoteException, FinderException;
```

The home interface can define further find methods according to the following conventions:

- Return type is the remote interface type or a collection type, which has the remote interface type as the content type
- Method always starts with the prefix "find"
- Throws the exception `java.rmi.RemoteException`
- Typically throws the exception `javax.ejb.FinderException`
- Parameters determine one or more EJB objects

Additionally, an entity bean's home interface can provide one or more `create()` methods, which returns an object reference of the bean's remote interface type. The arguments are application specific.

The create methods must comply with the following conventions:

- Return type is the remote interface type
- Method name is always "create", parameters can vary
- Throws the exception `java.rmi.RemoteException`
- Throws the exception `javax.ejb.CreateException`

The following example shows different types of finder and create methods. Required parts are shown in bold.

```
package vogel.transaction.chapter1.ejb;

public interface AccountHome extends javax.ejb.EJBHome {

  Account create( String accountId )
    throws java.rmi.RemoteException, javax.ejb.CreateException;

  Account create( String accountId, float initialBalance )
    throws java.rmi.RemoteException, javax.ejb.CreateException;

  Account findByPrimaryKey( String key )
    throws java.rmi.RemoteException, javax.ejb.FinderException;

  Enumeration findBySocialSecurityNumber( String socialSecurityNumber )
    throws java.rmi.RemoteException, javax.ejb.FinderException;

}
```

## Bean Implementation

The bean implementation is the principal work of a bean provider as it contains all of the application-specific semantics. A bean class implements the `SessionBean` or the `EntityBean` interface depending on its type. These interfaces extend the enterprise bean base interface `EnterpriseBean`.

### *Enterprise Bean Interface*

The enterprise bean interface just defines a common base interface; there are no methods defined.

```
package javax.ejb;

public interface EnterpriseBean extends Serializable {}
```

### *Session Bean*

A session bean implementation must implement the session bean interface and comply with a number of rules and naming conventions that define the relationship of this class to the remote and the home interface.

#### Session Bean Interface

The session bean interface `SessionBean` extends the interface `EnterpriseBean`. The methods of the session bean interface are closely associated with the life cycle of a session bean. To fully understand the semantics of the methods, we first have to take a look at the life cycle of session beans. During this process we introduce the methods of the session bean interface. Note that a session implementation must also implement methods corresponding to the home interface and to the remote interface. The home interface's `create()` methods have corresponding `ejbCreate()` methods in the implementation class.

The EJB specification defines *stateless* and *stateful* session beans.

**Stateless session bean.** The bean does not contain conversational state between method invocations. As a consequence, any session bean instance can be used for any client.

**Stateful session bean.** The bean contains conversational state that is kept across method invocations and transactions. Once a client has obtained a specific session bean, it must use this instance for the lifetime of the session. A client can, however, have multiple, distinguished sessions and hence multiple session bean instances.

### Life Cycle of a Stateless Session Bean

The life cycle of a stateless session is pretty simple, as shown in Figure 5.7. A new instance is created and the methods `setSessionContext()` and `ejbCreate()` are invoked on the session object. Now the new instance is in a pool of instances, which are ready to be invoked. Since the stateless session objects do not keep state, any of the instance can be used for any of the incoming method invocations. When an instance is removed from that pool, the method `ejbRemove()` is invoked on the session object.

Note that the creation and removal of session bean instances are not related to the `create()` and `remove()` methods on the home/remote interface. The life cycle of stateless session beans is governed by container policies.

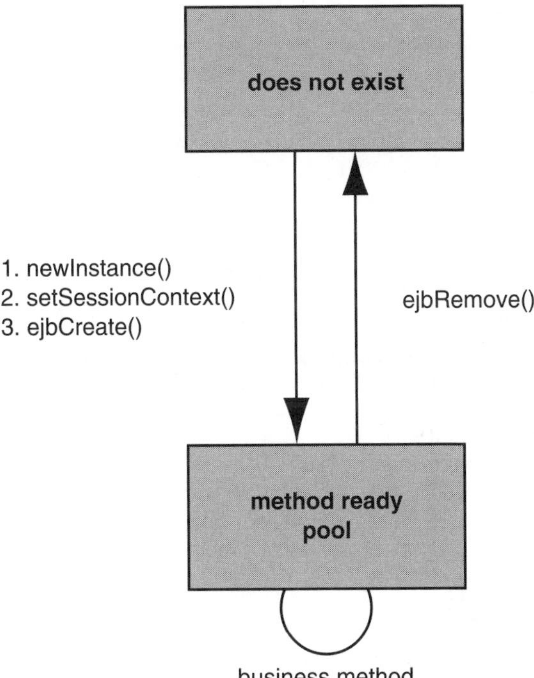


**Figure 5.7** Life cycle of a stateless session bean.

### Life Cycle of a Stateful Session Bean

Typically, the life of a session bean starts when a client invokes a `create()` method on the session bean's home interface (see Figure 5.8). The implementation of the home interface is provided by the container, based on the session bean implementation class. The container creates a new instance of the session bean, initializes it, and returns an object reference back to the client. During this process, first the method `setSessionContext()` and then the method `ejbCreate...()` are invoked on the session bean implementation (which implements the session bean interface). The bean provider can use these methods to initialize the session bean. Details of these methods are given later in the chapter. The state of the session bean is now *method ready.*

Once a client invokes a `remove()` method on the remote or home interface, the corresponding `ejbRemove()` method is invoked on the EJB object, to allow the bean provider to add application-specific cleanup code. Once the invocation is completed, the object is in a nonexistent

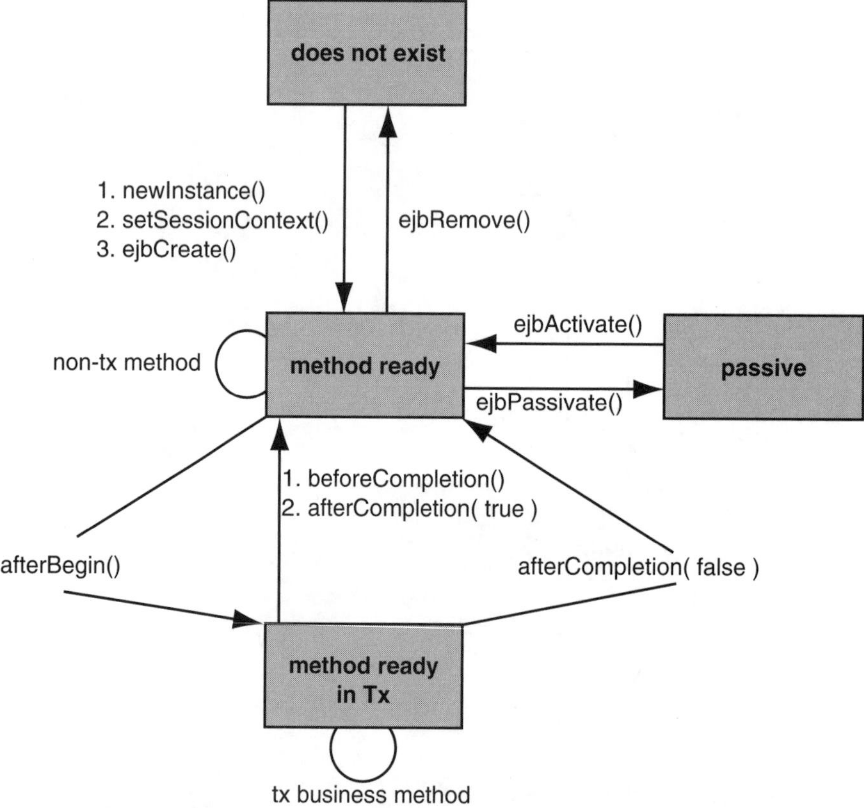


**Figure 5.8** Life cycle of a stateful session bean.

state again. When a client tries to invoke a method on a session object in this state, the exception `java.rmi.NoSuchObjectException` is thrown by the container.

The container can deactivate the session bean instance, typically for resource management reasons. For example, when a session object has not been used by a client for a certain time, the container stores reference and state of the session object on disk and frees the memory allocated by the bean. However, files or other operating system controlled resources that may have been opened by the session bean must be explicitly handled in the implementation. This can be done in the `ejbActivate()` and `ejbPassivate()` methods, which are triggered by the container. The instance is typically reactivated when the client makes the next call on the session bean's reference it holds. Then the container recreates the session object in memory. CORBA's object adapter provides similar activation and deactivation mechanisms.

When a method is invoked on the object in a transactional context, there are again a number of interception points for the bean provider. They are defined in the interface `SessionSynchronization`, which is explained below. The use of this interface is optional. The method `afterBegin()` is invoked after a method is invoked on the remote interface. That puts the EJB object in the state *method ready in TX*. Once the object is in this state it will accept the invocation of the method in this transaction context and only this. The commit of the transaction triggers the invocation of two methods, `beforeCompletion()` and `afterCompletion( true )`, on the EJB object. In the case of a rollback, the method `afterCompletion( false )` is invoked on the session object. As a result of the commit or rollback, the session object will be back in the *method ready* state.

A session bean's lifetime is bound to the lifetime of the container in which it is installed. Once the process, or JVM, in which the container is executed terminates, the session bean's reference usually becomes invalid. Once a session bean was passivated and its state persisted, a smart EJB server could re-activate the session bean in a different container.

### SessionBean Interface

The session bean interface defines the methods all session beans must implement.

```
package javax.ejb;

public interface SessionBean extends EnterpriseBean {

void setSessionContext(SessionContext sessionContext)
```

```
    throws RemoteException;

  void ejbRemove() throws RemoteException;

  void ejbActivate() throws RemoteException;

  void ejbPassivate() throws RemoteException;
}
```

The methods have the following semantics.

**`setSessionContext()`** sets a session context. The session context interface provides methods to access runtime properties of the context in which a session runs. Details about the session and EJB contexts are given later in the chapter when we explain the deployment of an enterprise bean. This method is typically implemented by storing the session context in a private variable of the session bean implementation class. The variable must be declared not-transient to retain its value of de-activation/re-activation cycles.

**`ejbRemove()`** notifies a session object that it is about to be removed. Whenever the container removes a session bean (for example, because a client invoked a remove operation on the remote or home interface), it calls this operation on the bean implementation.

**`ejbActivate()`** notifies a session object that it has been activated.

**`ejbPassivate()`** notifies a session object that it is about to be deactivated.

The activation and deactivation notifications allow a sophisticated bean implementation to manage resources, which they may control.

### Optional Session Synchronization Interface

The interface `SessionSynchronization` provides methods for session beans to get notified in the event of transaction synchronization. For example, implementing this interface allows a bean to synchronize cached data with the database within an ongoing transaction.

```
package javax.ejb;

public interface SessionSynchronization {

  void afterBegin() throws RemoteException;

  void beforeCompletion() throws RemoteException;

  void afterCompletion(boolean completionStatus) throws RemoteException;

}
```

The three methods are notifications from the container whenever a specific step in a transaction is completed.

**`afterBegin()`** notifies the session bean that a new transaction has begun. The session bean is already in a transaction and any work that is executed is within the scope of this transaction.

**`beforeCompletion()`** notifies the session bean that a client has completed work on the current transaction, but the resources involved have not yet been committed. The bean should now update the database with its cached values if there are any. If necessary, the session bean can force a rollback of the current transaction by invoking the method `setRollBackOnly()` on its session context.

**`afterCompletion()`** notifies the session bean that the current transaction has been completed. The parameter `completion-Status` indicates the outcome of the transaction. The value `true` means committed; `false` means rollback.

#### Session Bean Implementation

A session bean implementation must implement:

- The `SessionBean` interface
- Optionally, the `SessionSynchronization` interface
- Methods that correspond to the ones defined in the home interface
- Methods defined in the remote interface

We have already explained the typical implementations of the methods of the `SessionBean` interface. See Figure 5.9.

The home interface defines one or more create methods. For each of these methods we have to declare and implement a corresponding create method. The naming convention for the session bean's create methods corresponds to the one for the home interface. The create methods are called `ejbCreate()`. The parameters must match those defined in the home interface's corresponding create methods. This includes the exceptions. The return value is, however, `void` (and not remote interface specified in the home interface). The pattern for `ejbCreate()` method is

```
public void ejbCreate( <zero or more parameters> )
  throws RemoteException {
  // implementation
}
```

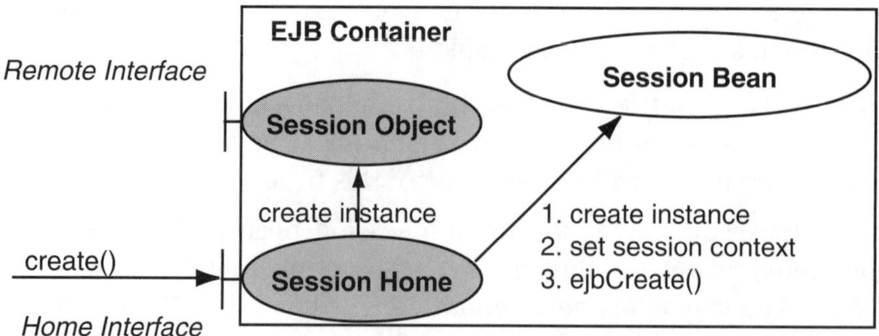


**Figure 5.9** Relationships of a session bean implementation.

Finally, we have to implement methods corresponding to the ones defined in the remote interface. Their signatures must exactly match those of the methods defined in the remote interface. The type safety is ensured by the container. There is no explicit "implements" relationship between the remote interface and the EJB implementation class. The container usually checks type safety at install time. Appropriate development tools for EJB should ensure the type safety at development time.

The constructor of the bean should not do anything; in fact, you can omit the constructor. All of the initialization of the bean is done in the `ejbCreate()` methods.

Finally, we revisit the example from Chapter 1.

```
package vogel.transaction.chapter1.ejb;

import java.rmi.RemoteException;

public class AtmBean implements SessionBean, Serializable{

  private SessionContext sessionContext;

  // application specific methods

  public void transfer(
    String sourceAccountId, String targetAccountId, float amount )
    throws RemoteException, InsufficientFundsException {


    //get the accounts
    ...
    // now that I got the accounts I make the transfer
    sourceAccount.debit( amount );
```

```
    targetAccount.credit( amount );
    return;
  }
```

ATMBean has no constructor and we have omitted some parts of the implementation of the transfer method. In the remainder of the code we provide a trivial implementation of an ebjCreate() method and the methods defined in the SessionBean interface.

```
// implement methods defined in SessionBean

 public void ejbCreate() throws RemoteException {

   System.out.println("ATM: create");

 }

 public void setSessionContext( SessionContext sessionContext ) {
   System.out.println("ATM: set session context");
   this.sessionContext = sessionContext;
 }

 public void ejbRemove() {
   System.out.println("ATM: remove");
 }

 public void ejbActivate() {
   System.out.println("ATM: activate");
 }

 public void ejbPassivate() {
   System.out.println("ATM: passivate");
 }
```

## *Entity Beans*

A entity bean implementation must implement the entity bean interface and comply with a number of rules and naming conventions that define the relationship of this class to the remote and the home interface.

### Life Cycle of an Entity Bean

The entity bean interface defines methods, similar to the ones in the session bean interface, which an entity bean must implement. To understand the meaning of the methods we must look at the life cycle of an entity bean, as shown in Figure 5.10.

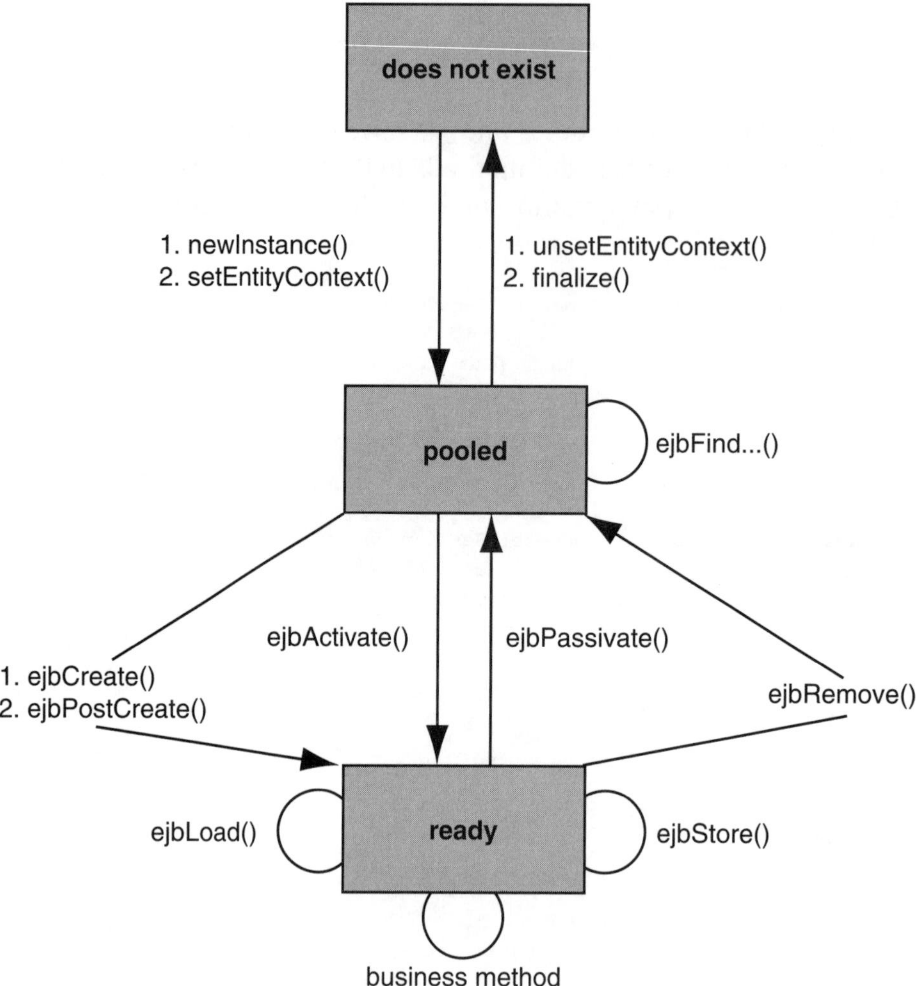


**Figure 5.10** Life cycle of an entity bean.

An instance of an entity bean is in one of the following three states:

**Nonexistent.** The instance does not exist.

**Pooled.** The instance exists but it is not associated with a particular EJB object entity; that is, there is no specific data associated with the instance.

**Ready.** The instance is associated with a particular EJB object entity; that is, there is specific data associated with the instance.

An instance of an entity bean is created by the container. The container sets the context of the instance by invoking `setEntityContext()` on the entity bean. The instance is now in the pooled state. All the instances in the pool are equal since they are not associated with any data. When and how many instances in a pool are created is up to the container implementation.

When a client invokes a finder method, the corresponding `ejbFind()` method is executed on an arbitrary object in the pooled state.

An instance moves from the pooled to the ready state when the container selects this instance to service a client's request on an entity object with no such instance in the ready state and in the proper transaction context. Then the container initializes the instance with the appropriate identity by invoking `ejbCreate()` and `ejbPostCreate()` on the instance. This is caused by a client invoking a create method on the home interface. An alternative way to move an instance from the pooled to the ready state is by `ejbActivate()`, which happens when an already existing object gets activated.

An entity object is moved back to the pooled state by deactivating it. This means that the instance is decoupled from the data represented by the entity. This happens when the transaction is completed or when the entity bean is removed; the method `ejbPassivate()` or `ejbRemove()` is invoked on the entity bean, respectively. When an unassociated instance is removed from the pool the method `unsetEntityContext()` is invoked on it.

When the instance is in the ready state, it is associated with a specific entity object. Clients can invoke the application-specific methods on the entity bean and the bean loads and stores its data as appropriate using the `ejbLoad()` and `ejbStore()` methods.

### Entity Bean Interface

The session bean interface is defined as shown next.

```
package javax.ejb;

public interface EntityBean extends EnterpriseBean {

  void setEntityContext(EntityContext entityContext) throws
RemoteException;

  void unsetEntityContext() throws RemoteException;

  void ejbRemove() throws RemoteException, RemoveException;

  void ejbActivate() throws RemoteException;

  void ejbPassivate() throws RemoteException;

  void ejbLoad() throws RemoteException;
```

```
  void ejbStore() throws RemoteException;
}
```

The methods have the following semantics.

**setEntityContext()** sets an entity context. The entity context interface provides methods to access properties of the runtime context in which an entity bean runs. Details about the entity and EJB contexts are given later in the chapter when we explain the deployment of an enterprise bean. This method is typically implemented by storing the session context in a private variable of the session bean implementation class.

**unsetEntityContext()** is called by the container before it terminates the life of the current instance of the entity bean. The bean can free resources that have been allocated during the `setEntityContext()` call.

**ejbRemove()** removes the database entry or entries associated with this particular entity bean.

**ejbActivate()** notifies an entity bean that it has been activated.

**ejbPassivate()** notifies an entity bean that it is about to be deactivated.

**ejbLoad()** refreshes the data the entity object represents from the database.

**ejbStore()** stores the data the entity object represents in the database.

#### Entity Bean Implementation

An entity bean implementation must implement:

- The EntityBean interface
- Methods that correspond to the ones defined in the home interface
- Methods that correspond to the ones defined in the remote interface

The amount of programming an enterprise bean provider has to do depends on the persistence policy, which is defined in the deployment descriptor. Persistence is the protocol or mechanism used to transfer the state of an entity bean to and from an underlying database. Note that the entity bean and the database may be connected via a legacy application.

The specification identifies two approaches to implement persistence:

**Bean-managed persistence.** The entity bean implementation is responsible for implementing the persistence. The bean provider writes the code to access the underlying database or application. These calls are placed in the methods `ejbCreate()`, `ejbFind...()`, `ejbRemove()`, `ejbLoad()`, and `ejbStore()`.

**Container-managed persistence.** The container is responsible for implementing the persistence. Instead of the bean provider implementing the database access code, the container is responsible for generating the appropriate code and its execution. The fields of the entity bean, which are managed by the container, must be specified in the deployment descriptor.

The obvious advantage of container-managed persistence is that the bean provider is freed from the task of writing database access code. That, however, requires sophisticated tools provided by the container. In many cases these tools imply an object relational mapping.

The example from Chapter 1 uses bean-managed persistence. We point out throughout the example which parts could have been omitted when using container-managed persistence.

The class `AccountBean` implements the interface `EntityBean`. We declare two variables for the entity context and the account balance; that is, the state of the bean. Note that you have to declare state variables, which are container-managed, as `public`. We don't declare a constructor. We also have a convenience function to obtain the primary key, the account identifier, from the entity context.

```
package vogel.transaction.chapter1.ejb;

import javax.ejb.*;
import java.sql.*;
import java.rmi.RemoteException;

public class AccountBean
  implements EntityBean {

  private EntityContext entityContext;
  public float balance;

  private String accountId() {
    return (String) entityContext.getPrimaryKey();
  }
```

The implementation of the application-specific methods, `credit()` and `debit()`, is straightforward: We just change the value of the state variable `balance`.

```
public void credit( float amount )
    throws RemoteException {

    balance = balance + amount;
    return;
  }

  public void debit( float amount )
    throws RemoteException, InsufficientFundsException {

    if( balance >= amount )
      balance = balance - amount;
    else
      throw new InsufficientFundsException();
    return;
  }
```

Now we implement the create and find methods corresponding to the ones defined in the home interface. For a container-managed implementation we would have trivial implementation, we only have to initial the state variables.

For the bean-managed implementation we have to supply the database access code. We use JDBC in this example. But other APIs, for example, to object databases or to legacy applications, can be used. The `ejbCreate()` method we implement with an SQL insert, the `ejbFindByPrimaryKey()` method with an SQL select.

```
public String ejbCreate( String accountId )
    throws RemoteException, CreateException {

    balance = 0;
    try {
      Statement statement = getStatement();
      ResultSet resultSet = statement.executeQuery(
        "insert into accounts values( '" + accountId + "', 0.0 )" );
      statement.close();
    }
    catch( Exception e ) {
      throw new RemoteException( e.toString() );
    }
    return accountId;
  }
```

```
public void ejbPostCreate( String accountId ) {
  return ;
}

public String ejbFindByPrimaryKey( String accountId )
  throws RemoteException, FinderException {

  try {
    Statement statement = getStatement();
    ResultSet resultSet = statement.executeQuery(
      "select balance from accounts where id = '" + accountId + "'" );
    if( resultSet.next() ) {
      balance = resultSet.getFloat(1);
    …
  return accountId;
}
```

Finally, we implement the methods defined in `EntityBean` interface. Setting and unsetting the entity context is straightforward. The implementation of the `ejbRemove()` method is provided by an SQL delete. We don't add code to the activation and passivation of the entity bean.

```
public void setEntityContext( EntityContext entityContext )
    throws RemoteException  {

    this.entityContext = entityContext;
  }

  public void unsetEntityContext() throws RemoteException {
    entityContext = null;
  }

  public void ejbRemove() throws RemoteException {
    try {
      Statement statement = getStatement();
      ResultSet resultSet = statement.executeQuery(
        "delete from accounts where id = '" + accountId() + "'" );
      statement.close();
    }
    catch( Exception e ) {

      throw new RemoteException( e.toString() );
    }
    return;
  }

  public void ejbActivate() throws RemoteException {}

  public void ejbPassivate() throws RemoteException {}
```

The ejbCreate(), ejbRemove(), ejbFind(), ejbLoad(), and ejbStore() methods are the biggest difference between container-managed and bean-managed implementation. For the container-managed case, we don't have to do anything; in the bean-managed case, we have to make the database calls. For example, we implement the ejbLoad() method with a SQL select and the ejbStore() method with a SQL update. We have also implemented a little helper method to obtain a SQL statement.

```
  public void ejbLoad()
    throws RemoteException {

    try {
      Statement statement = getStatement();
      ResultSet resultSet = statement.executeQuery(
        "select balance from accounts where id = '" +
        accountId() + "'" );
      if( resultSet.next() ) {
        balance = resultSet.getFloat(1);
        ...
    }
  }

  public void ejbStore()
    throws RemoteException {
    try {
      Statement statement = getStatement();
      ResultSet resultSet = statement.executeQuery(
        "update accounts set balance = " + balance +
        " where id = '" + accountId()  + "'");
      statement.close();
    }
    catch( Exception e ) {
      throw new RemoteException( e.toString() );
    }
  }

  private Statement getStatement() throws RemoteException {
    ...
  }
}
```

Furthermore, there are a number of rules and conventions to be observed:

**Concurrent access to entity beans.** The synchronization between concurrent invocations is managed by the container and is not the concern of the entity bean provider. The container typically uses one of the following strategies: database synchronization, or container synchronization. In the first case, the container provides multiple instances of the same entity bean and leaves the synchronization up to the database access calls in the `ejbCreate()`, `ejbRemove()`, `ejbLoad()`, and `ejbStore()` methods. In the second case, the container creates only one instance of the entity bean, which acquires an exclusive lock on the database. The concurrent invocations are serialized by the container.

**Reentrant entity beans.** By default, entity beans are not reentrant. When a call within the same transaction context arrives at the entity bean, the exception `java.rmi.RemoteException` is thrown. An entity bean can be declared reentrant in the deployment descriptor; however, special care needs to be taken in this case. The critical issue is that a container can generally not distinguish between a (loopback) call within the same transaction and a concurrent invocation (in the same transaction context) on that same entity bean. The second one is illegal and when the entity bean is marked reentrant it becomes the programmer's responsibility to ensure this rule.

## EJB Deployment

EJB deployer is responsible for taking an enterprise bean and deploying it in a certain context. The context determines the policies for executing the bean. These policies determine, for example, the transactional behavior or the access control of an enterprise bean.

EJB deployer would typically use wizard-like tools, provided by the container, to set the deployment descriptor for enterprise beans. The EJB specification version 1.0 defines serialized Java objects of the type `javax.ejb.deployment.SessionDescriptor` or `javax.ejb.deployment.EntityDescriptor`, depending on the type of the enterprise bean. The subsequent versions of the EJB specification prescribe XML for the definition of deployment descriptors. For both reasons, the change of the specification and the fact that a deployer uses tools, we omit the syntactical representation of the deployment descriptor. Instead, we focus on the content of the deployment information.

A deployment descriptor keeps information about the following:

- Transaction policies govern the transactional behavior of a bean.
- Access control policies govern the access to an enterprise bean.
- JNDI names set the name under which the home interface of the enterprise is registered.

- Type information defines the types, that is the name of the classes, for the home and remote interfaces, the primary key class (entity beans only), and the implementation class.
- Properties for enterprise beans with container-managed persistence provide the information required by the container to manage the persistence of a bean.

## Transaction Polices

Transaction policies cover two aspects: the transaction scope and the isolation levels.

### *Transaction Scope*

The EJB specification defines the values for the transactional scope:

**TX_NOT_SUPPORTED.** The enterprise bean does not support a global transaction.

**TX_SUPPORTS.** The enterprise bean supports a global transaction. If a caller makes an invocation in a transactional context, the container executes the invocation in the caller's transactional. If a caller has no association with a transaction, the container executes the invocation without a transaction.

**TX_MANDATORY.** An invocation on the enterprise bean requires a transactional context. If a caller makes an invocation in a transactional context, the container executes the invocation in the caller's transactional. If a caller has no association with a transaction, the container throws the exception `javax.jta.TransactionRequiredException`.

**TX_REQUIRED.** The enterprise bean requires a global transaction for the execution of an invocation. If a caller makes an invocation in a transactional context, the container executes the invocation in the caller's transactional. If a caller has no association with a transaction, the container creates a new transaction and executes the invocation in with this transaction.

**TX_REQUIRED_NEW.** The enterprise bean requires a new global transaction and executes the invocation with this transaction.

**TX_BEAN_MANAGED.** The transactional behavior is managed by the enterprise bean implementation using the `javax.transaction.CurrentTransaction`.

Transaction isolation levels are originally defined in the ANSI SQL specification. The concept has been adopted by the ODBC and JDBC standards and found its way in the EJB specification. Isolation level refers to the degree to which multiple interleaved transactions are prevented from interfering with each other in a multi-user database system. Ideally, one would like to have serializable transactions. That means that the interleaved execution of any set of concurrent transactions produces the same effect as a serial execution of the same transactions. There are three specific ways in which the serializability of a transaction may be violated.

**Dirty Read.** Transaction t1 modifies a row. Transaction t2 then reads the row. Now t1 performs a rollback and t2 has seen a row that never really existed.

**Non-repeatable Read.** Transaction t1 retrieves a row. Then transaction t2 updates this row and t1 retrieves the same row again. Transaction t1 has now retrieved the same row twice and has seen two different values for it.

**Phantoms.** Transaction t1 reads a set of rows that satisfy certain search conditions. Then transaction t2 inserts one or more rows that satisfy the same search condition. If transaction t1 repeats the read, it will see rows that did not exist previously. These rows are called phantoms.

The transaction isolation levels are defined based on the above defined permitted violations.

**TRANSACTION_READ_COMMITTED.** Does not allow dirty reads but allows the other two violations.

**TRANSACTION_READ_UNCOMMITTED.** Allows all three violations.

**TRANSACTION_REPEATABLE_READ.** Allows phantoms but not the other two violations.

**TRANSACTION_SERIALIZABLE.** Does not allow any of the three violations.

## Access Control

Access control is based on identities. There are three values you can set for enterprise bean defining with which identity it runs. These are:

**CLIENT_IDENTITY.** Runs the enterprise with the identity provided by the caller.

**SYSTEM_IDENTITY.** Runs the enterprise with a predefined system identity.

**SPECIFIED_IDENTITY.** Runs the enterprise with the identity specified in the deployment descriptor.

The deployment descriptor allows you to specify an access control entry. It can be defined for individual methods or for all methods of the enterprise bean. An access control entry associates a set of identities or roles with a set of methods, meaning that only the specified clients with the specified identities or roles can invoke those methods.

Note that the access control is type-based and not instance-based. That means you cannot formulate and enforce access control policies such as "only the creator of a session can access the session," or "only the portfolio owner and the financial consultant can access the portfolio."

### Naming

For each enterprise bean you must define a name under which its home interface is registered with JNDI. JNDI is a way to locate enterprise beans. The name is specified using the syntax for JNDI names.

### Typing

For each enterprise bean you must define a name of the classes for the home and the remote interface and for the bean implementation class. For entity beans you provide the name of the primary key class.

### Container-Managed Persistence

To enable container-managed persistence, you must specify the fields, which are managed by the container.

## Application Assembling

The task of an application assembler is to combine one or more enterprise beans with some additional components (servlets, applets, scripts, etc.). The result of the assembly process can be a complete application or another, more complex enterprise bean consisting of several enterprise beans. The EJB specification does not define much detail on the bean assembling. Generally, the client, which can be an application-level client or just another enterprise bean, has to do the following things:

**Locate the bean's home interface.** The EJB specification defines the JNDI as the API to locate home interfaces.

**Obtain an EJB object.** Create a session bean, or create or find an entity bean.

**Invoke the EJB object.** Invoking methods on the EJB object's remote interface.

## Locating the Home Interface

The EJB specification defines JNDI as the API for locating home interfaces. JNDI is intended to be implemented on top of different services. Examples include the CORBA's Naming Service, LDAP/X.500, flat file, and proprietary directory services. Figure 5.11 illustrates the different implementation choices. Typically, the EJB server provider selects a particular implementation of JNDI.

From the client's point of view, the selected technology doesn't matter. Client just needs to obtain an initial context and resolve the name to a home interface as shown in the following sample code. The initialization of the initial naming context factory is EJB container/server specific.

```
    AtmHome atmHome = null;
    try {
      Hashtable env = new Hashtable();
      env.put(javax.naming.Context.INITIAL_CONTEXT_FACTORY,
        "com.inprise.ejb.jndi.Context");
      javax.naming.Context root =
        new javax.naming.InitialContext(env);
      atmHome = (AtmHome) root.lookup("Atm");
  }
  catch( Exception ex ) {
    System.err.println(
      "Could not get home interface for ATM EJBs" + ex );
  }
```

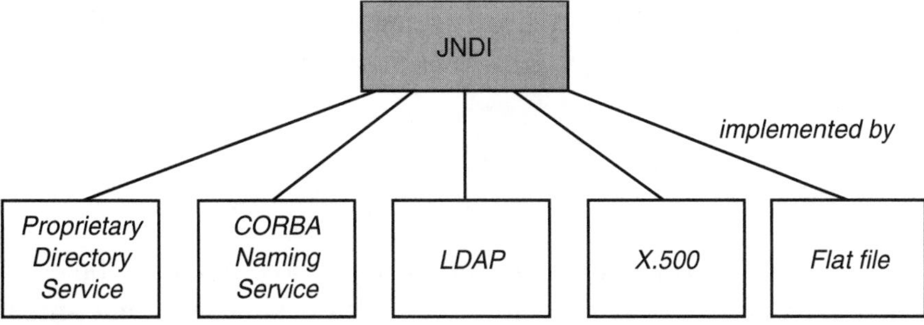


**Figure 5.11** JNDI and sample implementation.

The context's `lookup()` method returns an object of type `java.lang.Object`, which we have to cast to the expected type (for example, to the `AtmHome` interface).

## Obtaining the Remote Interface

Now that we have obtained the home interface of an enterprise bean we can get a reference to the enterprise bean's remote interface. We use the home's create or finder methods. Exactly which method we call depends on the type of the enterprise bean and the methods the enterprise bean provider has defined in the home interface.

### *Session Beans*

A client obtains a session bean by calling one of the create methods on the home interface. The default create method has no parameters; for example:

```
Atm atm = atmHome.create();
```

Stateless session beans have only create methods with no arguments. Stateful session beans can have a number of create methods. The additional parameters of these methods are used to initialize the session.

### *Entity Beans*

A client obtains an entity typically through a find operation. The default find method is

```
findByPrimaryKey( <key type> primaryKey )
```

The key type can be any Java class, which implements `Serializable`. The primary key class is set in the deployment description. For example, we can obtain an account entity bean by using an account identifier of the type `AccountPK.class`, which contains a string or integer which is the account number.

```
AccountPK accountPK = new AccountPK("1234-56-789");
Account source = accountHome.findByPrimaryKey( accountPK );
```

Again, the bean provider can define additional find methods to be used by a client. A client can also create entity beans using the home interface. However, note the different life spans of session and entity beans.

While a session bean is typically only valid for a client's session, an entity bean exists as long as its data is present in a database.

## Invoking Methods

The client can now invoke methods on the EJB as defined in the remote interface. For example, we invoke the transfer method on the ATM bean.

```
    // transfer some money from savings to checking
    atm.transfer( "savings", "checking", 100f );

    // cleaning up
    atm.remove();
}
catch( Exception ex ) {
    ...
}
```

The invocation of the `remove()` method is specific to session beans. A well-behaved client should always call the `remove()` method once it is finished with the session object. If the client doesn't do so, due to badly written code or due to a crash of the client program, the container will remove the object after a certain time. The timeout value is a deployment property. However, a client can also keep a handle to the session for future reference.

Clients of entity beans don't have to deal with this problem as entity beans are only associated with a client for the duration of a transaction and the container is in charge of their life cycles, including the activation and deactivation.

# CORBA and Enterprise JavaBeans

There are a number of aspects to the relationship between CORBA and Enterprise JavaBeans. Three important ones are the implementation of an EJB container/server with an ORB, the integration of legacy systems into an EJB middle tier, and the access of enterprise beans from non-Java components, specifically clients. The EJB specification is currently only concerned with the third aspect.

CORBA is a very suitable and natural platform on which to implement an EJB infrastructure. CORBA addresses all of the concerns of the EJB specification with the CORBA Core specification or the CORBA Services:

**Support for distribution.** CORBA Core and CORBA Naming Service

**Support for transactions.** CORBA Object Transaction Service

**Support for security.** CORBA Security Specification, including IIOP-over-SSL

Additionally, the CORBA allows the integration of non-Java components into an application. These components can be legacy systems and applications and different kinds of clients. Back-ends can be easily integrated using OTS and any programming language for which an IDL mapping exists. That, however, requires an EJB container, which provides OTS and IIOP APIs as we explained earlier in the chapter.

The EJB specification is concerned with the accessibility of enterprise beans from non-Java clients and provides an Enterprise JavaBean to CORBA mapping. The goals of the EJB/CORBA mapping are

- Interoperability between clients written in any CORBA-supported programming language and enterprise beans running on a CORBA-based EJB server.
- Enabling client programs to mix and match calls to CORBA objects and enterprise beans within the same transaction.
- Supporting distributed transactions involving multiple enterprise beans running on CORBA-based EJB servers provided by different vendors.

The mapping is based on the Java-to-IDL mapping. The specification has the following parts: mapping of distribution-related aspects, the mapping of naming conventions, the mapping of transactions, and the mapping of security. We explain each of these aspects in the following sections. Since the mapping uses new IDL features introduced by the OMG's Object-by-Value specification, interoperability with other programming languages requires CORBA 2.3-compliant ORBs.

## Mapping for Distribution

An enterprise bean has two interfaces that are remotely accessible: the remote interface and the home interface. Applying the Java/IDL mapping to these interfaces results in corresponding IDL specifications. The base classes defined in the EJB specification are mapped to IDL in the same manner.

We explain generation and use of IDL interfaces to enterprise with the ATM session bean introduced in Chapter 1. By applying the Java/IDL mapping to the home and the remote interface, we get the following IDL interface.

```
module vogel {
 module transaction {
  module chapter1 {
   module ejb {

    valuetype InsufficientFundsException : ::java::lang::Exception {};

    exception InsufficientFundsEx {
     ::vogel::transaction::chapter1::ejb::InsufficientFundsException value;
    };

    interface Atm : ::javax::ejb::EJBObject{

     void transfer (in string arg0, in string arg1, in float arg2)
      raises (::vogel::transaction::chapter1::ejb::InsufficientFundsEx);
    };

    interface AtmHome : ::javax::ejb::EJBHome {

     ::vogel::transaction::chapter1::ejb::Atm create ()
      raises (::javax::ejb::CreateEx);
    };
};};};};
```

## Mapping for Naming

A CORBA-based EJB runtime environment that wants to enable any CORBA clients to access enterprise beans must use the CORBA Naming Service for publishing and resolving the home interfaces of the enterprise beans. The runtime can use the CORBA Naming Service directly or indirectly via JNDI and its standard mapping to the CORBA Naming Service.

JNDI names have a string representation of the following form "directory1/directory2/.../directoryN/objectName". The CORBA Naming Service defines names as a sequence of name components.

```
typedef string Istring;

  struct NameComponent {
   Istring id;
   Istring kind;
  };

  typedef sequence<NameComponent> Name;
```

Each "/" separated name of a JNDI string name is mapped to a name component; the leftmost component is the first entry in the CORBA Naming Service name

A JNDI string name is relative to some naming context, which we call the *JNDI root context.* The JNDI root context corresponds to a CORBA Naming Service initial context. CORBA Naming Service names are relative to the CORBA initial context.

A CORBA program obtains an initial CORBA Naming Service naming context by calling resolve_initial_references("NameService") on the ORB (pseudo) object. The CORBA Naming Service does not prescribe a rooted graph for organizing naming context and, hence, the notion of a root context does not apply. Which context is returned by resolve_initial_references() depends on the initialization of the ORB.

For example, a C++ Client could locate the home interface to our `ATMSession` bean, which has been registered with a JNDI string name "vogel/transaction/chapter1/corbaEjb/atm". First we obtain initial naming context.

```
Object_ptr obj = orb->resolve_initial_refernces("NameService");
NamingContext initialNamingContext= NamingContext.narrow( obj );
if( current == NULL ) {
  cerr << "Couldn't initial naming context" << endl;
  exit( 1 );
}
```

Then we create a CORBA Naming Service name and initialize it according to the mapping explained previously.

```
Name name = new Name( 1 );
name[0].id = "atm";
name[0].kind = "";
```

Now we resolve the name on the initial naming context. We assume that we have initialized so that we have context of the naming domain of the enterprise bean. We narrow the resulting CORBA object to the expected type and make sure that the narrow was successful.

```
Object_ptr obj = initialNamingContext->resolve( name );
ATMSessionHome_ptr atmSessionHome = ATMSessionHome.narrow( obj );
if( atmSessionHome == NULL ) {
  cerr << "Couldn't narrow to ATMSessionHome" << endl;
  exit( 1 );
}
```

## Mapping for Transaction

A CORBA-based EJB runtime environment that wants to enable any CORBA client to participate in a transaction involving enterprise beans must use the CORBA Object Transaction Service for transaction control.

When an enterprise bean is deployed it can be installed with different transaction policies. The policy is defined in the enterprise bean's control descriptor. If the policy is TX_NOT_SUPPORTED, the enterprise does not support transactions, and we don't have to worry about the mapping of transactions to CORBA.

If the transaction policy is set to a different value, the enterprise bean must be instructed to interoperate with the CORBA Object Transaction Service. The following rules have been defined for transactional enterprise beans: A CORBA client invokes an enterprise through stubs generated from the IDL interfaces for the enterprise bean's remote and home interface. If the client is involved in a transaction, it uses the interfaces provided by CORBA Object Transaction Service. Details on the explicit transaction management are explained later in the chapter. For example, a C++ Client could invoke the `ATMSession` bean defined and located in the previous example.

```
try {
  …
  // obtain transaction current
  Object_ptr obj = orb->resolve_initial_refernces("Current");
  Current current = Current.narrow( obj );
  if( current == NULL ) {
    cerr << "Couldn't resolve current" << endl;
    exit( 1 );
  }

  // execute transaction
  try {
    current->begin();
    atmSession->transfer("checking", "saving", 100.00 );
    current->commit( 0 );
  } catch( … ) {
    current->rollback();
  }
}
catch( … ) {
  …
}
```

## Mapping for Security

Security aspects of the EJB specification are mainly focused on controlling the access to enterprise beans, as explained earlier in the chapter. CORBA defines a number of ways to define the identities, including the following cases:

**Plain IIOP.** CORBA's principal interface was deprecated in early 1998. The principal interface was intended for determining the identity of a client. However, the authors of the CORBA security services decided to choose a different approach.

The GIOP specification contains a component called *service context*, which is an array of an/value pair. The identifier is a CORBA long and the value is a sequence of octet. Among other purposes, entries in the service context can be used to identify a caller.

**Secure IIOP.** The CORBA security specification defines an opaque data type for the identity. The real type of the identity is determined by the chosen security mechanism; for example, GSS Kerberos, SPKM, or CSI-ECMA.

**IIOP over SSL.** SSL uses X.509 certificates to identify servers and, optionally, clients. When a server requests a client certificate, the server can use the certificate as a client identity.

CHAPTER

6

# Programming with EJB

In this chapter we use EJB to build the same flight-booking application as in Chapter 4, "Programming with OTS." In the case of EJB, the specification already defines the most significant design patterns: stateless and stateful session beans and entity beans. We have already introduced and explained these patterns in Chapter 1, "Quick Start to EJB, JTS, and OTS," and Chapter 5, "Understanding Enterprise JavaBeans." Although there are similarities between the CORBA/OTS patterns and the EJB patterns, it is important to note that CORBA design approaches are not directly applicable to EJB. In this chapter we explain some of the nuances in designing EJB applications.

This chapter has the following structure. First, we explain the EJB-based architecture of the application. Then we follow the tasks and roles defined in the EJB specification: providing Enterprise JavaBeans, assembling the application, deploying the Enterprise JavaBeans, and administrating the application.

## Application Architecture

We define the following enterprise beans for our flight-booking system as illustrated in Figure 6.1.

**Travel Agent** is a stateful session bean. It is the entry point for clients and also acts as a proxy for services provided by other enterprise beans which are not directly exposed to the client.

**Booking Business Object (BookingBO)** is a stateful session bean. It is the essential business object for the application. It coordinates the transactions between various enterprise beans associated with a flight booking, and caches data.

**Booking** is an entity bean. It represents a booking entry in the travel agent's database. This entry does not contain all the data for a booking, but the primary keys into the other databases where the remaining data is stored. The booking entity bean is implemented using bean-managed persistence.

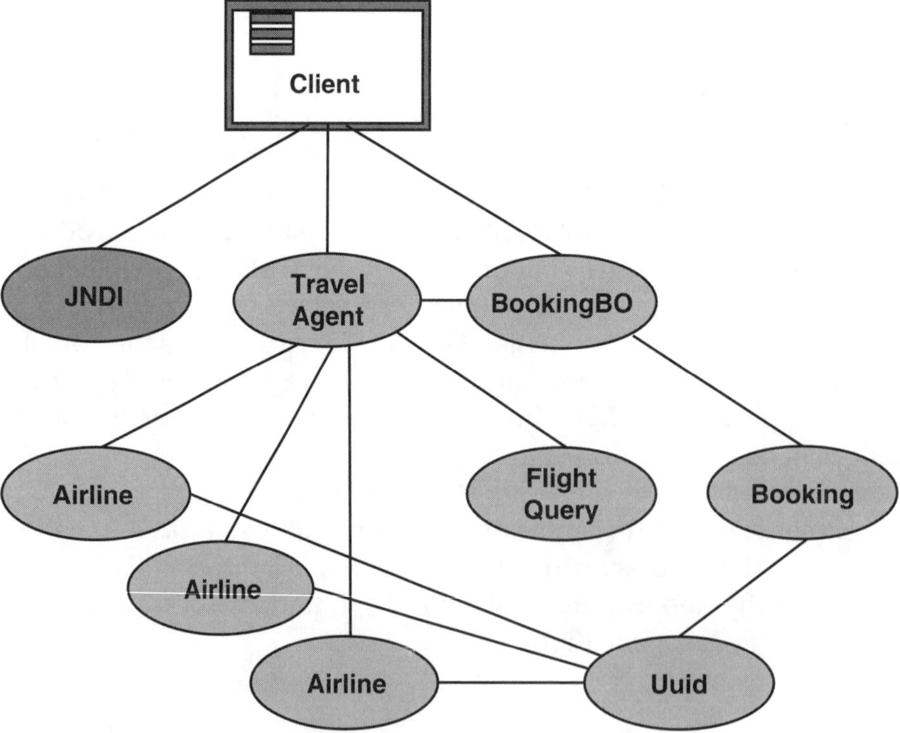


**Figure 6.1** Application architecture.

**Airline** is a stateless session bean. This enterprise bean provides access to an airline's database, including the capability of making and canceling bookings with this airline.

**Flight Query** is a stateless session bean. The query enterprise bean provides read-only access to a database, which stores the flight information for all airlines.

**Uuid** is an entity bean. The Uuid enterprise bean generates unique identifiers. It is implemented using container-managed persistence.

The EJB specification prescribes the Java Naming and Directory Interface (JNDI) as the API for locating the home interface. Figure 6.1 shows all the enterprise beans of the application as well as JNDI. It also illustrates the relationship between the various enterprise beans of the application.

A typical configuration would involve a number of different travel agent objects representing different agencies, a number of replicated query objects (replicated for load balancing and fault tolerance), and one or more airline objects for each airline. We explain configuration options in greater detail toward the end of the chapter.

We reuse the database tables we already defined and explained in Chapter 4, "Programming with OTS."

## Providing the Enterprise Beans

In this section, for each enterprise bean we specify the home and remote interfaces and explain their implementations. We also discuss design patterns and point out EJB-related design issues. The EJB specification defines a framework for building distributed applications. This is quite useful for a number of standard tasks. However, the framework restricts your capabilities for advanced design solutions.

### Java Classes for Data Types

Before we go into the design and implementation of the enterprise beans, we have to define a number of Java classes. These classes define the type of data, which is passed as parameters or as results of enterprise bean methods.

All of these types have been defined in a similar way as in the Chapter 4 example. There, the data types have been represented as IDL structs.

Here we define classes with public fields. These classes have a trivial and full-initializing constructor. The classes must implement `java.io.Serializable`, which indicates that they can be marshaled for remote invocations.

## *Airline Data Types*

There are a number of data types defined in the package `vogel.transaction.chapter6.airlines`. It contains data types and enterprise beans for airlines. We explain the data types in detail in the sections following. Each class defines a `toString()` method that creates a string representation of the respective class. For brevity, we have omitted repeating the explanation for this method in individual classes. Similarly, we have omitted the explanations of the constructors in each class.

### Simple Date

The class `SimpleDate` is defined in the package `vogel.transaction.chapter6.airlines`. The class has public fields for the day, month, year, hour, and minute to describe a simple date. The second constructor fully initializes the object. Finally, we have a `toString()` method, which creates a string representation of the simple date.

```
package vogel.transaction.chapter6.airlines;

public class SimpleDate
  implements java.io.Serializable {

  public int day;
  public int month;
  public int year;
  public int hour;
  public int minute;

  public SimpleDate() {}

  public SimpleDate(
    int day, int month, int year, int hour, int minute ){
    this.day = day;
    this.month = month;
    this.year = year;
    this.hour = hour;
    this.minute = minute;
  }

  public String toString() {
```

```
      return new String(
        month + "/" + day + "/" + year + " " +
        hour + ":" + minute );
    }
  }
```

### Person

The class `Person` is defined in the package `vogel.transaction.chapter6.airlines`. The class has public fields for title, first name, middle initial, and last name for describing a person.

```
package vogel.transaction.chapter6.airlines;

public class Person
  implements java.io.Serializable {

  public String title;
  public String firstName;
  public String middleInitial;
  public String lastName;

  ...
}
```

### Flight

The class `Flight` has public fields for the flight number, the departing and arriving airport, the departure and arrival date/time, the type of the aircraft, and the price for this leg. We have simplified the approach to pricing. Airlines have much more sophisticated rules to determine the price of a flight. Note that a flight just describes a direct connection from one airport to another. Often, a full flight is composed of multiple legs. A composite flight is described by an array of `Flight` objects.

```
package vogel.transaction.chapter6.airlines;

public class Flight
  implements java.io.Serializable {

  public String flightNumber;
  public String departingAirport;
  public String arrivingAirport;
  public SimpleDate departureDate;
  public SimpleDate arrivalDate;
  public String aircraft;
  public float price;
```

```
    ...
}
```

### Leg Record

The class `LegRecord` has public fields for the identifier for the leg, the flight, and the person associated with the flight.

```
package vogel.transaction.chapter6.airlines;

final public class LegRecord
  implements java.io.Serializable {

  public String id;
  public Flight leg;
  public Person passenger;


    ...
}
```

## *Travel Agent Data Types*

There are a number of data types defined in the package `vogel.transaction.chapter6.travelAgent`. This package contains data types and enterprise beans for travel agents.

### TA Booking Record

The class `TaBookingRecord` defines all the data, which is stored for a booking in the travel agent's database. The data is defined in the public fields, which are a label displayed for a booking, the identifier of the booking, the user id, and an array of airline identifiers for the price of a complete flight. The identifier is the primary key for the booking in the travel agent's database. The airline identifiers are primary keys for the respective airline's databases.

```
package vogel.transaction.chapter6.travelAgent;

final public class TaBookingRecord {

  public java.lang.String label;
  public java.lang.String id;
  public java.lang.String userId;
  public java.lang.String[] airlineIds;
```

```
    public float confirmedPrice;

    …
  }
```

### Booking Request

The class `BookingRequest` has public fields for the label displayed for the booking, an array of flight objects as described earlier, a person as described earlier, and a confirmed price for the whole flight. A booking request is sent from the client to the travel agent, which then handles the request by attempting to make the requested booking.

```
package vogel.transaction.chapter6.travelAgent;

import vogel.transaction.chapter6.airlines.*;

public class BookingRequest
  implements java.io.Serializable {

  public String label;
  public Flight[] aComposedFlight;
  public Person passenger;
  public float confirmedPrice;

  …
}
```

### Booking Record

The class `BookingRecord` extends `BookingRequest`. It defines additional public fields for the unique identifier of a booking, the user id for the person whom the booking is for, and a reference to the booking object and the booking business object (enterprise beans). The unique identifier is the primary key for the travel agent's database. A booking record contains the complete data associated with a booking.

```
package vogel.transaction.chapter6.travelAgent;

import vogel.transaction.chapter6.airlines.*;

public class BookingRecord
  extends BookingRequest
  implements java.io.Serializable {

  public String id;
  public String userId;
```

```
    public Booking bookingObj;
    public BookingBO bookingBoObj;
    ...
}
```

## Travel Agent

The travel agent is a stateful session bean. The travel agent provides a distinguished session object for each of the clients, as illustrated in Figure 6.2. The session bean's home interface provides the factory functionality, and the bean's remote interface provides the business functionality.

The interface and classes, which comprise the travel agent enterprise bean, are in the package `vogel.transaction.chapter6.travelAgent`.

### *Home Interface*

The home interface is a public Java interface that must extend `EJBHome`. The travel agent's home interface defines a single `create()` method. This must throw the exceptions `RemoteException` and `CreateException`.

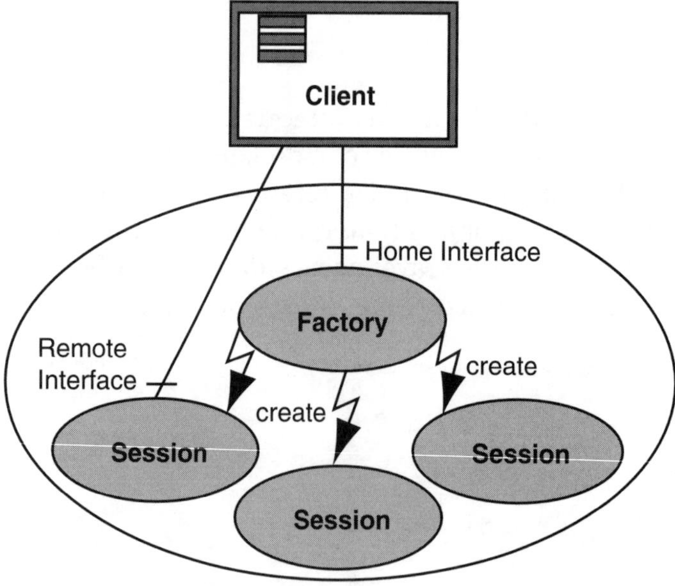


**Figure 6.2** Stateful session pattern.

```
package vogel.transaction.chapter6.travelAgent;

public interface TravelAgentHome extends javax.ejb.EJBHome {

  TravelAgent create(String userId, String password)
    throws java.rmi.RemoteException, javax.ejb.CreateException;
}
```

Usually, the `create()` method involves some authorization. Client authentication and instance-based access control are not within the scope of the EJB specification 1.0. Hence, we define two parameters for a user id and a password, which the session bean can use to authenticate the client and decide if the client is authorized to obtain a session. When sending passwords over the wire you should make certain that your communication channel is secured; for example, by an RMI over IIOP over SSL connection. Alternatively, X.500 client certificates could be used to identify the client. We would prefer that the EJB infrastructure take care of the client authentication and authorization.

### Remote Interface

The remote interface is a public Java interface that must extend `EJBObject`. It defines the application-specific or business methods of the enterprise bean. First we import the classes (for data types) from the package `vogel.transaction.chapter6.airlines`. These classes are used as parameters and result types for the methods of the remote interface.

```
package vogel.transaction.chapter6.travelAgent;

import vogel.transaction.chapter6.airlines.*;

public interface TravelAgent extends javax.ejb.EJBObject {

  public BookingBOHome getBookingBOHome()
    throws java.rmi.RemoteException;
```

The method `getBookingBOHome()` returns the reference to the home interface of the booking business object enterprise bean. This will allow the client to directly create and manipulate the booking business objects.

```
  public java.util.Vector findAllBookingRecords()
    throws java.rmi.RemoteException;
```

**DESIGN DISCUSSION—RETURNING VECTORS**

**Using vectors is a convenient programming practice in Java. The problem is that when a vector is defined in an external interface, the element type is not exposed. That means the contract between the enterprise bean and a client becomes weak. An alternative design is to use arrays, which are typed. That is equivalent to using CORBA sequences, which are mapped to Java arrays. Arrays, however, are not as convenient to use as vectors. Another design alternative would be to subclass the Java vector class by adding typed put and get methods. However, this again requires additional programming effort. The same discussion applies to other collection types.**

The method `findAllBookingRecords()` returns data about all bookings made by the user who is associated with this travel agent's session. The method returns a vector of booking records.

```
public java.util.Vector queryAvailableFlights(
    String from,
    String to,
    SimpleDate d )
    throws java.rmi.RemoteException;
}
```

The method `queryAvailableFlights()` returns a vector containing `Flight` objects. The travel agent is purely acting as a proxy to the flight query enterprise bean, which we explain next.

### Implementation

The implementation of the travel agent enterprise bean is provided by the class `TravelAgentBean`. A bean implementation class usually has a number of distinct parts.

**DESIGN DISCUSSION—PROXYING FUNCTIONALITY**

**The travel agent is acting as a proxy to the query enterprise bean. This design adds some overhead and may lead to some performance degradation due to an extra hop when a client accesses the query enterprise bean. The advantage of proxying is in the access control. The query enterprise bean may be provided and run by another business in a different security domain. In this domain, the customers of a specific travel agent and their access rights are unknown. Only travel agents and their access rights are covered by these security domains. Proxying allows you to extend access control from the query security domain to the travel agent's security domain.**

**Implementing home functionality.** The create and find methods as defined in the home interface provide factory type functionality. Note that the bean implementation class is not in an "implements" relationship to the home interface, and there is a set of rules that define the mapping between the methods in the home interface and the methods in the bean implementation class.

**Implementing remote functionality.** The implementation of the methods defined in the remote interface. Although the bean implementation class does not formally implement the remote interface, it keeps the names and signatures of the methods defined in the remote interface.

**Implementing the EJB specific interfaces.** A bean implementation class must implement the interfaces `javax.ejb.SessionBean` or `javax.ejb.EntityBean`, for session beans or entity beans, respectively. Optionally, the interface `javax.ejb.SessionSynchronization` may also be implemented. These interfaces are fully explained in Chapter 5, "Understanding Enterprise JavaBeans."

**Private supporting methods.** The bean implementation class can have any number of auxiliary methods. Although not required by the EJB specification, it is a good practice to declare these as `private`. Additionally, the bean implementation can be subclassed.

The class `TravelAgentBean` implements a stateful session bean, and hence must implement the interface `javax.ejb.SessionBean`. Optionally, the class may implement the interface `javax.ejb.SessionSynchronization`. This allows the bean implementer to intercept the transactions; for example, for persistifying cached values in the database. For simplicity, the travel agent implementation does not implement this interface.

```
package vogel.transaction.chapter6.travelAgent;

import vogel.transaction.chapter6.airlines.*;
import vogel.transaction.chapter6.schedule.*;

public class TravelAgentBean
  implements SessionBean {

  private SessionContext sessionContext;

  private javax.naming.Context root;
```

```
private Query query;
private BookingHome bookingHome;
private BookingBOHome bookingBOHome;

private String travelAgentName;

private String userId;
```

We declare a number of private variables. Usually, all session beans keep a reference to the session context. All of the other variables are application specific.

### Implementing the Home Interface

We have defined a single `create()` method in the travel agent's home interface. Correspondingly, we must implement an `ejbCreate()` method with the same arguments. The two methods differ, however, in the result type. While the `create()` method returns a reference to a remote interface, the `ejbCreate()` method returns `void`.

Note that the `ejbCreate()` method is used for the initialization for the new session instance. The current EJB specification does not allow for initializing the factory, which is implementing the home interface—that leads to a potential performance bottleneck. Instead of doing JNDI lookups once, we must repeat them every time we create a new session instance.

First, we get the environment as defined in the deployment descriptor. The JNDI specification does not specify the class for initializing a JNDI service. These classes vary from implementation to implementation. To keep our bean code portable we use an environment property to determine the name of that class. This allows us to adapt the bean to a different JNDI implementation by only changing values in the deployment descriptor. Once we have the property from the environment, we get the root context of our JNDI implementation.

```
public void ejbCreate( String userId, String password )
  throws RemoteException, CreateException {

  try {

    java.util.Hashtable env = new java.util.Hashtable();
    java.util.Properties properties = sessionContext.getEnvironment();
    String contextClassName =
      properties.getProperty("context-class-name");
    env.put( javax.naming.Context.INITIAL_CONTEXT_FACTORY,
      contextClassName );
    root = new javax.naming.InitialContext(env);
```

We also set the user id for the session. The EJB specification version 1.0 defines the method `getCallerIdentity()` on the interface `javax.ejb.EJBContext`. The specification of EJB security is currently under revision and does not address all security aspects. Specifically, the authentication of client identities is not addressed by the EJB specification.

In this `ejbCreate()` method we just provide the hooks to implement our own authentication. In this implementation we do not use the password to perform an authentication of the user. However, the identity could be checked against some security or directory service. You could make an IIOP call to the directory service defined and implemented in Chapter 4, "Programming with OTS." Alternatively, one could use a JNDI to an LDAP or other directory service.

```
this.userId = userId;
```

Often an object needs to know its identity in the same terms as it is known to external entities. For EJB, this is a JNDI name. The EJB specification does not provide an API for a bean instance to obtain its own name, which is defined in the deployment descriptor. To work around this problem we have copied the name in a property called "jndi-name" defined as part of the environment in the deployment descriptor. We obtain the value of the property and store it in an instance variable.

```
travelAgentName = properties.getProperty("jndi-name");
```

Next, we initialize the home interfaces and remote interfaces for the travel agent session. We already have the JNDI root context. We look up the query home interface to get a reference to the remote interface using the create() method. It only makes sense to get the remote interface for stateless session beans. For all other enterprise beans we get only the home interfaces. As you can see, we are already making use of the travel agent's name, which is used as a context name in our JNDI structure. Finally, we catch naming exceptions and convert them to remote exceptions. Create and remote exceptions are directly propagated to the caller.

```
QueryHome queryHome = (QueryHome) root.lookup( "Schedule/Query" );
query = queryHome.create();

bookingHome = (BookingHome) root.lookup(
  travelAgentName + "/BookingHome" );

bookingBOHome = (BookingBOHome) root.lookup(
```

```
        travelAgentName + "/BookingBOHome" );

    }
    catch( javax.naming.NamingException ne ) {
      java.rmi.RemoteException re = new java.rmi.RemoteException(
        "home interface not registered with JNDI: " + ne );
      throw re;
    }
    return;
  }
```

#### Implementing the Remote Interface

Now we implement the business methods defined in the remote interface. Although the implementation class is not in a formal *implement* relationship with the corresponding remote interface, the signatures of the methods are the same. The method `getBookingHome()` returns the home interface for booking business objects. Alternatively, a client could look up the interface in the naming service; however, it is more convenient for the client to just use the naming service for the initial boot strapping. We initialize the `bookingBOHome` interface in the `ejbCreate()` method as shown next.

```
public BookingBOHome getBookingHome()
    throws RemoteException {

    return bookingBOHome;
  }
```

The method `findAllBookingRecords()` allows a client to retrieve information about all bookings it has made in the past. The implementation has a number of steps: First, we invoke the find method `findAllBookings()` on the booking home interface. The booking home interface is initialized in the `ejbCreate()` method. The method `findAllBookings()` takes the user id as an argument and returns an enumeration of references to booking entity beans. Second, we create a booking business object for each of the booking entity beans. Third, we invoke the method `getBookingData()` on the booking business object and add the resulting `BookingRecord` objects to a vector. We also set the reference to the booking business object in the booking record. Finally, we return the vector.

We catch create and finder exceptions and propagate them by embedding them in a remote exception. Remote exceptions are propagated directly.

```
public java.util.Vector findAllBookingRecords()
  throws RemoteException {

  try {
    java.util.Vector v = new java.util.Vector();
    java.util.Enumeration bookingEnumeration =
      bookingHome.findAllBookings( userId );
    while( bookingEnumeration.hasMoreElements() ) {
      Booking b = (Booking) bookingEnumeration.nextElement();
      BookingBO bookingBO = bookingBOHome.create( b );
      BookingRecord bookingRecord = bookingBO.getBookingData();
      bookingRecord.bookingBoObj = bookingBO;
      v.addElement( bookingRecord );
      v.addElement(bookingBO.getBookingData());
    }
    return v;
  }
  catch( CreateException ce ) {
    throw new RemoteException( "cannot create booking BOs", ce );
  }
  catch( FinderException fe ) {
    throw new RemoteException( "cannot find bookings", fe );
  }
}
```

The method `queryAvailableFlights()` delegates the functionality to the query enterprise bean. We invoke the same method on the query's remote interface and return the resulting vector.

```
public Vector queryAvailableFlights(
  String from,
  String to,
  SimpleDate d )
  throws RemoteException {

  return query.queryAvailableFlights( from, to, d );

}
```

The method `getFlightIterator()` also proxies the functionality provided by the query enterprise bean. Again, we invoke the same method on the query's remote interface and return the resulting iterator, which is a stateful session bean as explained next.

```
public QueryIterator getFlightIterator(
  String from,
  String to,
  SimpleDate departureDate )
  throws java.rmi.RemoteException {
```

```
        return query.getFlightIterator( from, to, departureDate );
    }
```

### Implementing the SessionBean Interface

The interface SessionBean defines the following methods. These methods are called by the container on the enterprise bean at certain points in the bean's life cycle, as explained in Chapter 5. The implementation of these methods allows the programmer to customize the behavior in the enterprise bean's life cycle.

```
    void setSessionContext(SessionContext sessionContext)
        throws RemoteException {
        this.sessionContext = sessionContext;
    }
```

The method `setSessionContext()` is called by the container after a new session instance is created and before the method `ejbCreate()` is called. The typical implementation is to store reference to the session context. This allows the instance to access the environment and to control transactional behavior. The variable `sessionContext` should not be declared as transient to retain its value of deactivation and reactivation cycles.

Furthermore, there are methods that allow you to intercept the deactivation and reactivation of the bean instance. The methods `ejbPassivate()`and `ejbActivate()` allow the programmer to add custom code when a session object is deactivated or reactivated, respectively. Usually these methods are used to open and close custom resources. In our example, we do not have to add any custom code. The method `ejbRemove()` is invoked when the user calls `remove()`. The implementation of the method allows the programmer to add custom cleanup code, which we don't need in our example.

```
public void ejbActivate() throws RemoteException {}

    public void ejbPassivate() throws RemoteException {}

    public void ejbRemove() throws RemoteException {}
}
```

## Booking Entity

The booking bean is an entity bean. As for all kinds of enterprise beans, we must provide the home and the remote interface, and an implementation class for the enterprise bean. Since it is an entity bean, we must also provide a primary key class.

An entity bean is usually the runtime representation of one or multiple rows in a data storage. The booking entity bean represents one row in the travel agent's database. Note that the booking entity bean does not contain the full booking information. Further, data associated with a booking is stored in the airlines' databases and the flight query databases. The booking entity bean is complete in the sense that it keeps primary keys to other databases but does not access the associated data directly.

Figure 6.3 illustrates the scenario in which a flight is composed of two legs, serviced by United and Lufthansa, respectively. The travel agent database, and hence the booking entity bean, holds the primary keys for the other databases, depicted by the thin lines in Figure 6.3. Later in the chapter, we explain how the booking business object handles the different data sources.

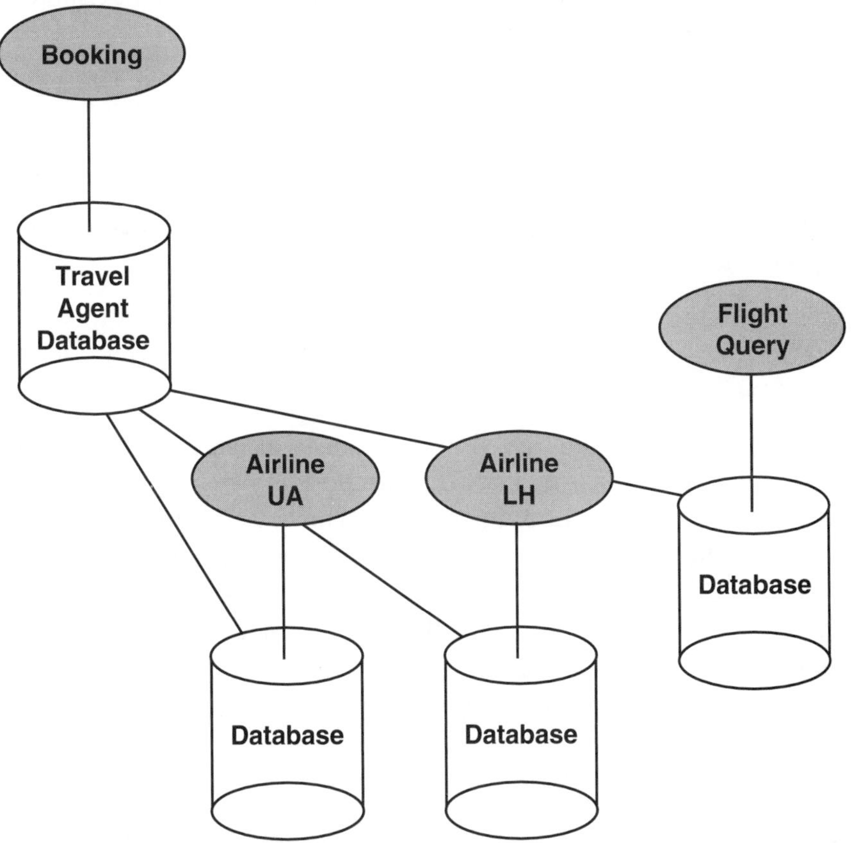


**Figure 6.3** Booking entity bean and its relationships.

### Home Interface

The home interface is defined as a public Java interface that extends `EJBHome`. Our booking home interface defines one `create()` and two `find()` methods. All methods must throw the exception `RemoteException`. The `create()` and the `find()` methods must throw the exceptions `CreateException` and `FinderException`, respectively.

```
package vogel.transaction.chapter6.travelAgent;

import vogel.transaction.chapter6.airlines.*;

public interface BookingHome extends javax.ejb.EJBHome {

  Booking create()
    throws java.rmi.RemoteException, javax.ejb.CreateException;
```

The `create()` method without an argument creates a noninitialized booking bean. The values are set with the business methods defined on the remote interface as shown here:

```
  Booking findByPrimaryKey( BookingPK key )
    throws java.rmi.RemoteException, javax.ejb.FinderException;
```

The method `findByPrimaryKey()` is required for all entity beans. It returns the entity bean identified by the primary key. The primary key class is defined here:

```
  java.util.Enumeration findAllBookings( String userId )
    throws java.rmi.RemoteException, javax.ejb.FinderException;
}
```

The EJB specification requires find methods to either return a specific object or a collection of objects. The method `findAllBookings()` returns an enumeration of booking objects. The enumeration type is the only JDK1.1 collection type. Java 2 provides a wider set of collection types including lists and sets. As a selection criterion for the find method, we specify the identifier of the person for whom the bookings are made. The enumeration is expected to contain references to the remote interface of `Booking` enterprise beans.

### Remote Interface

The remote interface is a public Java interface that extends `EJBObject`. It defines the application-specific or business methods of the enterprise bean. First, we import the classes from the package `vogel.transaction.chapter6.airlines`. These classes are used as parameters and result types for the methods of the remote interface.

```
package vogel.transaction.chapter6.travelAgent;

import vogel.transaction.chapter6.airlines.*;

public interface Booking extends javax.ejb.EJBObject {

  public TaBookingRecord getBookingData()
    throws java.rmi.RemoteException;
```

The method `getBookingData()` returns all the data associated with this booking.

```
  public void setBookingData( TaBookingRecord taBookingRecord )
    throws java.rmi.RemoteException;
}
```

The method `setBookingData()` overwrites the booking data.

## DESIGN DISCUSSION—FIND ALL

**A common design practice is to find all database entries that match a certain criterion; for example, the last name "Smith." Select some significant data like the complete name, social security number, and address, and present this data to the user for the selection of the entry of interest. Then the user obtains the complete entry. Using this design pattern with entity beans means:**

- Get all customers named "Smith":

```
Enumeration customerEnumeration =
  CustomerHome.findByLastName( "Smith" );
```

- Get significant data; for example, first name, middle initial, last name, and SSN.

```
while( customerEnumeration.hasNext() ) {
  Customer c = (Customer) nextElement();
  c.getMinimalCustomerData();
}
```

**Assuming that the customer object is designed and implemented as an entity bean with bean-managed persistence, the code just shown will result in 1 SQL select for findByLastName() and n SQL select and n SQL updates for getting the customer data, where n is the number of customers with the last name "Smith." A non-EJB implementation could have achieved the same effect with 1 SQL select and data caching. EJB containers providing container-managed persistence are not restricted by the specification and may provide optimized performance.**

### Primary Key Class

According to the EJB specification, the bean provider must define a primary key class for an entity bean. This class must implement `Serializable`. For container-managed entity beans, the specification states the following additional requirements:

- The class must be declared public.
- All fields must be declared public.
- The class must have a public default constructor.
- The names of the fields must be a subset of the names of the container-managed fields (container-managed fields only).

As primary key we use the public class `BookingPk`, which implements `Serializable`. The class defines a public variable `primaryKey` of type `String`. This variable is used as the primary key for the database table associated with a booking. The class has a public default constructor and a constructor, which allows for setting the value of the field.

```
package vogel.transaction.chapter6.travelAgent;

public class BookingPK
  implements java.io.Serializable {

  public String primaryKey;

  public BookingPK() {
  }

  public BookingPK( String id ) {
    primaryKey = id;
  }
}
```

### Implementation

The implementation of the booking enterprise bean is provided by the class `BookingBean`. The class `BookingBean` implements the interface `EntityBean`. We implement this bean with bean-managed persistence. The big difference between bean-managed persistence and container-managed persistence is that in bean-managed persistence, we provide the implementation of the methods to find, create, load, store, and remove beans. The implementation of the Uuid entity bean uses container-managed persistence and is shown later in the chapter.

We declare two private variables: one to keep the entity context of the bean instance, and one to keep the data associated with booking as `TaBookingRecord`.

```
package vogel.transaction.chapter6.travelAgent;

import vogel.transaction.chapter6.airlines.*;
import vogel.transaction.chapter6.schedule.*;

public class BookingBean
  implements EntityBean {

  private EntityContext entityContext;
  private TaBookingRecord taBookingRecord;
```

#### Implementing the Home Interface

The `create()` method defined in the home interface is implemented by the `ejbCreate()` method. It has no parameters. The method throws the exceptions `RemoteException` and `CreateException` as specified in the home interface.

The `ejbCreate()` method creates a new booking entity that only has a primary key but is not initialized with further data. We obtain a new primary key from the enterprise bean `Uuid` by issuing unique identifiers in the form of 8-character strings. We discuss the issue of generating identifiers and similar kind of services in an EJB context, which is somewhat problematic, later when we explain the Uuid enterprise bean.

To obtain a new id, we get the JNDI root context as explained earlier and look up the Uuid home interface. The Uuid enterprise bean is an entity bean, which is associated with a database table that has two columns: a primary key and an identifier. There is at most one entry in the table with a primary key equal to 1 and the identifier being the last identifier issued by the bean.

We get an entity bean by using the default find method. In the very rare case when the table is empty, the find method throws an exception and we create an entry using the create method. Once we have the reference to the remote interface we can invoke the method `newId()` to obtain a new identifier.

```
public BookingPK ejbCreate()
  throws RemoteException, CreateException {
  try {

    java.util.Hashtable env = new java.util.Hashtable();
```

```
java.util.Properties properties = entityContext.getEnvironment();
String contextClassName =
  properties.getProperty("context-class-name");
env.put( javax.naming.Context.INITIAL_CONTEXT_FACTORY,
  contextClassName );
javax.naming.Context root = new javax.naming.InitialContext(env);
UuidHome uuidHome = (UuidHome) root.lookup( "Apex/UuidHome" );
UuidPK pk = new UuidPK( "1" );
Uuid uuid;
try {
  uuid = uuidHome.findByPrimaryKey( pk );
}
catch( FinderException fe ) {
  uuid = uuidHome.create();
}
String id =  uuid.newId();
```

There is a potential race condition in the preceding code. When two clients try to get an identifier at the same time and their find methods fail, the following could happen: The first client succeeds with the create. Consequently, the second client fails with the create and hence would not obtain the uuid remote interface and hence no identifier. We have not addressed this problem in the code as it would occur only once when bootstrapping the system and we don't consider the effect critical.

Next we store the new id in the travel agent's database. You could defer this database operation to the time when the complete record is stored, but the EJB entity bean pattern requires us to create a database entry in the `ejbCreate()` method. Otherwise, the subsequent `ejbLoad()` method will fail.

We obtain a SQL connection and then create a statement. We insert a new row in the table, which only contains the primary key. Upon the completion of the SQL insert we return a primary key for the newly created bean. The implementation of the primary key class is explained later in the chapter.

```
    Connection connection = getConnection();
    Statement statement = connection.createStatement();
    statement.executeUpdate(
      "insert into ta_booking ( id ) values( '" + id + "' )" );
    statement.close();
    connection.close();

    return new BookingPK( id );
  }
  catch( javax.naming.NamingException ne ) {
    throw new RemoteException(
```

```
        "Booking - ejbCreate(): naming error: " + ne );
    }
    catch( java.sql.SQLException se ) {
      throw new RemoteException(
        "Booking - ejbCreate(): database access error: " + se );
    }
  }
```

We catch naming and SQL exceptions and convert them to remote exceptions. Remote and create exceptions are propagated directly.

We also have to implement a corresponding `ejbPostCreate()` method. That method provides access to the object reference of the newly created entity bean. In our example, we leave the method implementation empty.

```
public void ejbPostCreate(){}
```

The `ejbFindByPrimaryKey()` method implements the home interface's `findByPrimaryKey()` method, and it throws the exceptions `RemoteException` and `FinderException`. Unlike `findByPrimaryKey()`,`ejbFindByPrimaryKey()` returns the primary key of the entity bean instead of the object reference.

```
public BookingPK ejbFindByPrimaryKey( BookingPK pk )
  throws RemoteException, FinderException {

  String bookingId = pk.primaryKey;
```

First, we extract the primary key from the primary key object. Then we get a SQL connection and a statement and create a SQL select. Now we execute the select query and process the results by converting the database types in our application to the specific data types. We do not really process the result set, we just make sure that there is a matching entry in the result set. If the result is null or empty we throw a finder exception. In the case of an occurring SQL exception we throw a remote exception. Finally, we return the primary key.

```
  try {
    Connection connection = getConnection();
    Statement statement = connection.createStatement();
    ResultSet resultSet = statement.executeQuery(
      "select * from TA_BOOKING where ID = '" + bookingId + "'"  );
    if( !resultSet.next() ) {
      System.out.println("no entries in result set");
      throw new FinderException("no entries in result set");
    }
```

```
        statement.close();
        connection.close();
      }
      catch( java.sql.SQLException se) {
        throw new RemoteException(
          "Booking - ejbFindByPrimaryKey(): database access error: " +
          se );
      }
      return pk;
    }
```

The `ejbFindAllBookings()` method implements the home interface's `findByAllBookings()` method. It throws the exceptions `RemoteException` and `FinderException` as specified in the home interface's corresponding method. Note that method `ejbFindByPrimaryKey()` returns an enumeration of primary keys instead of an enumeration of object reference as specified in home's find method.

We declare and create a vector to collect primary keys from the database. We obtain a connection and create a statement. Then we execute our select query.

```
  public java.util.Enumeration ejbFindAllBookings( String userId )
      throws RemoteException, FinderException {

      java.util.Vector pkVector = new java.util.Vector();
      try {
        Connection connection = getConnection();
        Statement statement = connection.createStatement();
        ResultSet resultSet = statement.executeQuery(
          "select ID from TA_BOOKING where USERID = '" + userId + "'"  );
```

We check to see if the result is null, and if so, we throw an exception. Otherwise, we loop through the result set, extract the identifiers for the matching bookings, and create primary key objects from them. We put the primary keys in the vector. Once we are finished with the result set, we close the statement and the connection. Now we must convert the vector to an enumeration.

```
  while( resultSet.next() ) {
          String id = resultSet.getString(1);
          BookingPK pk = new BookingPK( id );
          pkVector.addElement( pk );
        }
        statement.close();
        connection.close();

        return pkVector.elements();
```

```
    }
    catch( java.sql.SQLException se) {
      throw new RemoteException(
        "Booking - ejbCreate(): database access error: " + se );
    }
  }
```

### Implementing the Remote Interface

The business methods on the entity bean's remote interface, `setBookingData()` and `getBookingData()`, allow us to set and get the data associated with the entity bean. Their implementations are straightforward. We just return or update the booking bean's `taBookingRecord` variable. The persistence of the values is handled by the bean's `ejbLoad()` and `ejbStore()` methods, which are explained later in the chapter.

```
public TaBookingRecord getBookingData()
    throws RemoteException {

    return taBookingRecord;
  }

  public void setBookingData( TaBookingRecord taBookingRecord )
    throws RemoteException {

    this.taBookingRecord = taBookingRecord;
    return;
  }
```

### Implementing the EntityBean Interface

The methods defined in the interface `EntityBean` determine the bean's life cycle. Specifically, they deal with the manipulation of the entity context, the loading and storing of the entity bean's data, and the deletion of an entity bean.

The method `setEntityContext()` is invoked by the container when an entity is created and put into the ready pool. A typical implementation of this method is to store the entity context in an instance variable. The method `unsetEntityContext()` is invoked by the container when an entity bean ceases to exist. The usual implementation of this method is to set the entity context instance variable to null. Note that these methods are not associated with a particular data represented by an entity bean.

```
  public void setEntityContext( EntityContext entityContext )
    throws RemoteException  {

    this.entityContext = entityContext;
  }

  public void unsetEntityContext() throws RemoteException {

    entityContext = null;
  }
```

The method `ejbLoad()` is invoked by the container before a business method can be executed. It gets the most recent values from the travel agent's database. We get a connection and create a statement. Then we execute a select query, which is determined by the primary key. If the result is null, a remote exception is raised.

```
  public void ejbLoad()throws RemoteException {

    try {
      Connection connection = getConnection();
      Statement statement = connection.createStatement();

      ResultSet resultSet = statement.executeQuery(
        "select * from TA_BOOKING where ID = '" +
        (String)((BookingPK) entityContext.getPrimaryKey()).primaryKey +
        "'"  );
```

Now we get the data from the result set. We expect only one entry in the result entry. We create a new instance of the type `TaBooking-Record` and initialize it with data from the result set. The database stores the booking id issued by an airline for various legs of a flight in a single string. We extract the various 10-character segments and store them in an array. Finally, we close the statement and the connection. When a SQL exception occurs we propagate it as a remote exception.

```
      resultSet.next();

      taBookingRecord = new TaBookingRecord();

      taBookingRecord.id = resultSet.getString(1);
      taBookingRecord.label = resultSet.getString(2);
      taBookingRecord.userId = resultSet.getString(3);
      taBookingRecord.confirmedPrice = resultSet.getInt(5);

      String airlineIds = resultSet.getString(4);
      if( airlineIds != null ) {
        airlineIds = airlineIds.trim();
        int length = airlineIds.length() / 10;
```

```
      taBookingRecord.airlineIds = new String[ length ];
      for( int i = 0; i < length; i++ ) {
        taBookingRecord.airlineIds[i] =
          airlineIds.substring( i*10, (i+1)*10 );
      }
    }
    statement.close();
    connection.close();
    return;
  }
  catch( java.sql.SQLException se) {
    throw new RemoteException(
      "Booking ejbLoad(): database access error: " + se );
  }
}
```

The method `ejbStore()` stores an entity bean's data once a transaction is completed. We get a connection and a statement and execute a SQL update. According to our convention, we concatenate the identifiers for the various airline bookings associated into a single string, which is stored in the column `legIds`.

```
public void ejbStore()throws RemoteException {

  try {
    Connection connection = getConnection();
    Statement statement = connection.createStatement();

    String legIds = new String();
    for( int i = 0; i < taBookingRecord.airlineIds.length; i++ ) {
      legIds = legIds.concat( taBookingRecord.airlineIds[i] );
    }

    String sqlUpdate = new String(
      "update TA_BOOKING " +
      "set label = '" + taBookingRecord.label + "', " +
      "userId = '" + taBookingRecord.userId + "', " +
      "legIds = '" + legIds + "', " +
      "price = '" + taBookingRecord.confirmedPrice + "' " +
      "where id = '" + taBookingRecord.id + "'" );

    statement.executeUpdate( sqlUpdate );

    statement.close();
    connection.close();
  }
  catch( java.sql.SQLException se ) {
    throw new RemoteException(
      "Booking ejbStore(): database access error: ", se);
  }
}
```

Removing an entity bean means to delete its corresponding entry from the database. In the implementation of the method `ejbRemove()`, we get a connection, a statement, and execute a SQL delete, which is determined by the entity bean's primary key. We obtain the primary key from the entity context.

```
public void ejbRemove() throws RemoteException {
  try {
    Connection connection = getConnection();
    Statement statement = connection.createStatement();
    String sqlDelete = new String(
      "delete from TA_BOOKING where ID = " +
     (String)((BookingPK) entityContext.getPrimaryKey()).primaryKey );
    statement.executeUpdate( sqlDelete );
    statement.close();
    connection.close();
  }
  catch( java.sql.SQLException se ) {
    throw new RemoteException(
      "Booking ejbRemove(): database access error: ", se);
  }
}
```

Activation and deactivation of entity beans have different semantics compared with session beans. Activation means to move a bean instance from the pool to the ready state, and deactivation means to return it to the pool. Activation is immediately followed by `ejbLoad()`, and passivation follows the `ejbStore()`. The methods `ejbActivate()` and `ejbPassivate()` allow you to intercept the activation and deactivation of an entity bean. We don't have any use of these interception points and consequently do not implement the methods.

```
public void ejbActivate() throws java.rmi.RemoteException {}
public void ejbPassivate() throws java.rmi.RemoteException {}
```

### Implementing Private Methods

We have put the code for obtaining a JDBC connection in a private method. The implementation allows for controlling the URL for the database and the user and password via properties set in the deployment descriptor.

```
private Connection getConnection()
  throws java.sql.SQLException {
```

```
    java.util.Properties properties = entityContext.getEnvironment();
    String url = properties.getProperty("db-url");
    String username = properties.getProperty("db-username");
    String password = properties.getProperty("db-password");
    return DriverManager.getConnection(url, username, password);
}
```

## Booking Business Object

Earlier we explained the booking entity bean, which is a simple representation of data stored in the travel agent's database. The BookingBO enterprise bean introduced in this section is a complex business object that coordinates various data sources and caches data associated with a booking.

There are a number of similarities between the characteristics of the booking business object and the entity bean pattern. However, the entity model is too specialized to be applied for the complex business objects. Hence, we have specified the booking business object as a stateful session bean. Figure 6.4 illustrates the relationships among the booking business object, the booking entity bean, and other enterprise beans and data sources.

As illustrated in Figure 6.4, a booking business object `BookingBO` is created through its factory caused by the invocation of a create method on the home interface. The `BookingBO` session keeps a reference to the booking entity and caches the booking data. It also queries the other data sources, through their stateless session beans, and keeps the data in cache.

**DESIGN DISCUSSION—COMPLEX BUSINESS OBJECTS WITH EJB**

**While entity beans provide a database access layer, and stateful session beans provide client access layer, there is often a need for complex business objects between these two tiers. Complex business objects typically combine data from potentially different data sources with business logic. Business objects often cache data.**

**Some of the features defined in the entity bean's pattern like the create, find, and remove methods are very suitable for business objects. However, the pattern definition is too rigid for more general business objects.**

**Stateful session beans provide a reasonable but not a perfect design solution for such business objects.**

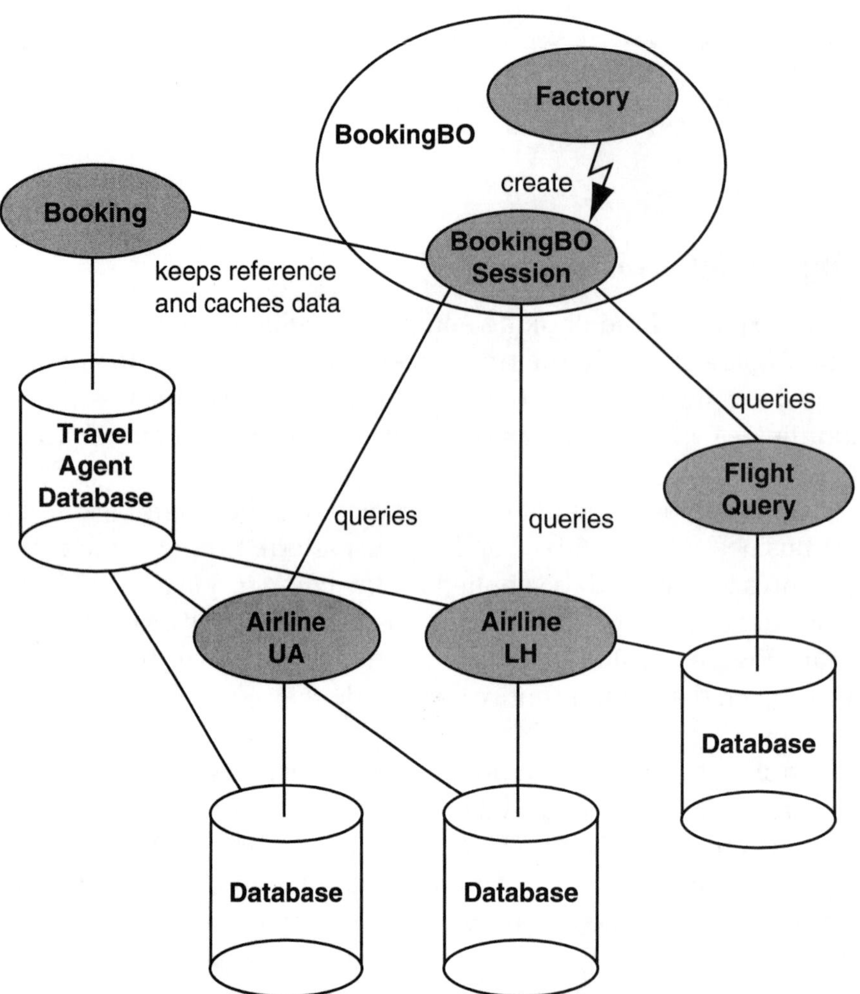


**Figure 6.4** Booking business object and its relationships.

## *Home Interface*

The home interface is defined as a public Java interface that extends `EJBHome`. The BookingBO home interface defines two `create()` methods. All methods on the home interface must throw the exception `RemoteException`. The `create()` method must also throw the exception `CreateException`.

```
package vogel.transaction.chapter6.travelAgent;

public interface BookingBOHome extends javax.ejb.EJBHome {
```

```
  BookingBO create( BookingRequest bookingRequest )
    throws java.rmi.RemoteException, javax.ejb.CreateException;
```

The preceding `create()` method creates a new BookingBO instance, which is initialized with the data from the booking request.

```
    BookingBO create( Booking booking )
    throws java.rmi.RemoteException, javax.ejb.CreateException;
}
```

The second `create()` method creates a BookingBO instance, which is initialized with data from the various databases. The reference to the booking entity is used to locate the appropriate data sources; in fact, it is more a finder method than a create method. However, the convention for session beans does not allow for finder methods on the home interface.

### *Remote Interface*

The remote interface is a public Java interface that extends `EJBObject`. It defines the application-specific or business methods of the enterprise bean. First, we import the classes from the package `vogel.transaction.chapter6.airlines`. These classes are used as parameters and result types for the methods of the remote interface.

```
package vogel.transaction.chapter6.travelAgent;

import vogel.transaction.chapter6.airlines.*;

public interface BookingBO extends javax.ejb.EJBObject {

  public BookingRecord getBookingData()
    throws java.rmi.RemoteException;

  public void setBookingData( BookingRecord bookingRecord )
    throws java.rmi.RemoteException;
}
```

The remote interface defines two business methods for accessing and modifying the data associated with a booking. If appropriate, there can be similar set and get methods added for a finer-grained access.

### *Implementation*

The class `BookingBOBean` provides the implementation of the booking business object enterprise bean. This business object is concerned with managing different data sources represented by entity beans (travel agent booking), stateless session beans (airlines and query), and caching data in the middle tier. We define a number of instance variables to hold the data.

```
package vogel.transaction.chapter6.travelAgent;

import vogel.transaction.chapter6.airlines.*;
import vogel.transaction.chapter6.schedule.*;

public class BookingBOBean
  implements SessionBean {

  private SessionContext sessionContext;
  private javax.naming.Context root;
  private Query query;
  private BookingHome bookingHome;
  private java.util.Hashtable airlines;
  private BookingRecord bookingRecord;
```

### Implementing the Home Interface

We have defined two `create()` methods, one to create a totally new booking business object and the other one to create a booking business object from the data stored in the different databases. Correspondingly, we have two `ejbCreate()` methods. The method to create a new booking business object takes a booking request and the user id as arguments. First, we initialize the home interfaces and stateless sessions, which we need to invoke. This is done in the private method `initializeHomes()`, which is explained later in the chapter. Then we create a new travel agent record and initialize it with the data available from the booking request.

```
public void ejbCreate( BookingRequest bookingRequest, String userId )
    throws java.rmi.RemoteException, javax.ejb.CreateException {

    initializeHomes();

    Booking booking = bookingHome.create();

    TaBookingRecord taBookingRecord = new TaBookingRecord();
    taBookingRecord.id  =
      ((BookingPK) booking.getPrimaryKey()).primaryKey;
    taBookingRecord.confirmedPrice = bookingRequest.confirmedPrice;
    taBookingRecord.label = bookingRequest.label;
    taBookingRecord.airlineIds =
      new String[ bookingRequest.aComposedFlight.length ];
    taBookingRecord.userId = userId;
```

The user identification is done using a user id that needs to be resolved. The user id is only meaningful in the travel agent's domain, and is not known to the airlines. One way to obtain user information would be to look up a person's record via JNDI; for example, from a LDAP server. However, when JNDI is front-ending a CORBA Naming Service, this approach does not work. Alternatively, one could make another database lookup using a stateless session bean. In the case where JNDI lookup fails, we use a hard-coded default solution.

```
try {
  bookingRequest.passenger = = (Person) root.lookup(
   "Apex/Customers/" + userId );
}
catch( javax.naming.NamingException ne ) {
  bookingRequest.passenger =
    new Person( "Mr", "Andreas", "", "Vogel" );
}
```

Now we go ahead and book the different legs with the associated airlines. We create and initialize a leg record. We get the airline id, which is formed by the first two characters of the flight number; for example, "UA" from "UA3208." Then we get the corresponding airline remote interface from a hashtable and book the leg with the airline. As a result, we get a booking id for the leg from the airline, which we store as a travel agent booking record.

```
      for( int i = 0; i <  bookingRequest.aComposedFlight.length; i++ ) {
        LegRecord legRecord = new LegRecord();
        legRecord.passenger = bookingRequest.passenger;
        legRecord.leg = bookingRequest.aComposedFlight[i];

        String airlineId =
          bookingRequest.aComposedFlight[i].flightNumber.substring(
            0, 2 );
        Airline airline = (Airline) airlines.get( airlineId );
        taBookingRecord.airlineIds[i] = airline.bookLeg( legRecord );
      }
      booking.setBookingData( taBookingRecord );
    }
    return;
  }
```

After we loop through all the legs of the flight and make the bookings with the airlines, we store the booking in the travel agent's database by invoking the method `setBookingData()` on the booking entity bean. Create and remote exceptions are directly propagated.

The other `ejbCreate()` method creates a booking business object from existing booking data. It takes a reference to a booking entity object (most likely obtained through a finder method on the booking home interface). We start by initializing homes and stateless sessions. Then we invoke the `getBookingData()` method on the booking entity bean, which returns a travel agent booking record. We create a new booking record and initialize it with the data from the travel agent booking record.

```
public void ejbCreate( Booking booking )
  throws java.rmi.RemoteException, javax.ejb.CreateException {

  initializeHomes();

  TaBookingRecord taBookingRecord = booking.getBookingData();

  bookingRecord = new BookingRecord();
  bookingRecord.confirmedPrice = taBookingRecord.confirmedPrice;
  bookingRecord.id = taBookingRecord.id;
  bookingRecord.label = taBookingRecord.label;
  bookingRecord.userId = taBookingRecord.userId;
```

Now we get the airline's booking ids for each of the flight's legs. Again we extract the airline id and obtain the airline session from the airline's hashtable. On the airline's remote interface, we invoke the method `lookUpById()`, which returns leg record for this id.

```
  bookingRecord.aComposedFlight =
    new Flight[taBookingRecord.airlineIds.length];
  for( int i = 0; i < taBookingRecord.airlineIds.length; i++ ) {
    String airlineId = taBookingRecord.airlineIds[i].substring(0,2);
    if( airlines.containsKey( airlineId ) ) {
      Airline airline = (Airline) airlines.get( airlineId );
      LegRecord legRecord =
        airline.lookUpById( taBookingRecord.airlineIds[i] );
      if( i == 0 ) {
        bookingRecord.passenger = legRecord.passenger;
      }
```

If we are in the loop's first iteration, we obtain the passenger data from the leg record and copy it into the booking record. Then we get the flight object from the leg record. However, the flight object is not complete since we decided not to store redundant data in the airline database. So we obtain the remaining data from the query enterprise bean by invoking the method `getFlight()` on its remote interface. A flight is uniquely determined by the flight number and the departure date.

```
        bookingRecord.aComposedFlight[i] = legRecord.leg;
        Flight f1 = query.getFlight(
          legRecord.leg.flightNumber, legRecord.leg.departureDate );
        bookingRecord.aComposedFlight[i].aircraft = f1.aircraft;
        bookingRecord.aComposedFlight[i].arrivalDate = f1.arrivalDate;
        bookingRecord.aComposedFlight[i].arrivingAirport =
          f1.arrivingAirport;
        bookingRecord.aComposedFlight[i].departingAirport =
          f1.departingAirport;
        bookingRecord.aComposedFlight[i].departureDate =
          f1.departureDate;
      }
    }
    return;
  }
```

#### Implementing the Remote Interface

The remote interface defines methods to get and set a booking record. The implementation of the method `getBookingData()` is straightforward. It just returns the instance variable `bookingRecord`.

```
  public BookingRecord getBookingData()
    throws java.rmi.RemoteException {

    return bookingRecord;
  }
```

The method `setBookingData()` overwrites the value of the instance variable `bookingRecord`. Then we create a new travel agent booking record and initialize it with the data from the booking record.

```
  public void setBookingData( BookingRecord bookingRecord )
    throws java.rmi.RemoteException {

    this.bookingRecord = bookingRecord;
    try {
      TaBookingRecord taBookingRecord = new TaBookingRecord();
      taBookingRecord.id  = bookingRecord.id;
      taBookingRecord.confirmedPrice = bookingRecord.confirmedPrice;
      taBookingRecord.label = bookingRecord.label;
      taBookingRecord.airlineIds =
        new String[ bookingRecord.aComposedFlight.length ];
      taBookingRecord.userId = bookingRecord.userId;
```

Now we make new bookings for the legs. We loop through the legs and invoke `bookLeg()` for each leg on the appropriate airline. Finally, we set the new booking on the booking entity bean.

```
        for( int i = 0; i <  bookingRecord.aComposedFlight.length; i++ ) {
          LegRecord legRecord = new LegRecord();
          legRecord.passenger = bookingRecord.passenger;
          legRecord.leg = bookingRecord.aComposedFlight[i];
          String airlineId =
            bookingRecord.aComposedFlight[i].flightNumber.substring( 0, 2 );
          Airline airline = (Airline) airlines.get( airlineId );
          taBookingRecord.airlineIds[i] = airline.bookLeg( legRecord );
        }
        bookingRecord.bookingObj.setBookingData( taBookingRecord );
      }
      return;
    }
```

Remote exceptions are propagated directly.

### Implementing the SessionBean Interface

The interface `SessionBean` is implemented by the class `Business-BOBean`. The method `setSessionContext()` stores the session context in an instance variable, and the implementations of the other methods are left empty.

```
public void setSessionContext(SessionContext context)
    throws java.rmi.RemoteException {

    sessionContext = context;
}
```

The `ejbRemove()` method cancels a booking by deleting the associated booking business object. As shown in the code, we must cancel all the legs booked with the airlines. There we obtain an instance of the appropriate airline and invoke the `removeLeg()` on it. We do not implement the method for intercepting the deactivation and reactivation of the session bean.

```
public void ejbRemove() throws java.rmi.RemoteException{
  try {
    // get the booking bean
    Booking booking = bookingRecord.bookingObj;

    // remove airline bookings
    for( int i = 0; i < bookingRecord.aComposedFlight.length; i ++ ) {

      String flightNumber =
        bookingRecord.aComposedFlight[i].flightNumber;
      String airlineId = flightNumber.substring( 0, 2 );
      Airline airline = (Airline) airlines.get( airlineId );
      TaBookingRecord taBookingRecord = booking.getBookingData();
```

```
      airline.removeLeg( taBookingRecord.airlineIds[i] );
    }

    // remove entity bean, that is,
    // remove entry in the travel agent database
    booking.remove();
  }
  catch( javax.ejb.RemoveException re ) {
    throw new java.rmi.RemoteException(
      "could remove booking" + bookingRecord.id, re  );
  }
}
public void ejbActivate() throws java.rmi.RemoteException{}
public void ejbPassivate() throws java.rmi.RemoteException{}
```

### Implementing Private Methods

The private method initialize is used by various home interfaces and remote interfaces of stateless session beans. We start with the usual JNDI initialization and lookup of the home interfaces. The new issue addressed in the method is the use of the `list()` methods on a JNDI context, which is used to find all airlines. Airlines are expected to be registered in the "Airlines" context.

```
private void initialize()
  throws java.rmi.RemoteException, javax.ejb.CreateException {

  try {
    java.util.Hashtable env = new java.util.Hashtable();
    java.util.Properties properties = sessionContext.getEnvironment();
    String contextClassName =
      properties.getProperty("context-class-name");
    env.put( javax.naming.Context.INITIAL_CONTEXT_FACTORY,
      contextClassName );
    root = new javax.naming.InitialContext(env);

    QueryHome queryHome = (QueryHome) root.lookup( "Schedule/Query" );
    query = queryHome.create();

    bookingHome = (BookingHome) root.lookup( "Apex/BookingHome" );

    airlines = new java.util.Hashtable();
    javax.naming.NamingEnumeration airlineNamingEnumeration =
      root.list( "Airlines" );
    while( airlineNamingEnumeration.hasMore() ) {
      javax.naming.Binding binding =
        (javax.naming.Binding) airlineNamingEnumeration.next();
      String name = binding.getName();
      AirlineHome airlineHome = (AirlineHome) binding.getObject();
```

```
        airlines.put( name, airlineHome.create() );
      }
    }
    catch( javax.naming.NamingException ne ) {
      java.rmi.RemoteException re = new java.rmi.RemoteException(
        "JNDI problem: " + ne );
    return;
  }
```

## Flight Query

The flight query is a stateless session bean. It is defined and implemented in the package `vogel.transaction.chapter6.schedule`. The home interface of a stateless session bean lets you create a session on which you can invoke the enterprise bean's business methods. The session object does not keep state information between invocations. In fact, it is quite common that every time you make an invocation on the session object, you end up with a different instance. Figure 6.5 illustrates the stateless session bean pattern.

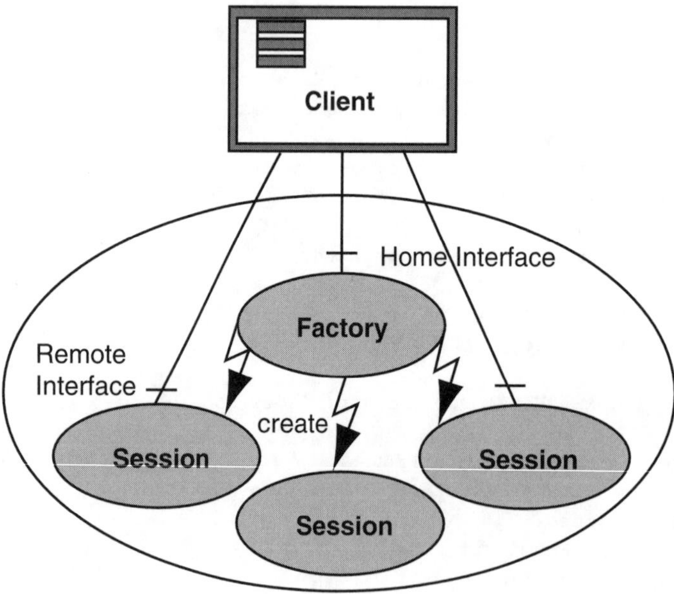


**Figure 6.5** Stateless session bean.

### *Home Interface*

The home interface is a public Java interface that extends `EJBHome`. Our query home interface defines a single `create()` method as required for stateless session beans. This method must throw the exception `Remote-Exception` and it also throws the exception `CreateException`.

```
package vogel.transaction.chapter6.schedule;

public interface QueryHome extends javax.ejb.EJBHome {

  Query create()
    throws java.rmi.RemoteException, javax.ejb.CreateException;
}
```

### *Remote Interface*

The remote interface is also a public Java interface that extends `EJB-Object`. It defines the application-specific or business methods of the enterprise bean. First, we import the classes (for data types) from the package `vogel.transaction.chapter6.airlines`. These classes are used as parameters and result types for the methods of the remote interface.

```
package vogel.transaction.chapter6.schedule;

import vogel.transaction.chapter6.airlines.*;

public interface Query extends javax.ejb.EJBObject {

  public java.util.Vector queryAvailableFlights(
    String from,
    String to,
    SimpleDate departureDate )
    throws java.rmi.RemoteException;

  public QueryIterator getFlightIterator(
    String from,
    String to,
    SimpleDate departureDate )
    throws java.rmi.RemoteException;

  public Flight getFlight(
    String flightNumber,
    SimpleDate departureDate )
    throws java.rmi.RemoteException;
}
```

The method queryAvailableFlights() returns a vector of flights, which match the departure and arrival airport and are in a certain interval around the specified departure date. We already discussed the pros and cons of using vectors versus arrays.

The method getFlightIterator() executes the method queryAvailableFlights(), but it returns an iterator instead of the data itself. The iterator is a stateful session bean, which is explained later in the chapter.

The method getFlight() returns flights, which are uniquely identified by the flight number and the departure date.

## *Implementation*

The implementation of the flight query enterprise bean is provided by the class QueryBean. We hard-code two search policies within the class. The variable departureTimeInterval is the time in hours, which is considered for the search, before and after the requested departure time. The changeTimeInterval is the time usually required to make a connecting flight.

```
package vogel.transaction.chapter6.schedule;

import vogel.transaction.chapter6.airlines.*;

public class QueryBean
  implements SessionBean {

  private SessionContext sessionContext;

  private int departureTimeInterval = 2;
  private int changeTimeInterval = 60;

  private QueryIteratorHome queryIteratorHome;
```

### Implementing the Home Interface

Since the flight query is a stateless session bean, we must implement ejbCreate() method with no parameters. Usually there's not much to be done in a stateless session bean's ejbCreate() method. Here we initialize the query iterator of the home interface via JNDI in the usual way:

```
public void ejbCreate()
  throws CreateException {

  try {
```

```
      java.util.Hashtable env = new java.util.Hashtable();
      java.util.Properties properties = sessionContext.getEnvironment();
      String contextClassName =
        properties.getProperty("context-class-name");
      env.put( javax.naming.Context.INITIAL_CONTEXT_FACTORY,
        contextClassName );
      javax.naming.Context root = new javax.naming.InitialContext(env);
      queryIteratorHome = (QueryIteratorHome)
        root.lookup( "Schedule/QueryIterator" );
    }
    catch( javax.naming.NamingException ne ) {
      throw new javax.ejb.CreateException(
        "Cannot get query iterator home");
    }
    return;
  }
```

### Implementing the Remote Interface

The remote interface defines three business methods: `queryAvailableFlights()`, `getFlightIterator()`, and `getFlight()`.

The implementation of the method `queryAvailableFlights()` involves the creation, execution, and processing of a number of queries to find flights that satisfy the request. The request is expressed by source and destination airports and a departure date.

```
public Vector queryAvailableFlights(
  String from,
  String to,
  SimpleDate departureDate )
  throws RemoteException {

  int i, j;
  String[] selectStatements = new String[3];
  ResultSet[] resultSets = new ResultSet[3];
  Statement[] statements = new Statement[3];
  Flight[][] flights = null;
  Vector flightVector = new Vector();
```

We create the three SQL queries for nonstop, one-hop, and two-hop connections. We use the request data and the policies defined previously to construct the query.

```
selectStatements[0] =
   "select * from flight_type ft, flight_instance fi where " +
   " ft.from_airport = '" + from + "' and " +
   " ft.to_airport = '" + to + "' and " +
   " ft.flight_number = fi.flight_number and " +
```

```
 " fi.departure_date = to_date('" +
 departureDate.month + "-" + departureDate.day + "-" +
 departureDate.year + "', 'MM-DD-YY') and " +
 " ft.departure_hour - " + departureTimeInterval +
 " <= " + departureDate.hour + " and" +
 " ft.departure_hour + " + departureTimeInterval +
 " >= " + departureDate.hour );

selectStatements[1] =
 "select * from flight_type ft1, flight_instance fi1," +
 " flight_type ft2, flight_instance fi2 where " +
 " ft1.from_airport = '" + from + "' and " +
 " ft2.to_airport = '" + to + "' and " +
 " ft1.to_airport = ft2.from_airport and " +
 " ft1.flight_number = fi1.flight_number and " +
 " ft2.flight_number = fi2.flight_number and " +
 " fi1.departure_date = to_date('" +
 departureDate.month + "-" + departureDate.day + "-" +
 departureDate.year + "', 'MM-DD-YY') and" +
 " ft1.departure_hour - " + departureTimeInterval +
 " < " + departureDate.hour + " and" +
 " ft1.departure_hour + " + departureTimeInterval +
 " > " + departureDate.hour + " and" +
 " (ft2.departure_hour * 60 + ft2.departure_minute) -" +
 " (ft1.arrival_hour * 60 + ft1.arrival_minute) > " +
 changeTimeInterval );

selectStatements[2] =     "select * from flight_type ft1,
 flight_instance fi1," +
 " flight_type ft2, flight_instance fi2," +
 " flight_type ft3, flight_instance fi3 where " +
 " ft1.from_airport = '" + from + "' and " +
 " ft3.to_airport = '" + to + "' and " +
 " ft1.to_airport = ft2.from_airport and " +
 " ft2.to_airport = ft3.from_airport and " +
 " ft1.flight_number = fi1.flight_number and " +
 " ft2.flight_number = fi2.flight_number and " +
 " ft3.flight_number = fi3.flight_number and " +
 " fi1.departure_date = to_date('" +
 departureDate.month + "-" + departureDate.day + "-" +
 departureDate.year + "', 'MM-DD-YY') and" +
 " ft1.departure_hour - " + departureTimeInterval +
 " < " + departureDate.hour + " and" +
 " ft1.departure_hour + " + departureTimeInterval +
 " > " + departureDate.hour + " and" +
 " (ft2.departure_hour * 60 + ft2.departure_minute) -" +
 " (ft1.arrival_hour * 60 + ft1.arrival_minute) > " +
 changeTimeInterval + " and " +
 " (ft3.departure_hour * 60 + ft3.departure_minute) -" +
 " (ft2.arrival_hour * 60 + ft2.arrival_minute) > " +
 changeTimeInterval );
```

An example of a query for a two-hop query from San Francisco to Frankfurt for January 1, 1999 around 8:00 A.M. is

```
select * from
flight_type ft1, flight_instance fi1,
flight_type ft2, flight_instance fi2 where
ft1.from_airport = 'SFO' and
ft2.to_airport = 'FRA' and
ft1.to_airport = ft2.from_airport and
ft1.flight_number = fi1.flight_number and
ft2.flight_number = fi2.flight_number and
fi1.departure_date = to_date('1-1-99', 'MM-DD-YY') and
ft1.departure_hour - 2 < 8 and ft1.departure_hour + 2 > 8 and
(ft2.departure_hour * 60 + ft2.departure_minute) Ò
  (ft1.arrival_hour * 60 + ft1.arrival_minute) > 60
```

Now that we have created the SQL queries, we proceed in the usual manner by getting a connection, creating statements, and executing the queries.

```
try {
  Connection connection = getConnection();
  for( i = 0; i < 3; i++ ) {
    try {
      statements[i] = connection.createStatement();
      resultSets[i] =
        statements[i].executeQuery(selectStatements[i]);
    }
    catch( Exception ex ) {
      throw new RemoteException(
        "no connection with " + i + " stops", ex );
    }
  }
```

After we successfully make the queries, we process the result sets. We go through each of the three result sets and copy the data into the flight objects. We collect all flight objects in the flight vector.

```
Timestamp timestamp;
for( i = 0; i < 3; i++ ) {
  if( resultSets[i] == null ) {
    System.out.println("no connection with " + i + " legs");
  }
  else {
    while( resultSets[i].next() ) {
      Flight[] flight = new Flight[i+1];
      for( j = 0; j < i+1; j++ ) {
        flight[j] =  new Flight();
        flight[j].flightNumber = resultSets[i].getString(11*j+1);
        flight[j].departingAirport =
```

```
                resultSets[i].getString(11*j+2);
              flight[j].arrivingAirport =
                resultSets[i].getString(11*j+3);
              timestamp = resultSets[i].getTimestamp(11*j+9);
              flight[j].departureDate = new SimpleDate(
                timestamp.getDate(),
                timestamp.getMonth() + 1,
                timestamp.getYear(),
                resultSets[i].getInt( 11*j+4 ),
                resultSets[i].getInt( 11*j+5 ) );
              timestamp = resultSets[i].getTimestamp(11*j+10);
              flight[j].arrivalDate = new SimpleDate(
                timestamp.getDate(),
                timestamp.getMonth() + 1,
                timestamp.getYear(),
                resultSets[i].getInt( 11*j+6 ),
                resultSets[i].getInt( 11*j+7 ) );
              flight[j].aircraft = resultSets[i].getString( 11*j+11 );
            }
            flightVector.addElement( flight );
          }
        }
      }
```

Finally, we close the statements and the connection and return the flight vector. Exceptions are converted and propagated as remote exceptions.

```
      for( i = 0; i < 3; i++ ) {
        statement[i].close();
      }
      connection.close();
      return flightVector;
    }
    catch( Exception e) {
      throw new RemoteException("database access error", e);
    }
  }
```

The method `getFlightIterator()` does the same as the method `getAvailableFlights()`, but instead of returning all the data in a single package, it returns an iterator from which the available flights can be obtained. We use `getAvailableFlights()` to get the flight information. The returned vector is converted into an array. This array is used as an argument for the iterator home interface's `create()` method. We then return the iterator. A possible create exception is converted and propagated as a remote exception.

```
  public QueryIterator getFlightIterator(
    String from,
```

```
        String to,
        SimpleDate departureDate )
        throws java.rmi.RemoteException {

        try {
          java.util.Vector v = queryAvailableFlights(
            from, to, departureDate );
          Flight[][] flights = new Flight[ v.size() ][];
          v.copyInto( flights );
          QueryIterator queryIterator = queryIteratorHome.create( flights );
          return queryIterator;
        }
        catch( javax.ejb.CreateException ce ) {
          throw new java.rmi.RemoteException(
            "Cannot create query iterator", ce );
        }
      }
```

The method `getFlight()` returns a flight object for a flight uniquely identified by the flight number and the departure date. The implementation is straightforward. We construct a SQL select query, get a connection and a statement, and execute the query. Then we process the result set by copying the relevant data into a flight object, which we finally return.

```
public Flight getFlight( String flightNumber, SimpleDate d )
 throws RemoteException {

 int i, j;
 String sqlSelect;
 ResultSet resultSet;
 Statement statement;
 Flight flight = null;
 Connection c = null;

 sqlSelect = new String(
   "select * from FLIGHT_TYPE ft, FLIGHT_INSTANCE fi where " +
   "ft.flight_number = '" + flightNumber +"' and " +
   "fi.flight_number = '" + flightNumber +"' and " +
   "fi.departure_date = to_date('" +
   d.month + "-" + d.day + "-" + d.year + "', 'MM-DD-YY')" );

 try {
   Connection connection = getConnection();
   statement = connection.createStatement();
   resultSet = statement.executeQuery( sqlSelect );

   Timestamp timestamp;
   resultSet.next();

   flight =  new Flight();
```

```
            flight.flightNumber = resultSet.getString(1);
            flight.departingAirport = resultSet.getString(2);
            flight.arrivingAirport = resultSet.getString(3);
            timestamp = resultSet.getTimestamp(9);
            flight.departureDate = new SimpleDate(
              timestamp.getDate(),
              timestamp.getMonth() + 1,
              timestamp.getYear(),
              resultSet.getInt( 4 ),
              resultSet.getInt( 5 ) );
            timestamp = resultSet.getTimestamp(10);
            flight.arrivalDate = new SimpleDate(
              timestamp.getDate(),
              timestamp.getMonth() + 1,
                timestamp.getYear(),
              resultSet.getInt( 6 ),
              resultSet.getInt( 7 ) );
            flight.aircraft = resultSet.getString( 11 );

            connection.close();
          }
          catch( Exception ex ) {
            throw new RemoteException(
              "Query getFlight(): database access problem");
          }
          return flight;
        }
```

### Implementing the SessionBean Interface

The interface `SessionBean` is implemented by the class `Query`. The method `setSessionContext()` stores the session context in an instance variable and the implementations of the other methods are left empty.

### Implementing Private Methods

We have put the code for obtaining a JDBC connection in a private method. The implementation allows for controlling the URL for the database and the username and password via properties set in the deployment descriptor.

```
        private Connection getConnection()
          throws java.sql.SQLException {

          java.util.Properties properties = entityContext.getEnvironment();
          String url = properties.getProperty("db-url");
          String username = properties.getProperty("db-username");
          String password = properties.getProperty("db-password");
```

```
    return DriverManager.getConnection(url, username, password);
}
```

## Iterators with EJB

Iterators are a proven design pattern for handling large amounts of data in distributed objects environments. The Enterprise JavaBeans Specification does not directly support the iterator pattern. In this section we explain how iterators can be designed and implemented using a combination of stateless and stateful session beans.

We added the method `getFlightIterator()` to the flight's query remote interface. It takes the same parameters as the method `getAvailableFlights()`, but it returns a reference to the remote interface of a stateful session bean called `QueryIterator`. Figure 6.6 illustrates the relationship between the two enterprise beans.

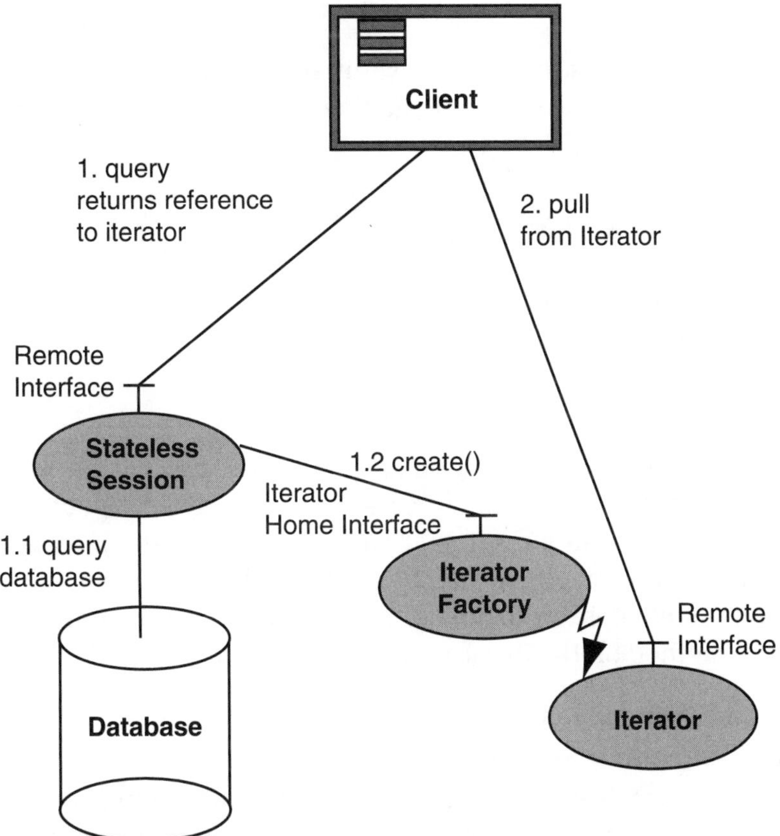


**Figure 6.6** Iterators with EJB.

## Home Interface

The home interface is a public Java interface that extends `EJBHome`. The iterator home interface defines a single `create()` method. This method must throw the exception `RemoteException` and it also throws the exception `CreateException`. The `create()` method takes a single argument of type `Flight[][]`, which is the handle to the data the iterator is managing.

```
package vogel.transaction.chapter6.schedule;

public interface QueryIteratorHome extends javax.ejb.EJBHome {

  Query create( Flight[][] flights )
    throws java.rmi.RemoteException, javax.ejb.CreateException;
}
```

## Remote Interface

The remote interface is also a public Java interface that extends `EJBObject`. It defines the iterator-specific methods of the enterprise bean.

```
package vogel.transaction.chapter6.schedule;

import vogel.transaction.chapter6.airlines.*;

public interface QueryIterator extends javax.ejb.EJBObject {

  Flight[][] nextN( int n )
    throws java.rmi.RemoteException, EmptyException;
}
```

We only define a single method `nextN()`, which returns an array of $n$ matching flights. Iterators also have a `remove()` method, which we don't have to explicitly define as it is already specified in the interface `EJBObject`. Furthermore, the session bean's time-out mechanism takes care of removing stale iterator instances in case the user did not invoke the `remove()` method on the iterator bean.

### Implementing the SessionBean Interface

The interface `SessionBean` is implemented by the class `QueryIterator`. The method `setSessionContext()` stores the session context in an instance variable, and the implementations of the other methods are left empty.

### *Implementation*

The implementation of the flight query enterprise bean is provided by the class QueryIteratorBean. We declare the usual session context and variables to keep the state of the iterator, which are the flights, the counter of flights already returned, and a flag indicating if all elements have been returned.

```
package vogel.transaction.chapter6.schedule;

import vogel.transaction.chapter6.airlines.*;
import vogel.transaction.chapter6.schedule.*;

public class QueryIteratorBean
  implements SessionBean {

  private SessionContext sessionContext;
  private Flight[][] flights;
  private int counter = 0;
  private boolean empty = false;
```

#### Implementing the Home Interface

The home interface defined a single create() method that takes a two-dimensional flight array as an argument. The ejbCreate() method has the same signature and its implementation is assigning the reference of the passed array to an instance variable.

```
  public void ejbCreate( Flight[][] f )
    throws java.rmi.RemoteException {

    flights = f;
    return;
  }
```

#### Implementing the Remote Interface

The remote interface defines a single business method, nextN(). It takes an integer as an argument and returns an array of composed flights. The semantics is that it returns as many composed flights as specified in the argument, or as many as the iterator holds if there are less than requested. If all flights are obtained from the iterator, it will throw EmptyException.

```
  public Flight[][] nextN( int n )
    throws java.rmi.RemoteException, EmptyException {
```

```
        if( empty ) {
          throw new EmptyException();
        }

        Flight[][] f;
        try {
          if( counter + n >= flights.length ) {
            f = new Flight[flights.length - counter][];
            empty = true;
          }
          else {
            f = new Flight[n][];
          }
          for( int i = 0; i < n && i < flights.length - counter; i++ ) {
            f[i] = flights[ counter + i ];
          }
          counter = counter + n;
          return f;
        }
        catch( Exception e ) {
          throw new java.rmi.RemoteException("Iteraor failure: ", e );
        }
      }
```

## Airline

The airline is a stateless session enterprise bean. It is defined and implemented in the package `vogel.transaction.chapter6.airline`. We have already discussed stateless session beans for the flight query; hence, we focus here on the specifics of the airline bean.

### *Home Interface*

The home interface defined is a public Java interface that extends `EJBHome`. Our query home interface defines a single `create()` method as required for stateless session beans. This method must throw the exceptions `RemoteException` and `CreateException`.

```
package vogel.transaction.chapter6.airlines;

public interface AirlineHome extends javax.ejb.EJBHome {

  Airline create()
    throws java.rmi.RemoteException, javax.ejb.CreateException;

}
```

### Remote Interface

The remote interface is also a public Java interface that extends `EJBObject`. It defines the application-specific or business methods of the enterprise bean. First we import classes (for data types) from the package `vogel.transaction.chapter6.airlines`. These classes are used as parameters and result types for the methods of the remote interface.

```
package vogel.transaction.chapter6.airlines;

public interface Airline extends javax.ejb.EJBObject {

  public String bookLeg( LegRecord legRecord )
    throws java.rmi.RemoteException;

  public LegRecord lookUpById( String confirmationNumber )
    throws java.rmi.RemoteException;

  public void removeLeg( String id )
    throws java.rmi.RemoteException;
}
```

The method `bookLeg()` books a leg with the airline represented by the enterprise bean. The leg record contains information about the flight and the person who is traveling.

The method `lookUpById()` returns a leg record for the flight, which is uniquely identified by the airline's confirmation number.

The method `removeLeg()` deletes a leg record for the flight, which is uniquely identified by the airline's confirmation number.

### Implementation

The implementation of the airline enterprise bean is provided by the class `AirlineBean`. Besides the session context, we declare variables for the uuid home interface and for the airline name.

```
package vogel.transaction.chapter6.airlines;

import javax.ejb.*;
import java.util.Vector;
import java.sql.*;
import vogel.transaction.chapter6.travelAgent.*;

public class AirlineBean
  implements SessionBean {
```

```
private SessionContext sessionContext;
private UuidHome uuidHome;
private String airlineName;
```

### Implementing the Home Interface

The home interface of a stateless session bean allows only for a single `create()` method that has no parameters. The corresponding `ejbCreate()` method is used to obtain the home interface of the uuid entity bean similar to what we have seen before. We also create a primary key for the Uuid entity bean, which is explained in detail later in the chapter.

```
public void ejbCreate()
  throws java.rmi.RemoteException, javax.ejb.CreateException {

  try {
    java.util.Hashtable env = new java.util.Hashtable();
    java.util.Properties properties = sessionContext.getEnvironment();
    String contextClassName =
      properties.getProperty("context-class-name");
    env.put( javax.naming.Context.INITIAL_CONTEXT_FACTORY,
      contextClassName );
    javax.naming.Context root = new javax.naming.InitialContext(env);

    uuidHome = (UuidHome) root.lookup( "Apex/UuidHome" );
    pk = new UuidPK( "1" );
    uuid = newId();
```

We also obtain the JNDI name of the bean through an environment property following a private naming convention as we already motivated and explained for the travel agent.

```
    airlineName = properties.getProperty("jndi-name");

    return;
  } catch( Exception ex ) {
    System.err.println( ex );
    throw new javax.ejb.CreateException(
      "problem at ejbCreate(): " + ex );
  }
}
```

### Implementing the Remote Interface

The remote interface defines two methods. The method `bookLeg()` books a leg with the airline represented by the enterprise bean. The leg record contains information about the flight and the person who is traveling. First, we get a new unique identifier from the method `newId()`, which is explained later in the chapter. Then the implementation follows the now well-known pattern: Create the SQL insert statement, get the connection, create the statement, execute the query and close statement and connection. Finally, we return the identifier for the booked leg.

```
public String bookLeg( LegRecord legRecord )
  throws java.rmi.RemoteException {

  String sqlInsert;
  Statement statement;
  Connection connection;

  String confirmationNumber = newId();

  sqlInsert = new String(
    "INSERT INTO FLIGHT_BOOKING VALUES( '" +
    legRecord.passenger.title + "' , '" +
    legRecord.passenger.firstName + "', '" +
    legRecord.passenger.middleInitial + "', '" +
    legRecord.passenger.lastName + "', '" +
    legRecord.leg.flightNumber + "', " +
    "TO_DATE( '" +
    legRecord.leg.departureDate.month + "-" +
    legRecord.leg.departureDate.day + "-" +
    legRecord.leg.departureDate.year + "'" +
    ", 'MM-DD-YY')," +
    legRecord.leg.price +  ", '" +
    confirmationNumber + "' )" );

  try {
    connection = getConnection();
    statement = connection.createStatement();
    statement.executeUpdate(sqlInsert);
    statement.close();
    connection.close();
  }
  catch( Exception ex ) {
    throw new java.rmi.RemoteException( "Error at query" + ex );
  }
  return confirmationNumber;
}
```

The method `lookUpById()` returns a leg record for the flight, which is uniquely identified by the airline's confirmation number. The implementation is a simple wrapper around the SQL select.

```
public LegRecord lookUpById( String id )
  throws java.rmi.RemoteException {
```

```
    int i, j;
    String sqlSelect;
    ResultSet resultSet;
    Statement statement;
    Connection connection;
    LegRecord legRecord;

    sqlSelect = new String(
      "select * from FLIGHT_BOOKING where CONFIRMATIONNUMBER = '" +
      id + "'" );

    try {
      connection = getConnection();
statement = connection.createStatement();
      resultSet = statement.executeQuery(sqlSelect);
Timestamp timestamp;
resultSet.next();

      legRecord = new LegRecord();
      legRecord.passenger = new Person();
      legRecord.leg = new Flight();
      legRecord.passenger.title = resultSet.getString(1);
      legRecord.passenger.firstName = resultSet.getString(2);
      legRecord.passenger.middleInitial = resultSet.getString(3);
      if( legRecord.passenger.middleInitial == null )
        legRecord.passenger.middleInitial = "";
      legRecord.passenger.lastName = resultSet.getString(4);
      legRecord.leg.flightNumber = resultSet.getString(5);
      timestamp = resultSet.getTimestamp(6);
      legRecord.leg.departureDate = new SimpleDate(
        timestamp.getDate(),
        timestamp.getMonth() + 1,
        timestamp.getYear(),
        -1, // undefined - implicitly defined through flight number
        -1  // undefined - implicitly defined through flight number
      );
      legRecord.leg.price = resultSet.getInt(7);
      legRecord.id = resultSet.getString(8);
```

We only process the expected, first element of the result set. There are, however, fields in the leg record for which we have no data. We complete the leg record with dummy data. The data can be accessed via the query bean in a way similar to what the booking business object does. We explained this earlier.

```
      legRecord.leg.aircraft = "";
      legRecord.leg.arrivalDate = new SimpleDate(
        -1, -1, -1, -1, -1 );
      legRecord.leg.arrivingAirport = "";
```

```
        legRecord.leg.departingAirport = "";

        statement.close();
        connection.close();
      }
      catch( Exception ex ) {
        throw new java.rmi.RemoteException(
          "database access error: " + ex );
      }
      return legRecord;
    }
```

The method `removeLeg()` cancels a leg record for the flight, which is uniquely identified by the airline's confirmation number. The implementation is a simple wrapper around the SQL delete.

```
    public void removeLeg( String id )
      throws java.rmi.RemoteException {

      try {
        Connection connection = getConnection();
        Statement statement = connection.createStatement();
        String sqlDelete =
          "delete from FLIGHT_BOOKING where CONFIRMATIONNUMBER = " + id;
        System.err.println( "Airline removeLeg(): " + sqlDelete );
        statement.executeUpdate( sqlDelete );
        statement.close();
        connection.close();
      }
      catch( Exception e ) {
        System.err.println("Airline removeLeg(): database access error: "
          + e);
        throw new java.rmi.RemoteException(
          "Airline removeLeg(): database access error: ", e);
      }
```

### Implementing the SessionBean Interface

We have the usual, trivial implementation of the methods defined in the `SessionBean` interface.

### Implementing Private Methods

We have two private methods: `getConnection()` and `newId()`. We have omitted the details of `getConnection()` here. The method `newId()` returns a unique identifier for the airline. As explained previously, we try to find a uuid entity with the well-known key "1". If this fails, because we are the very first to request a uuid, we will create a new entity bean. Once we have the bean, we invoke `newId()` on its remote interface. We return the resulting id prefixed with the airline identifier such as "UA" or "LH".

```
private String newId()
    throws java.rmi.RemoteException {

    String id;
    try {
      uuid = uuidHome.findByPrimaryKey( pk );
    }
    catch( FinderException fe ) {
      uuid = uuidHome.create();
    }
    id =  uuid.newId();
    return airlineName + id;
  }
```

## Uuid

The Uuid bean is an entity enterprise bean. It is defined and implemented in the package `vogel.transaction.chapter6.travelAgent`. We've already discussed entity beans for the booking. The Uuid bean is, however, implemented using container-managed persistence.

### *Home Interface*

The home interface is defined as a public Java interface that extends `EJBHome`. Query home interface defines a single `create()` method with no parameters and the `findByPrimaryKey()` method.

```
package vogel.transaction.chapter6.travelAgent;

public interface UuidHome extends javax.ejb.EJBHome {

  Uuid create()
    throws java.rmi.RemoteException, javax.ejb.CreateException;

  Uuid findByPrimaryKey( UuidPK key )
    throws java.rmi.RemoteException, javax.ejb.FinderException;
}
```

### *Remote Interface*

The remote interface is also a public Java interface that extends `EJBObject`. It defines the application-specific or business methods of the enterprise bean.

```
public interface Uuid extends javax.ejb.EJBObject {

  public String newId()
    throws java.rmi.RemoteException;
}
```

The method `newId()` returns a new unique identifier in the form of an 8-character string.

### Primary Key Class

The primary key class follows the pattern introduced with the primary key for bookings. The primary key contained by this class is of type `String`.

```
public class UuidPK
  implements java.io.Serializable {

  public String primaryKey;

  public UuidPK() {
  }

  public UuidPK( String id ) {
    primaryKey = id;
  }
}
```

### Implementation

The implementation of the uuid enterprise bean is provided by the class `UuidBean`. We implemented it using container-managed persistence. Publicly declared fields, which are declared accordingly in the deployment descriptor, are container managed. They must include all public fields from the bean's primary key class; in our case, this is `String primaryKey`.

```
public class UuidBean
  implements javax.ejb.EntityBean {

  private javax.ejb.EntityContext entityContext;

  // container managed fields
  public long lastId;
  public String primaryKey;
```

### Implementing the Home Interface

Since the Uuid bean is implemented as a container-managed bean, there are a few subtleties. First, the `ejbCreate()` method returns void instead of a primary key. Second, we don't provide the implementation of the `ejbFindByPrimaryKey()` method; the container provides it.

In the implementation of the `ejbCreate()` method we create the very first identifier, which is set to the current time in seconds.

```
public void ejbCreate()
  throws java.rmi.RemoteException, javax.ejb.CreateException {

  primaryKey = new String("1");
  long t = System.currentTimeMillis();
  lastId = t / 1000;
  return;
}
```

The implementation of the `ejbPostCreate()` method is left empty.

```
public void ejbPostCreate() {}
```

### Implementing the Remote Interface

The business method returns unique identifiers in the form of 8-character strings. New identifiers are created by adding 1 to the last identifier.

```
public String newId() {

  StringBuffer sb = new StringBuffer( Long.toString( lastId++ ) );
  sb.setLength( 8 );
  String id = new String( sb );
  return id;
}
```

### Implementing the EntityBean Interface

For all the other methods, we must only provide trivial implementation—the work is taken over by the container.

```
public void setEntityContext( javax.ejb.EntityContext entityContext ){}
public void unsetEntityContext() throws java.rmi.RemoteException{}
public void ejbRemove() throws java.rmi.RemoteException{}
public void ejbActivate() throws java.rmi.RemoteException{}
public void ejbPassivate() throws java.rmi.RemoteException{}
public void ejbLoad()throws java.rmi.RemoteException{}
public void ejbStore()throws java.rmi.RemoteException{}
```

# Assembling the Application

Assembling an application involves two tasks: the assembly of enterprise beans into more complex applications, and the design and implementation of a corresponding client.

## Server-Side Composition

The current version of the EJB specification identifies only the server-side application assembly as a task, but does not provide any specifics about the assembly process. In our example, we have done the assembly manually by designing and implementing the session beans for the booking business object and the travel agent.

## Client Types

There can be a wide variety of clients that interface with enterprise bean-based applications. Figure 6.7 summarizes the most common clients.

- Java applets and applications, which directly access JNDI and the enterprise beans via RMI.
- COM clients that access JNDI and enterprise beans via a bridge; for example, a COM-CORBA bridge in conjunction with an EJB container, which provides RMI-over-IIOP access.
- Browser clients driven by dynamic HTML generated by a servlet (or other Web server backend) that acts as the client to JNDI and the enterprise beans.

Other aspects of clients apply as they do for the CORBA/OTS applications, which we discussed in Chapter 4, "Programming with OTS." Specifically, this includes the transaction origination.

## Client Implementation

We have implemented the same client that we used for the CORBA/OTS example in Chapter 4. We have fully reused the GUI code and just substituted the remote calls. We walk through a typical use case and show the corresponding code segments from the client.

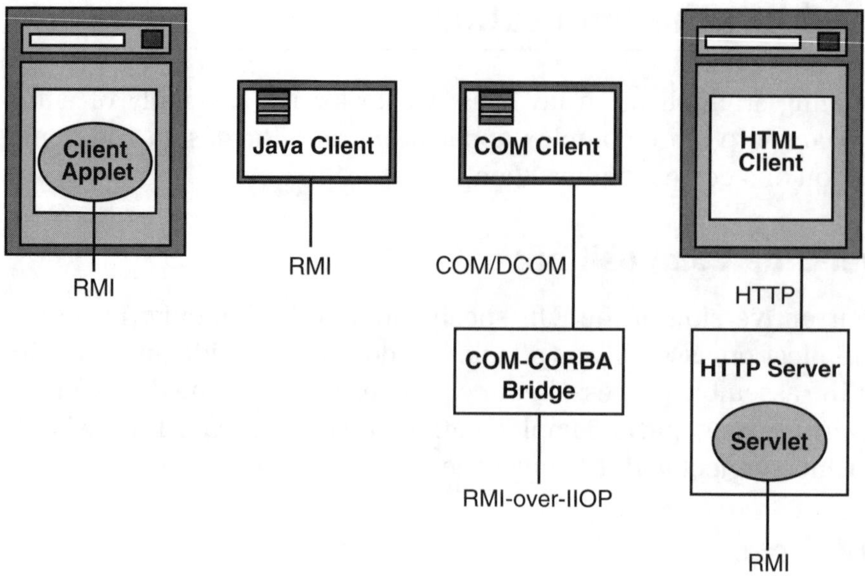


**Figure 6.7** Various client configurations.

## *Login*

To produce the login window as shown in Figure 6.8, we have to find the available travel agents. First, we get the initial context of JNDI.

```
Hashtable env = new Hashtable();
env.put(javax.naming.Context.INITIAL_CONTEXT_FACTORY,
  "com.inprise.ejb.jndi.Context");
root = new javax.naming.InitialContext(env);
```

Then we list all the travel agents. Travel agents are expected to be bound to the context "TravelAgents." We go through the returned enumeration and collect all the names and references and store them in a hashtable.

```
javax.naming.NamingEnumeration taNamingEnumeration =
  root.list( "TravelAgents" );
travelAgents = new java.util.Hashtable();

while( taNamingEnumeration.hasMore() ) {
  try {
    javax.naming.Binding binding =
      (javax.naming.Binding) taNamingEnumeration.next();
    String name = binding.getName();
    agentNames.addElement( name );
```

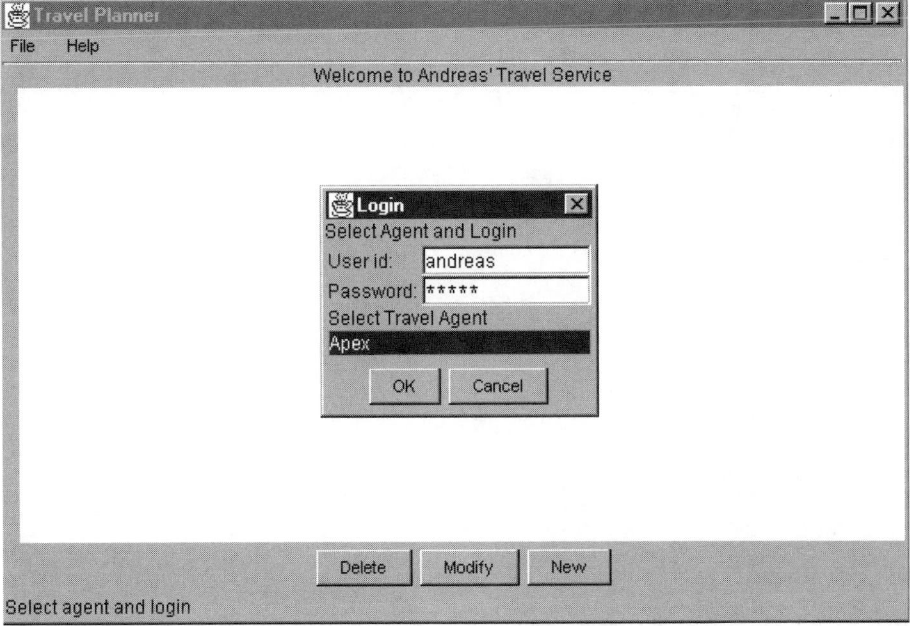


**Figure 6.8** Client–login.

```
            travelAgents.put( name, binding.getObject() );
          }
          catch( Exception ex ) {
            System.err.println("JNDI problem: " + ex );
          }
        }
```

Once we have selected a travel agent, we invoke the `create()` method on the travel agent's home interface. This is the login process.

```
taf.session = travelAgentHome.create( userId, password );
```

### *Get Bookings*

To obtain information about bookings made earlier, we invoke the method `findAllBookingRecords()` on the travel agent's session bean. The resulting vector contains the booking records, which fully describe a booking. Figure 6.9 illustrates the client GUI after a successful login showing prior bookings on the left side of the screen.

```
bookingRecordVector = session.findAllBookingRecords();
```

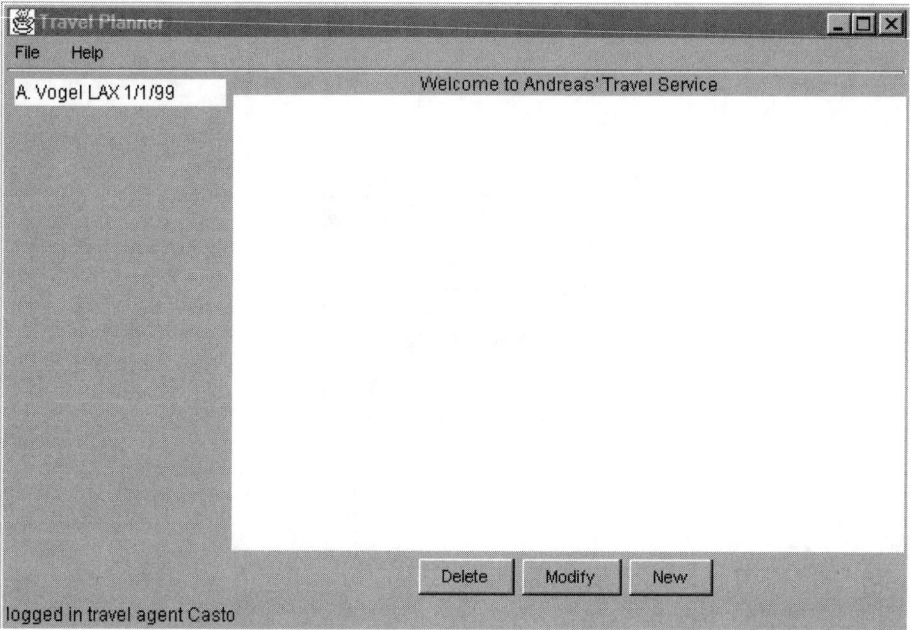


**Figure 6.9** Client—after successful login.

## *Make Queries*

There are two ways to make queries. One way is to get all available flights in one hit. We obtain the input data from the GUI and call the method `queryAvailableFlights()` on the travel agent session object.

```
SimpleDate d = new SimpleDate(
  Integer.parseInt( dayTextField.getText()),
  Integer.parseInt( monthTextField.getText()),
  Integer.parseInt( yearTextField.getText()),
  Integer.parseInt( hourTextField.getText()),
  0 );

flights = taf.session.queryAvailableFlights(
  fromTextField.getText(),
  toTextField.getText(),
  d );
```

Alternatively, we can use the query iterator. We invoke `getFlight-Iterator()` on the travel agent's session bean. Then we call `nextN()` on the iterator until we receive an `EmptyException` to get all the available flights, which we store in a vector. We then invoke the `remove()` method on the iterator.

```
QueryIterator queryIterator = taf.query.getFlightIterator(
   fromTextField.getText(),
   toTextField.getText(),
   d );
 flights = new Vector();
 try {
   Flight[][] f;
   while( true ) {
     f = queryIterator.nextN( 1 );
     System.err.println("got " + f.length + " flights");
     System.err.println("Flight[0][0]: " + f[0][0].flightNumber );
     flights.addElement( f[0] );
   }
 }
 catch( EmptyException ee ) {
   // got everything from the iterator, so clean up
   queryIterator.remove();
 }
```

## *Make Bookings*

Figure 6.10 shows the client window to make bookings. Inside the client code, we first obtain the `BookingBOHome` interface from the travel

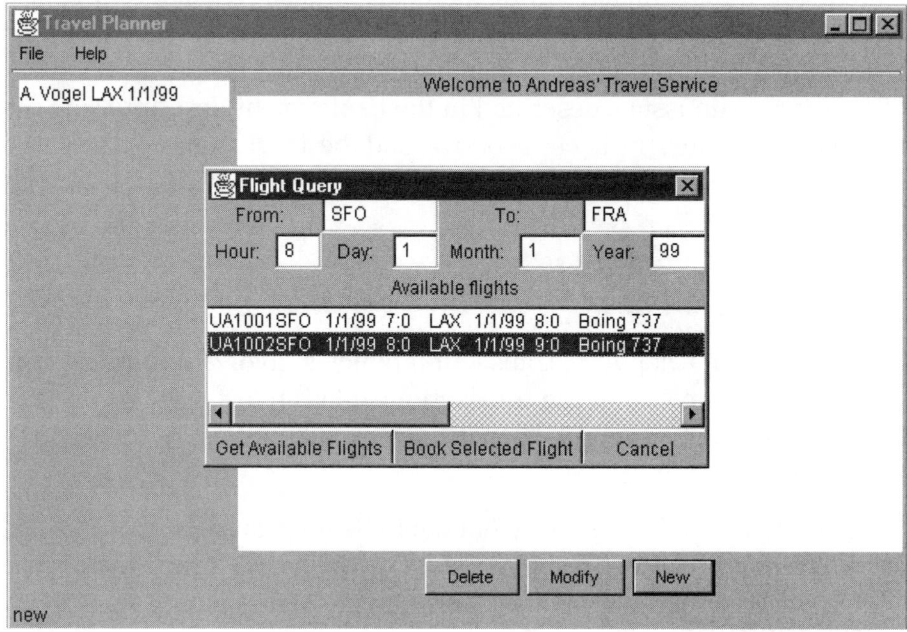


**Figure 6.10** Client–get available flights.

agent session. Then we call the `create()` method on the home interface and supply a booking request as an argument.

```
BookingBOHome bookingBOHome = taf.session.getBookingHome();
BookingBO booking = bookingBOHome.create( bookingRequest );
```

## Deploying the Enterprise Beans

In this section we explain and discuss the deployment policies and properties for the various beans. The EJB specification version 1.0 defines serialized instances of the class `DeploymentDescriptor` as the format for providing deployment information. Subsequent versions of the EJB specification will define XML instead. We abstract from the syntactical representation, as we do not expect the deployer to be confronted with it anyway. Instead, EJB server vendors will provide GUI wizards, which will guide a deployer through the setting of the deployment policies and properties.

The EJB specification suggests that deploying enterprise beans is largely decoupled from providing them. This is not the case for all the policies and properties. Specifically, transaction policies are quite closely related to the implementation of the bean. It seems realistic to expect that the bean provider determines some of the deployment descriptor, while the deployer fills in the remaining policies and properties.

The three main issues described in the deployment descriptor are the transaction policies, the access control, and the JNDI names of the enterprise beans. We explain setting for each of these in separate sections next.

### Transaction Policies

As introduced in Chapter 5, transaction policies involve the transaction management policies and the transaction isolation level. We go through all the enterprise beans and discuss the various options for transaction policies.

**Travel Agent.** The travel agent could be the transaction originator, which requires the policy TX_REQUIRES_NEW. If the client is the transaction originator, the travel agent must have the policy TX_REQUIRED. To support both cases, the travel agent would have the policy TX_REQUIRED, which means it uses the client's transaction context or creates a new one when the client makes a nontransactional call.

You can simply set one of the policies for the whole bean. However, specifically considering performance, a more fine-grained selection is possible. It would be sufficient to only require a transaction, an existing or a new one, for booking methods. You would select one of three policies discussed earlier. The read operations do not require to be executed in the context of a transaction. The policy could be either TX_SUPPORTED or TX_NOT_SUPPORTED.

**Booking Business Object.** The booking business object is either the transaction originator or it extends a transaction. At least, its write methods, the `create( BookingRequest bookingRequest )` and the `setBookingData()` method, require a transaction context. Following the argumentation presented for the travel agent, the policies TX_REQUIRES_NEW or TX_REQUIRED could be applied. The other methods should have the policies TX_SUPPORTED or TX_NOT_SUPPORTED.

**Booking Entity.** The booking entity bean is expected to be invoked by an object, which already requires a transaction context. Hence, it should have the transaction policy TX_REQUIRED. This applies in particular to the method `setBookingData()`.

**Airline.** The airline session bean is in the same category as the booking entity bean.

**Query.** The query session bean only provides read operations and hence does not require transactions. The policies TX_SUPPORTED or TX_NOT_SUPPORTED should be used.

**Uuid.** The uuid entity bean is in the same category as the query session bean.

We have not considered using the policy TX_BEAN_MANAGED as this would require handling all the transactional issues right in the application code. This policy should only be used when the container-managed transactions create a serious roadblock for the application.

## Access Control Policies

In our example, we have not addressed access control. We did this for two major reasons: First, the security aspects of the EJB specification are about to change as we write this. Second, what we really need for this example is instance-based access control, such as "only the creator of a booking, the traveler and employees of the travel agency are allowed to access and modify bookings made by the creator," which is neither in the scope of the current EJB specification nor on the EJB road map.

## Naming

We use the following names to register our enterprise beans:

**Travel Agent.** There can be multiple travel agents. They are expected to be registered in the context "TravelAgents." We use the names "Apex" and "Casto."

**Booking Business Object.** There can be multiple booking business objects, usually one home per travel agent. They are expected to be registered in the context "BookingBO." The names should match those of the associated travel agents.

**Booking Entity.** There can be multiple booking business objects, usually one home per travel agent. They are expected to be registered in the context "Booking." The names should match those of the associated travel agents.

**Airline.** There can be multiple airlines. They are expected to be registered in the context "Airlines." We use the airlines United "UA" and Lufthansa "LH."

**Query.** There can be multiple queries. They are expected to be registered in the context "Schedule." We only use a single instance and call it "Query."

**Uuid.** The uuid is registered as "Apex/Uuid."

A thought-out naming scheme and disciplined usage of it is important for larger applications. The key problem of JNDI as with any other white-page style naming service is that it is not type safe. Specifically, when using the JNDI `list()` method, one may end up with references of the wrong type. A yellow-page style directory like the CORBA Object Trading Service overcomes this problem.

## Deployment Properties for Container-Managed Persistence

To enable container-managed persistence we have to provide some information in the deployment descriptor. This includes the names of the container-managed fields. For the uuid enterprise bean we declare the fields "primaryKey" and "lastId" as container-managed.

### Miscellaneous Deployment Properties

Miscellaneous deployment properties include the class names for the home and the remote interface, for the bean implementation class, the time-out for stateful and stateless session beans, and the reentrant flag and the primary key class name for entity beans.

### Deployment Properties for Portability

During the implementation of our enterprise beans we mentioned a few times that we use deployment properties to increase the portability of our components. To abstract from the JNDI initialization class we use a property "context-class-name." To abstract from the database we use properties called "db-url", "db-username", and "db-password" to determine the URL, the username, and the password for database connection, respectively.

## Administration of Enterprise JavaBeans

Since the EJB specification is extremely vague about the administration, management, and operation of EJB applications and their containers and servers, there is not much we can do in the context of the EJB specification. However, this important issue is addressed by the leading EJB vendors. Please refer to their products' documentation for further information.

## Configuration Alternatives

The application, as we have it designed and built, can be configured in different ways to suit different purposes. The smallest entity of configuration is an enterprise bean. There are two aspects of the configuration. The first one is how many distinguishable instances of an enterprise bean (that is, of the home interface) should be created. The second aspect is how to distribute all instances over different containers, servers, processors, machines, and so forth.

The first aspect is addressed by the deployment descriptor. For each distinguishable instance of an enterprise bean you must have a separate entry in the deployment descriptor.

The second aspect is more complex. A contributing factor is that the EJB specification does not define what exactly an EJB container is and what an EJB server is and how they relate to physical entities such as processors and machines. The jar file, however, which contains one or multiple enterprise beans, is the smallest entity for configuration over different containers.

In our example we have distributed the application over multiple containers. The primary container is hosting all the travel agent-related enterprise beans. It is also hosting the JNDI implementation. The second container hosts the query enterprise bean and the query iterator. The third hosts two instances of the airline entity bean. Alternatively, one could deploy all the enterprise beans in a single container.

All the configuration issues for distributed objects discussed in this book and elsewhere apply to enterprise beans, too. We will have to wait and see what configuration features will be added by the various EJB server vendors and how useful they will be.

# Index

## P